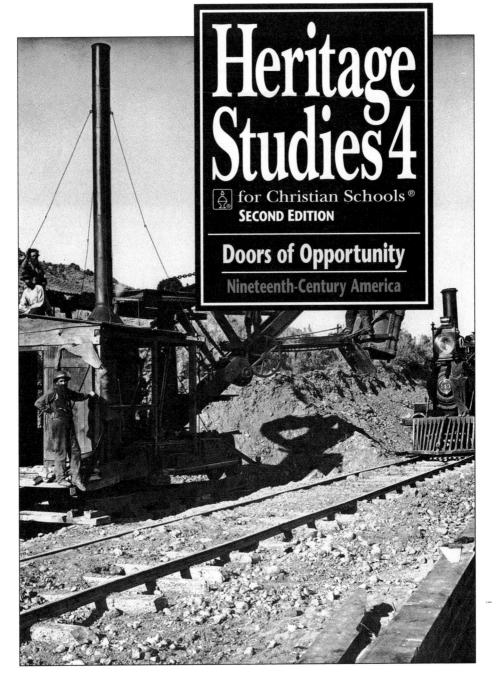

Heritage Studies 4

for Christian Schools®
SECOND EDITION

Doors of Opportunity
Nineteenth-Century America

Kimberly H. Pascoe and Dawn L. Watkins

Bob Jones University Press, Greenville, S

This textbook was written by members of the faculty and staff of Bob Jones University. Standing for the "old-time religion" and the absolute authority of the Bible since 1927, Bob Jones University is the world's leading Fundamentalist Christian university. The staff of the University is devoted to educating Christian men and women to be servants of Jesus Christ in all walks of life.

Providing unparalleled academic excellence, Bob Jones University prepares its students through its offering of over one hundred majors, while its fervent spiritual emphasis prepares their minds and hearts for service and devotion to the Lord Jesus Christ.

If you would like more information about the spiritual and academic opportunities available at Bob Jones University, please call

1-800-BJ-AND-ME (1-800-252-6363).
www.bju.edu

NOTE:

The fact that materials produced by other publishers may be referred to in this volume does not constitute an endorsement by Bob Jones University Press of the content or theological position of materials produced by such publishers. The position of the Bob Jones University Press, and the University itself, is well known. Any references and ancillary materials are listed as an aid to the student or the teacher and in an attempt to maintain the accepted academic standards of the publishing industry.

HERITAGE STUDIES 4 for Christian Schools® Second Edition
Doors of Opportunity: Nineteenth Century America

Kimberly H. Pascoe
Dawn L. Watkins

Produced in cooperation with the Bob Jones University Department of Social Studies Education, the College of Arts and Science, and Bob Jones Elementary School.

Monopoly is a registered trademark of the Parker Brothers Division of General Mills Fun Group Inc.

© 1997, 1999 Bob Jones University Press
Greenville, South Carolina 29614
First Edition © 1985 Bob Jones University Press

ISBN 0-89084-916-1

15   14   13   12   11   10   9   8   7   6   5   4

Contents

Geography

American History

Government

Economics

World History

Culture

The Continents

Ten seconds . . . five . . . two, one. Into space you shoot, an astronaut in the space shuttle. The first few minutes are filled with checking the equipment. But soon enough you reach the height of two hundred miles, and the shuttle begins to orbit, or circle, the earth.

From space, the earth looks mostly blue because it is mostly covered with water. In the blue you can see brown patches of land. Over all are swirling white clouds.

If you traveled on to the moon, you could look back and see the whole earth. Then the earth would look like a big blue ball, a *sphere*.

You may never have the opportunity to see the shape of the earth from space. But you can get an idea of how the earth looks. You can look at photographs. And you can use maps— flat pictures of the earth— and globes— models of the earth.

Like the earth, a globe is a sphere. It shows how the earth's water and land look. We divide the water into four oceans and the land into seven continents. Find all the oceans and continents on the globe.

Asia is the largest continent. It is connected to one of the smallest continents, Europe. Some *geographers,* people who study the earth, think these two continents should be just one. They call the one large continent *Eurasia.* Do you think that is an appropriate name?

The Arctic Ocean is the smallest ocean. Which ocean do you think is the biggest? The Pacific Ocean is the largest and the deepest. In some places, it is almost seven miles deep. All seven continents could fit into the space the Pacific takes up.

The North Pole is the northern-most point on the earth. It is in the Arctic Ocean. The southernmost point on the earth is called the *South Pole.* You can find it on the continent of Antarctica.

Halfway between the North and South Poles, an imaginary line circles the earth, the *equator.* The equator divides the earth into two half spheres, or *hemispheres:* the Northern Hemisphere and the Southern Hemisphere. Find the continent on which you live on the maps below. Which hemisphere do you live in?

Most of the land on earth is in the Northern Hemisphere. All of North America, Asia, and Europe are in the Northern Hemisphere. Parts of Africa and South America are also north of the equator. Which continents are found completely within the Southern Hemisphere?

Northern Hemisphere

Southern Hemisphere

4

You cannot see the whole globe at one time. When you look at a globe, you can see about one half—a hemisphere. To see the other hemisphere, you must turn the globe. We divide the earth into hemispheres to make it easier to study.

There is a second way to divide the earth into hemispheres. Geographers draw a line from the North Pole to the South Pole and another line back to the North Pole again. These lines divide the Eastern Hemisphere from the Western Hemisphere.

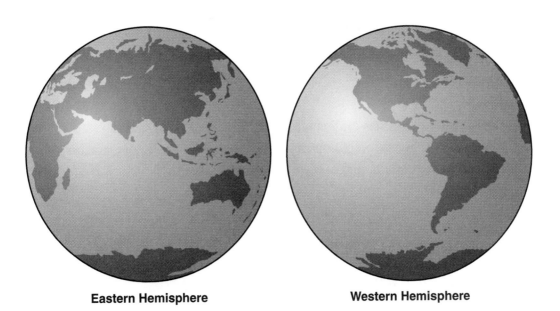

Eastern Hemisphere   **Western Hemisphere**

These lines have names too. One line runs from the North Pole to the South Pole through the Atlantic Ocean. It passes through England. This line is called the *prime meridian.* On the other side of the globe, the second line runs through the Pacific Ocean. It is called the *international date line.* Together these lines circle the globe from north to south, just as the equator circles the globe from east to west. When the earth is divided in this way, in which hemisphere is your country located?

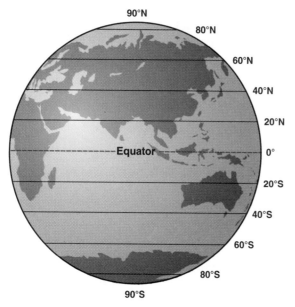

Parallels of latitude

Parallels and Meridians

The equator, prime meridian, and international date line are just three of the lines that geographers draw on globes and maps. Most globes and maps have many more lines on them, running north/south and east/west. Together the lines form a grid on the earth. The grid helps to locate places.

One set of the lines circles the globe from east to west. Each line is *parallel* to the equator. That means that each line is always an equal distance from the equator and every other line in this set. They are *parallels of latitude*.

The second set of lines runs along the globe from north to south. These lines are called *meridians of longitude*. Meridians are different from parallels in two ways. First, each meridian is drawn only half way around the globe. It takes two meridians to complete a circle. And meridians are not always an equal distance apart. All the meridians meet at both the North and the South Poles. Where are the meridians most far apart from each other?

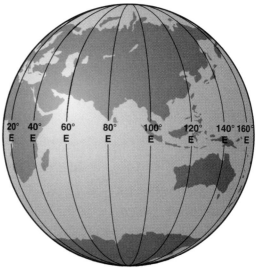

Meridians of longitude

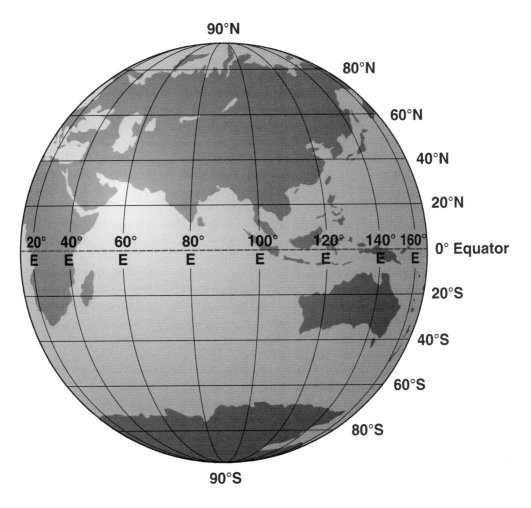

The number given to each parallel of latitude tells how far it is north or south of the equator. On the map above, the first parallel south of the equator is 20°S. We say it is 20 degrees south latitude. What label is given to the first parallel north of the equator? It is 20°N. The North Pole is 90°N. Can you guess the latitude of the South Pole?

Except for the prime meridian and the international date line, meridians of longitude are labeled with numbers and directions too. Each meridian east of the prime meridian is labeled in degrees east longitude. The meridians west of the prime meridian are labeled in degrees west longitude. East and west longitude meet at 180°, the international date line.

To Find Places Using Latitude and Longitude

1. Get a globe, a flat map of the world, a pencil, and a piece of paper.

2. Find the equator and the prime meridian on the globe. Put one finger on each line. Follow the lines to the spot where they meet, 0° latitude, 0° longitude. Is it found on a continent or in an ocean? Do the same thing on the world map. Do the lines meet in the same spot?

3. You can find any place on the earth using latitude and longitude. Follow the lines to where 20°S meets 40°W. What continent are you on?

4. Think of a latitude and a longitude. Let your Heritage Studies partner find the place where the two lines meet on the globe or map. Make a list of latitude and longitude pairs, always writing the latitude first. Can your partner find these places? Can you find the latitude and longitude of your hometown?

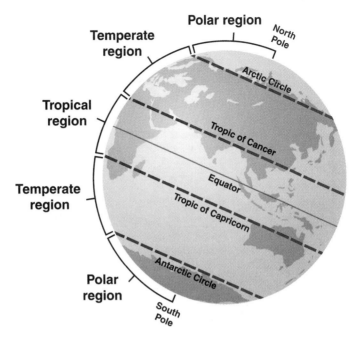

Sun

Climates of the Continents

What is the weather like where you live? Is it always the same? We can know much about a place when we know the kind of climate it has. *Climate* is the normal condition of the atmosphere near the earth's surface in a particular place.

You can find many different climates on each continent. In South America, you can find a hot, wet climate in the rain forest. You can find a desert in which rain has fallen just once in four hundred years. And high in the Andes Mountains, you can find the ground covered with snow all year. What causes these differences in climate?

How far a place is from the equator will affect its climate. Near the equator, the sun's light shines directly, or straight, on the land. The direct sunshine makes the land near the equator hot year-round. Would you like to live in a place that is always hot? We use two parallels of latitude to mark the boundaries of this hot-weather land. The lines are $23\frac{1}{2}°$N and $23\frac{1}{2}°$S. In the Northern Hemisphere the line is called the tropic of Cancer. Can you find the name of the line in the Southern Hemisphere? The area between these two lines is known as the *Tropics*.

9

$66\frac{1}{2}°N$

$23\frac{1}{2}°N$

$23\frac{1}{2}°S$

$66\frac{1}{2}°S$

If it is hottest near the equator, what do you think the climate is like at the poles? The poles are the coldest places on the earth. We use two more parallels of latitude to mark these cold areas. Both parallels are $66\frac{1}{2}°$ from the equator. North of the equator, the parallel is called the Arctic Circle. To the south, it is the Antarctic Circle.

The parallels at $23\frac{1}{2}°$ from the equator are called the Tropics. Most of the land on the earth falls between the Tropics and the Arctic or Antarctic Circles. Here the climate changes with the seasons. Places near the Tropics are warmer, but no place is always hot or cold.

How far a place is from an ocean or a large sea will also affect its climate. The hot summer sun warms the land quickly, but water warms up more slowly. The water stays cooler longer. Land near the cool water stays cooler too. During the winter, the opposite happens. The land loses heat quickly and becomes cool. But water loses heat slowly, so land near the water stays warmer as long as the water is warm. Which region would you like to visit?

Matthew Fontaine Maury
(1806-73)

Matthew Maury joined the United States Navy. He sailed all over the world. On his many trips, Maury remembered a verse his father had read from the Bible about "paths" in the sea. If the Bible said that there were paths in the sea, Matthew was sure sailors could find them.

When Maury hurt his leg in a terrible accident and could no longer work on the ships, he stayed in the navy. He remembered the paths of the seas. With the help of other sailors, he was able to find and map one of these paths. Ships following this path shortened a seventy-day trip to twenty-four days!

Soon ship captains from many countries were sending Maury the information he needed to map his paths. It took thousands of observations and years of hard work. The paths, or *currents*, Maury mapped made ocean travel quicker, smoother, and safer. Even today ships use the maps made by Lt. Matthew Maury, "the Pathfinder of the Seas."

> *"Thou madest him to have dominion over the works of thy hands; thou hast put all things under his feet: all sheep and oxen, yea, and the beasts of the field; the fowl of the air, and the fish of the sea, and whatsoever passeth through the paths of the seas."*
>
> **Psalm 8:6-8**

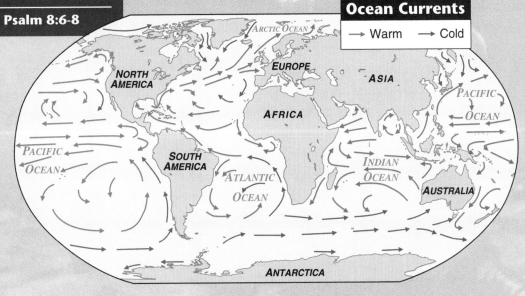

Ocean Currents
→ Warm   → Cold

Ocean water does not stay in one place. It moves in *currents,* like rivers. Some currents are cold, and some are warm. Cold currents begin near the poles and flow toward the equator. Where do you think warm currents begin? Currents also help to heat or cool the nearby land. Look at the map of ocean currents on the previous page. What lands do you think are warmed by currents? What places are cooled?

Air temperature is a major influence on climate. Few plants can take temperatures over 120°F (50°C) for more than a few minutes. But many tropical plants will die if exposed to freezing temperatures even briefly. Photosynthesis, by which plants make food, operates best in most plants between freezing and 80°F (25°C); higher and lower temperatures slow down plant activity. Temperature also influences animal activities, such as hibernation and migration, although no one knows exactly how. Look at this map; what else influences climate?

ARCTIC OCEAN

NORTH AMERICA

PACIFIC OCEAN

ATLANTIC OCEAN

SOUTH AMERICA

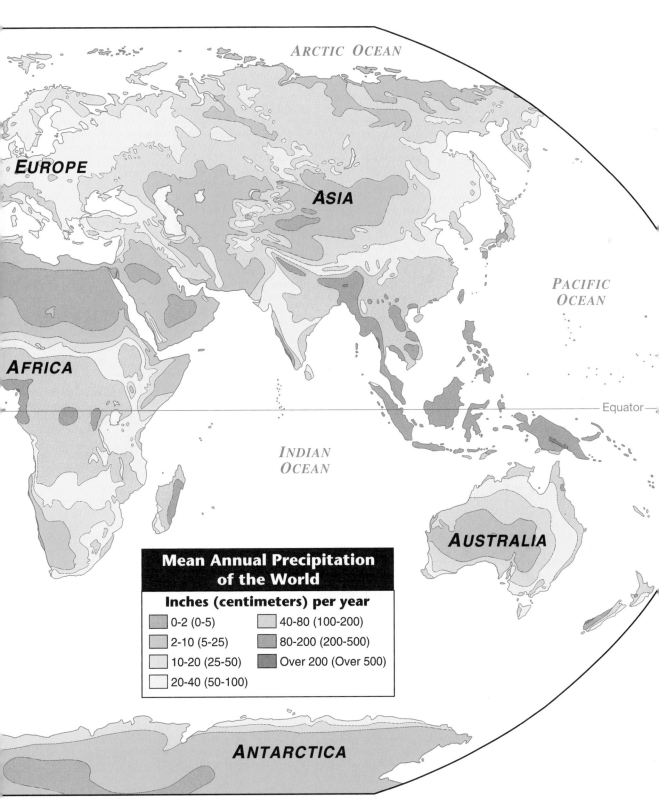

ARCTIC OCEAN

EUROPE

ASIA

PACIFIC
OCEAN

AFRICA

Equator

INDIAN
OCEAN

AUSTRALIA

**Mean Annual Precipitation
of the World**

Inches (centimeters) per year

0-2 (0-5)	40-80 (100-200)
2-10 (5-25)	80-200 (200-500)
10-20 (25-50)	Over 200 (Over 500)
20-40 (50-100)	

ANTARCTICA

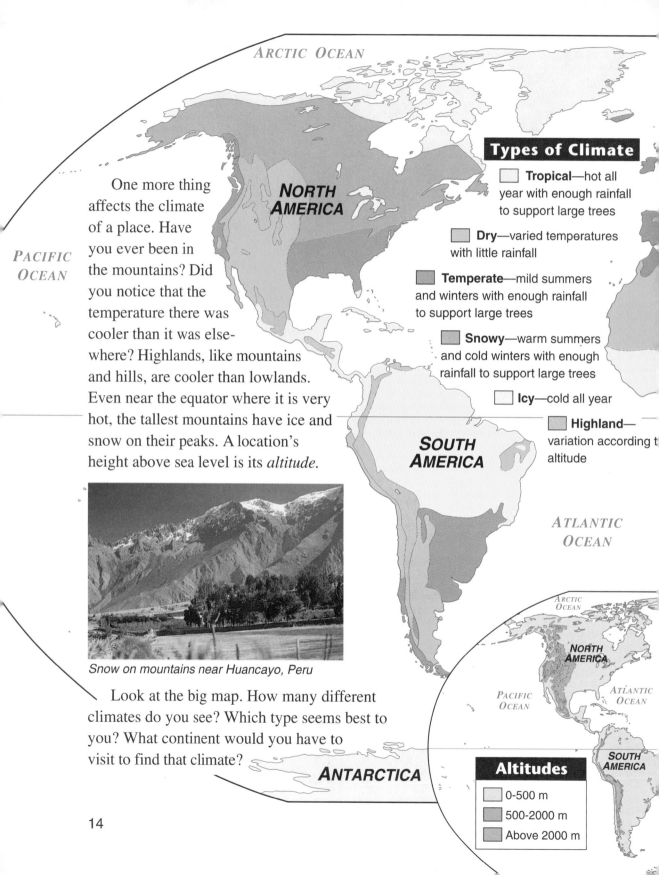

ARCTIC OCEAN

NORTH AMERICA

PACIFIC OCEAN

Types of Climate

Tropical—hot all year with enough rainfall to support large trees

Dry—varied temperatures with little rainfall

Temperate—mild summers and winters with enough rainfall to support large trees

Snowy—warm summers and cold winters with enough rainfall to support large trees

Icy—cold all year

Highland—variation according t altitude

One more thing affects the climate of a place. Have you ever been in the mountains? Did you notice that the temperature there was cooler than it was else-where? Highlands, like mountains and hills, are cooler than lowlands. Even near the equator where it is very hot, the tallest mountains have ice and snow on their peaks. A location's height above sea level is its *altitude*.

SOUTH AMERICA

ATLANTIC OCEAN

Snow on mountains near Huancayo, Peru

Look at the big map. How many different climates do you see? Which type seems best to you? What continent would you have to visit to find that climate?

ANTARCTICA

ARCTIC OCEAN

NORTH AMERICA

PACIFIC OCEAN

ATLANTIC OCEAN

SOUTH AMERICA

Altitudes

0-500 m

500-2000 m

Above 2000 m

14

ARCTIC OCEAN

EUROPE

ASIA

PACIFIC
OCEAN

AFRICA

Equator

INDIAN
OCEAN

AUSTRALIA

ARCTIC OCEAN

ASIA

EUROPE

PACIFIC
OCEAN

AFRICA

Equator

INDIAN
OCEAN

AUSTRALIA

15

Pretend that you live in the mountains and your best friend lives in the lowlands. How might your homes be different? How would the way you dress be different? What if you lived in the Tropics and the friend lived near the North Pole? The climate in which you live will help you decide what kind of house you live in, what kind of clothes you wear, and even what kind of food you eat.

Houses over water in Singapore

Three friends in Alaska

Three friends in South America

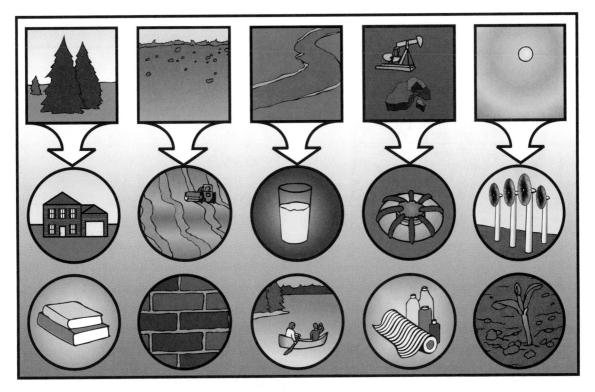

Natural Resources

Climate is not the only thing that determines how, or even whether, people live in a certain place. The natural resources of an area help people decide whether a place is good for living. *Natural resources* are the things God put on the earth for man to use and enjoy. How long do you think a list of natural resources would be?

This chart shows just a few of the natural resources God has given us. Could you find all of these resources in all places on the earth? Each *region,* or part of a continent, has its own natural resources. Which natural resources are found near your home? No natural resource, not even the sun, can be found in every region. Caves never get any sun. And in the Arctic and Antarctic Circles, the sun shines only during six months of the year. What other resources might you find in such places instead?

Victoria Falls, the world's highest

Exploring the Continents

We know that the tallest mountain in the world is Mount Everest. It is found between the countries of Nepal and China, on the continent of Asia. We know that the longest river is the Nile River on the African continent, and the largest island is Greenland. Today we know many things about the world in which we live. But men have not always known as much. How did they find out such things?

Do you remember how people in Europe learned about North and South America? Christopher Columbus sailed for Asia but instead found a land new to him. Later other explorers came. They learned about the land by looking around. They learned more from the people who had lived in the land for hundreds of years. When the explorers returned to their homes, they told about what they had learned.

Men have learned about the other continents in much the same way. Explorers have visited parts of Europe, Africa, Australia, and Asia. But for a very long time, no explorer had ever visited the seventh continent, Antarctica. In fact, until 1820 no one even knew that Antarctica was there. Would you like to explore unknown places?

Mount Everest in Nepal

Antarctica
December 14, 1911

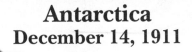

An Antarctic landscape

Roald Amundsen, a Norwegian explorer, rechecks his navigation equipment. This is it, at last, after two months of hard trekking—the South Pole. Perhaps he thinks of being famous.

He plants his country's flag over the spot. He smiles at his four assistants and glances over the Eskimo dogs that have pulled the four sleds into history.

One month and three days later, Robert F. Scott and his team from Great Britain will arrive at the Pole, only to find Amundsen's tent and flag already there.

A landform map shows how the surface of an area looks. Look at this landform map of part of the earth. It shows the surface of the earth the way it would look if there were no water on it.

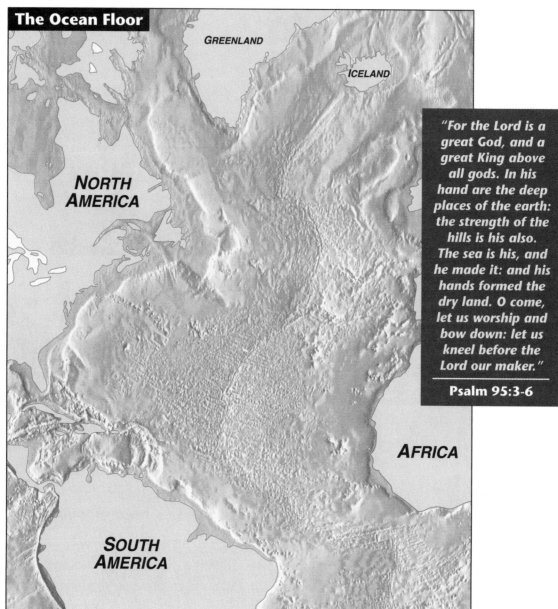

The Ocean Floor

GREENLAND

ICELAND

NORTH AMERICA

SOUTH AMERICA

AFRICA

"For the Lord is a great God, and a great King above all gods. In his hand are the deep places of the earth: the strength of the hills is his also. The sea is his, and he made it: and his hands formed the dry land. O come, let us worship and bow down: let us kneel before the Lord our maker."

Psalm 95:3-6

2

Through the Golden Door

The New Colossus

by Emma Lazarus

Not like the brazen giant of Greek fame,
With conquering limbs astride from land to land;
Here at our sea-washed, sunset gates shall stand
A mighty woman with a torch, whose flame
Is the imprisoned lightning, and her name
Mother of Exiles. From her beacon-hand
Glows world-wide welcome; her mild eyes command
The air-bridged harbor that twin cities frame.
"Keep, ancient lands, your storied pomp!" cries she
With silent lips. "Give me your tired, your poor,
Your huddled masses yearning to breathe free,
The wretched refuse of your teeming shore.
Send these, the homeless, tempest-tost, to me,
I lift my lamp beside the golden door!"

After Columbus discovered America, people were inspired by the idea of a New World. They listened to the tales told by Columbus and other explorers. And they dreamed about a place full of forests and clear, blue lakes. There land and food were free for the taking. Why would such a place be so appealing?

Many people were interested in this new land because it seemed so different from where they were living. Some decided to become *emigrants,* people who move away from their old country to live in a new place. When they reached America, these brave pioneers became *immigrants.* Immigrants are those who go into a new country. They hoped to build a new home in the New World.

The United States is a nation of immigrants. Some Americans are immigrants themselves. Others are the children, grandchildren, or great-grandchildren of immigrants. Only one group of people has lived in America long enough to be thought of as native Americans. Can you tell which people? The American Indians are native Americans. Their people have lived in America for several thousand years.

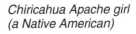

*Chiricahua Apache girl
(a Native American)*

The Spanish built another fort, the Fort of Saint Mark, in St. Augustine in the 1600s.

The First Immigrants

Spanish immigrants built the first lasting settlement on the land that became the United States. They built a fort at St. Augustine, Florida, in 1565. Later, Spanish immigrants built towns in the Southwest. Today those settlements are part of Texas, New Mexico, Arizona, and California. Many of the Spanish immigrants planned to make their fortune and then go back to Spain.

Soon immigrants came from other countries; they were French, Dutch, and Swedish. They too planned to make as much money as they could and then return to their old homes. Many did. But a few decided to stay in their new homes. What might have made them change their minds?

Other immigrants came with the plan to stay in the New World. These immigrants settled in the East. They built towns up and down the Atlantic coast. These towns were part of thirteen colonies that belonged to England. Where do you think most of these immigrants came from?

A Norwegian immigrant

24

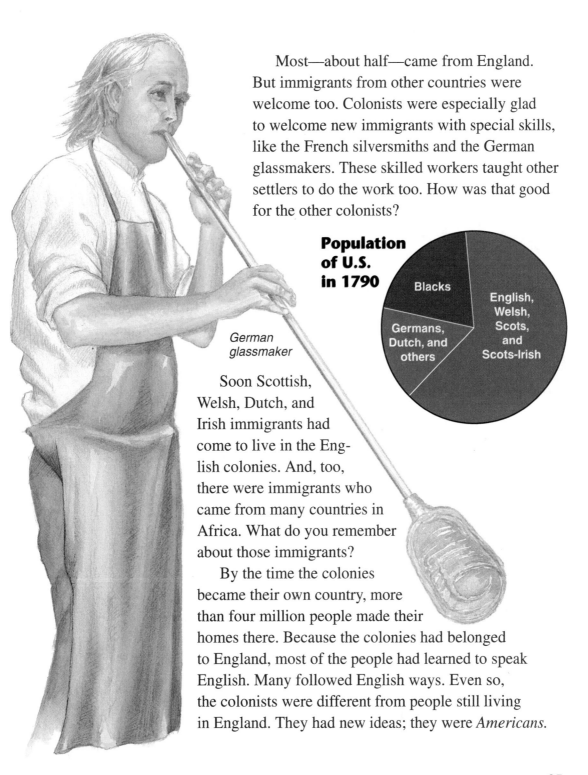

Most—about half—came from England. But immigrants from other countries were welcome too. Colonists were especially glad to welcome new immigrants with special skills, like the French silversmiths and the German glassmakers. These skilled workers taught other settlers to do the work too. How was that good for the other colonists?

Population of U.S. in 1790

Blacks

Germans, Dutch, and others

English, Welsh, Scots, and Scots-Irish

German glassmaker

Soon Scottish, Welsh, Dutch, and Irish immigrants had come to live in the English colonies. And, too, there were immigrants who came from many countries in Africa. What do you remember about those immigrants?

By the time the colonies became their own country, more than four million people made their homes there. Because the colonies had belonged to England, most of the people had learned to speak English. Many followed English ways. Even so, the colonists were different from people still living in England. They had new ideas; they were *Americans*.

Reasons for Coming to America

Why would a person or a family or a whole community travel hundreds, even thousands, of miles to live in a strange place? Most immigrants to America have answered those questions in one of three ways.

Some came to find a better life. They had heard that America had plenty of land. Everyone could get a job there and no one had to be hungry. Everyone had the same chance—the poor as well as the rich.

Separatists came to Plymouth.

Others came to find freedom to worship God as they believed they should. The Separatists came for this reason in 1620. Later, Quakers and Roman Catholics and Huguenots and others came too.

Some came for a different freedom: *political* freedom. In most countries, people could not say whether they thought laws were good or bad. They might be put in jail or even killed for questioning them.

Thanks to the words of the Declaration of Independence, Americans believe that "all men are created equal." The Bill of Rights promises freedom to every person in America. The words of the Declaration of Independence and the Bill of Rights still "echo" around the world, drawing immigrants to America.

The Declaration of Independence

IN CONGRESS, JULY 4, 1776.

The unanimous Declaration of the thirteen united States of America.

A crowded European city in the 1800s

Fewer immigrants came after the colonies became a country. At first, people in Europe did not believe that the American ideas of freedom could work. They thought that other countries would try to take over the new United States.

Soon, wars between France and England and between England and the United States kept people at home. It was not safe to travel across the ocean when countries were at war. Can you think why such travel would be dangerous?

After 1820, immigrants began coming to America again. Where do you think these immigrants came from? Many came from the same countries that sent the earliest immigrants. Some others came from Norway, and a few came from Canada. Which immigrants had the shortest trip?

Most immigrants who came during this time came to find a better life. In many countries of Europe, *landlords,* or landowners, forced the peasant farmers to move from their land. These poor farmers moved to the already crowded cities and towns. They hoped to find jobs there. But soon there were no jobs to find. Those who could scrape a bit of money together packed up their families and headed to America.

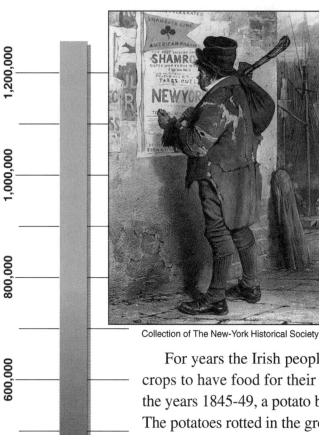

An Irish worker dreams of going to America.

Collection of The New-York Historical Society

The flow of immigrants into America was slow and steady for about thirty years. Then something terrible happened in Ireland that changed the flow into a flood.

For years the Irish people had planted potato crops to have food for their families. But during the years 1845-49, a potato blight struck the crops. The potatoes rotted in the ground. Suddenly the people in Ireland had no food to eat.

Many Irish people died from hunger. Those who did live made plans to leave their homeland. Between 1850 and 1860, as many immigrants came to America as had come in all the thirty years before. More than two million immigrants came; most were from Ireland.

The New Immigrants

Immigration slowed down almost to a stop in the years between 1860 and 1865. What do you think was the cause? During these years, Americans were at war with Americans. The horrible, bloody Civil War kept many would-be immigrants at home.

Irish Immigration to America 1836-65

1,200,000

1,000,000

800,000

600,000

400,000

200,000

0

1836-45

1846-55

1856-65

As soon as peace was made between the North and the South, immigrants were again ready to come. For a while, most still came from the same countries of northern Europe. But more and more, immigrants began coming from different countries as well. What other countries do you think some immigrants came from?

These *new immigrants,* as they were called, came from countries in the south and east of Europe. They too had heard about the opportunities in America. When railroads were built through countries like Austria-Hungary, Russia, and Italy, the people finally had an easy way to travel. They rode the trains to cities on the coast. There they boarded ships bound for America.

Above: Austro-Hungarian immigrants

Left: Immigrants from Europe

Life in America was not as easy for these new immigrants as it had been for the first ones who came. Many of the early immigrants spoke the English language. They did things the same ways that the English settlers did. They looked and dressed the same. How would being like the people already in America help an immigrant who had just arrived?

The new immigrants were different in every way. They spoke languages that were much different from English. They ate different kinds of foods. They wore clothes that were strange and brightly colored. They were poorer too.

One more thing set many of these new immigrants apart: religion. The new immigrants were Roman Catholic or Jewish. But most Americans were *Protestant*. They went to churches that had separated from the Catholic Church. Why might this difference cause problems?

To be sure, many Jews and Roman Catholics had made their homes in America before the new immigrants came. But never before had so many come so quickly. Some Protestants feared that they would soon be outnumbered. Then the Catholics or the Jews might try to take away the freedom of all Americans to worship God as they thought they should. It had happened before in other countries. Do you think the Protestants were right to be afraid?

Many of the Jewish immigrants came from Russia. Like the Irish immigrants who had come thirty years before, the Russian Jews were forced to leave their homeland. But it was not hunger that made them leave. The Jewish people were blamed for everything that went wrong in Russia. The *czar,* Russia's king, encouraged his people to persecute the Jews.

The Russian Jews gave a name to the persecutions—*pogroms*—and they lived in constant fear. They never knew when a pogrom might happen or what small thing might cause one. The czar's soldiers and the townspeople burned the homes and businesses owned by Jews. They stole and ruined all that the Jewish people had worked for. With nowhere else to go, the Russian Jews turned to America. Can you think of others who were persecuted for their beliefs and came to America?

The Isaak family, Russian immigrants

Immigrants arriving with a few possessions from their old country

Leaving the Old Country

To many people in Europe, America seemed like a wonderful, golden place. And living in the old country was often horrible. But making the decision to leave the place that had been home for so many years was not easy. How would you have felt about making such a decision?

Once the decision was made, the emigrants began making plans. First, money had to be raised to pay for a ticket. Sometimes money was needed to pay for food on the ship as well. A whole family might have to put their money together. They would send one person to America, hoping that he would make a good living. Then he could send money back for the rest of the family to make the trip.

What things would you have taken to America? Nearly every emigrant took with him some clothing. If there was room left in the suitcase, trunk, or basket, some other things could go too. Perhaps a place could be found for a special doll or a favorite book. When Bessie Jane Priest came from England, she brought a bracelet her uncle had given her. Like many mothers, she probably brought pots and pans so that she could cook for her family in their new home.

To Study Your Family History

1. Get a notebook and a pencil, or a cassette tape and a tape recorder.

2. Find out something new and interesting about your family history from one of the following sources:

   a. An older family member, such as a grandparent, aunt, or uncle.
   b. An old family Bible.
   c. Newspaper clippings.
   d. A bundle of old letters.
   e. Old photographs.
   f. Special family books, such as diaries, baby books, or autograph books.

3. In your notebook, record the things you find out. If you talk to an older family member, try to use a tape recorder. Then write a page telling the family story you learned. Be sure to include details like the year, the place, and the names and ages of the family members in the story.

4. Share your family information with your classmates. Then put your written work in a folder or scrapbook. If you like, find out about more family stories and add them to the folder or scrapbook too.

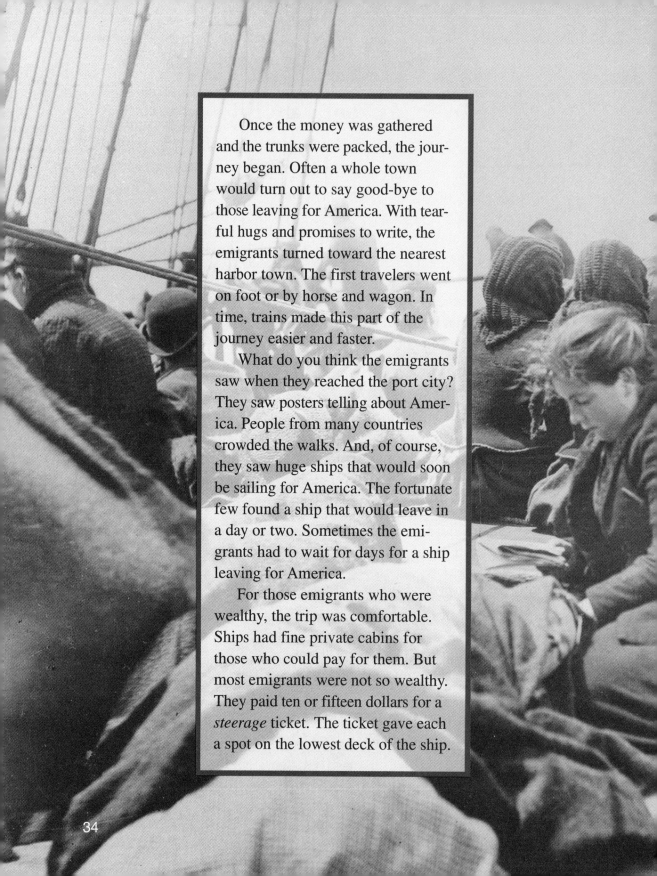

Once the money was gathered and the trunks were packed, the journey began. Often a whole town would turn out to say good-bye to those leaving for America. With tearful hugs and promises to write, the emigrants turned toward the nearest harbor town. The first travelers went on foot or by horse and wagon. In time, trains made this part of the journey easier and faster.

What do you think the emigrants saw when they reached the port city? They saw posters telling about America. People from many countries crowded the walks. And, of course, they saw huge ships that would soon be sailing for America. The fortunate few found a ship that would leave in a day or two. Sometimes the emigrants had to wait for days for a ship leaving for America.

For those emigrants who were wealthy, the trip was comfortable. Ships had fine private cabins for those who could pay for them. But most emigrants were not so wealthy. They paid ten or fifteen dollars for a *steerage* ticket. The ticket gave each a spot on the lowest deck of the ship.

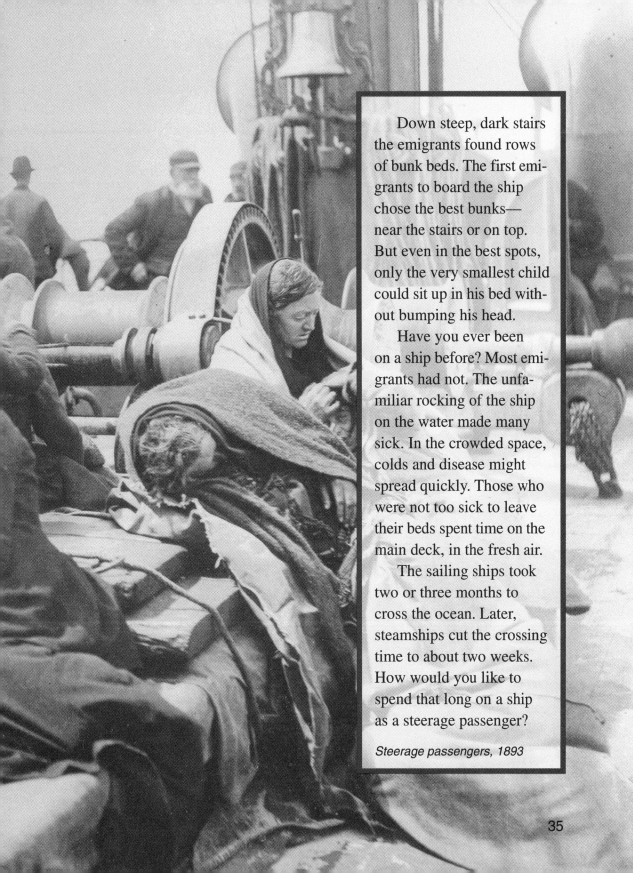

Down steep, dark stairs the emigrants found rows of bunk beds. The first emigrants to board the ship chose the best bunks— near the stairs or on top. But even in the best spots, only the very smallest child could sit up in his bed without bumping his head.

Have you ever been on a ship before? Most emigrants had not. The unfamiliar rocking of the ship on the water made many sick. In the crowded space, colds and disease might spread quickly. Those who were not too sick to leave their beds spent time on the main deck, in the fresh air.

The sailing ships took two or three months to cross the ocean. Later, steamships cut the crossing time to about two weeks. How would you like to spend that long on a ship as a steerage passenger?

Steerage passengers, 1893

35

What excitement filled the crowded ship when land was finally sighted. America, at last! But where exactly would the immigrants be when they stepped off the ship? Look at the map. How many different cities does it show? Immigrants came into America in all these places. But most came to New York City.

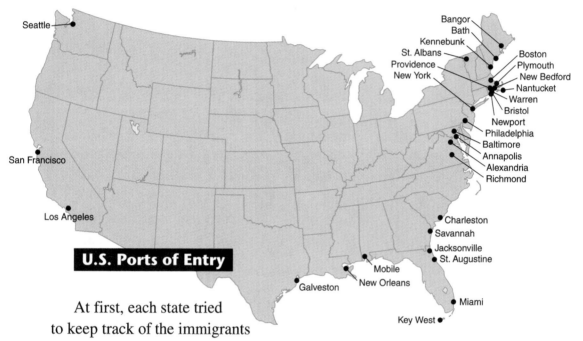

U.S. Ports of Entry

At first, each state tried to keep track of the immigrants that came to their part of America. Ship captains gave a list of their passengers to state officers. But not much was done to help or welcome the immigrants to their new country. Instead, some immigrants got an unfriendly welcome from thieves. They were robbed, and a few were even killed. With more and more immigrants coming all the time, the United States needed a better way of welcoming them.

In 1855, the first official station for receiving immigrants into the United States was opened. At Castle Garden in New York City, immigrants could exchange their money for American money. They could buy railroad tickets to take them to other parts of the country. And if they were sick after their long trip, they could see a doctor.

Sculpting Statues

Most statues are carefully carved from a stone called *marble*. It is smooth and strong. The person who carves the statue is called a *sculptor*. He uses special tools to sculpt, or carve, the stone. What other things can statues be made from?

Frédéric Auguste Bartholdi was well known in his country of France. He liked to sculpt big statues. His first statue was twelve feet tall! He tried to make each statue he carved bigger and better than the one before.

A friend told Bartholdi about his idea for a gift from the people of France to the people of America. Such a statue would make a wonderful gift for the hundredth birthday of the United States.

Building the left hand of the Statue of Liberty

Bartholdi began to work. He drew many sketches of his ideas. Finally he had a drawing that he liked. He called his statue "Liberty Enlightening the World."

It took many years to sculpt the statue to liberty. Because Bartholdi wanted to make it huge, he did not make the statue from stone. He shaped each part from wood, then carefully hammered copper sheets over the wood until it was shaped just right. A skeleton of iron and steel held the copper parts in place.

Americans put the statue on an island in New York Harbor. For millions of immigrants, it was the first thing "American" they saw. The Statue of Liberty stood for American freedom and liberty.

Castle Garden served for thirty-five years as an immigration station. During those years more than eight million immigrants passed through its doors. In time the number of immigrants grew too great for the small building. A bigger immigration station had to be built.

Ellis Island

The United States built a new place for receiving immigrants on Ellis Island. It opened in 1892. Its many buildings covered the whole island. A hospital gave the sick immigrants a place to stay while they received care. Many immigrants got their first taste of American food in the Ellis Island dining room.

Not every immigrant who came to Ellis Island visited the hospital or ate in the dining room. But everyone had to pass through the main building. The huge building looked like a castle to the immigrants. The workers in their uniforms reminded them of soldiers in the old country. The workers shouted orders at the immigrants in English. Do you think the immigrants understood the words?

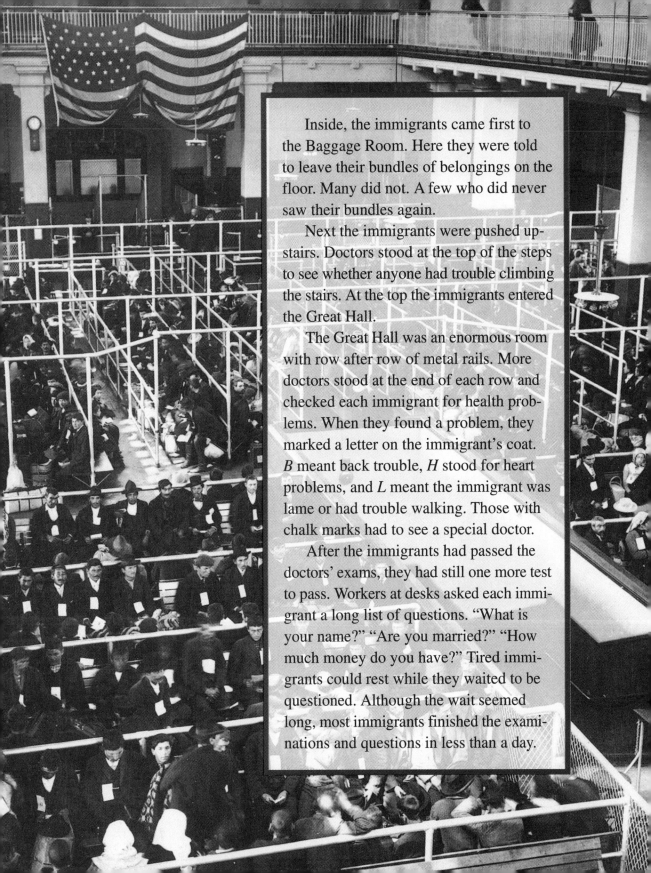

Inside, the immigrants came first to the Baggage Room. Here they were told to leave their bundles of belongings on the floor. Many did not. A few who did never saw their bundles again.

Next the immigrants were pushed upstairs. Doctors stood at the top of the steps to see whether anyone had trouble climbing the stairs. At the top the immigrants entered the Great Hall.

The Great Hall was an enormous room with row after row of metal rails. More doctors stood at the end of each row and checked each immigrant for health problems. When they found a problem, they marked a letter on the immigrant's coat. *B* meant back trouble, *H* stood for heart problems, and *L* meant the immigrant was lame or had trouble walking. Those with chalk marks had to see a special doctor.

After the immigrants had passed the doctors' exams, they had still one more test to pass. Workers at desks asked each immigrant a long list of questions. "What is your name?" "Are you married?" "How much money do you have?" Tired immigrants could rest while they waited to be questioned. Although the wait seemed long, most immigrants finished the examinations and questions in less than a day.

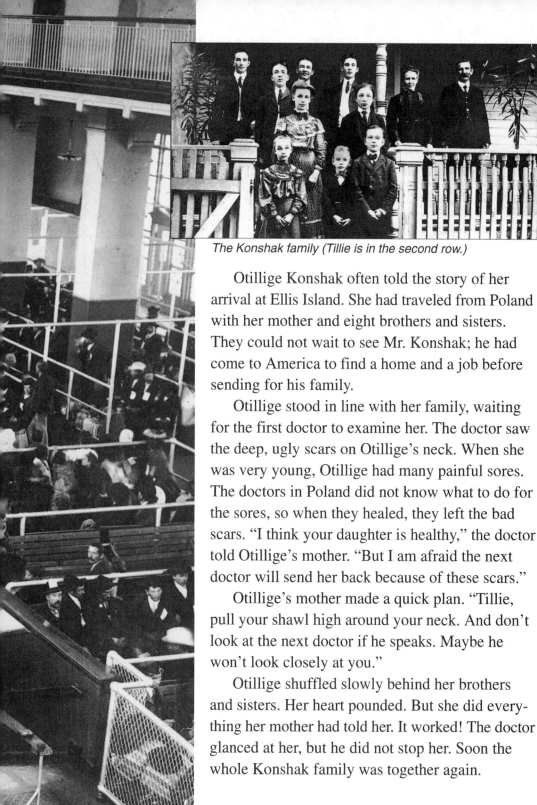

The Konshak family (Tillie is in the second row.)

Otillige Konshak often told the story of her arrival at Ellis Island. She had traveled from Poland with her mother and eight brothers and sisters. They could not wait to see Mr. Konshak; he had come to America to find a home and a job before sending for his family.

Otillige stood in line with her family, waiting for the first doctor to examine her. The doctor saw the deep, ugly scars on Otillige's neck. When she was very young, Otillige had many painful sores. The doctors in Poland did not know what to do for the sores, so when they healed, they left the bad scars. "I think your daughter is healthy," the doctor told Otillige's mother. "But I am afraid the next doctor will send her back because of these scars."

Otillige's mother made a quick plan. "Tillie, pull your shawl high around your neck. And don't look at the next doctor if he speaks. Maybe he won't look closely at you."

Otillige shuffled slowly behind her brothers and sisters. Her heart pounded. But she did everything her mother had told her. It worked! The doctor glanced at her, but he did not stop her. Soon the whole Konshak family was together again.

Ellis Island
April 17, 1907

On this day 11,000 people are waiting on Ellis Island, or on ships nearby, to find out whether they can enter the United States.

This young Jewish girl has left Russia with her family. They wanted to escape the pogroms, cruel persecutions encouraged by the czar.

She is twelve—old enough to be sent back to Russia alone if she does not pass the examinations.

So far, she has passed every examination without receiving a chalk mark on her coat. She has seen others with many different marks given them by the doctors. Even though she does not know what they mean, she knows the marks are not good.

This is the most dreaded examination. The inspector will turn back her eyelids with a metal hook so that he can look beneath them.

A Fresh Start

The examinations passed and the questions answered, the golden door to America swung wide open. Now the hard work of making a new life in a strange land began for each immigrant. Where would he go? Would he find work? Would he be accepted by his new neighbors?

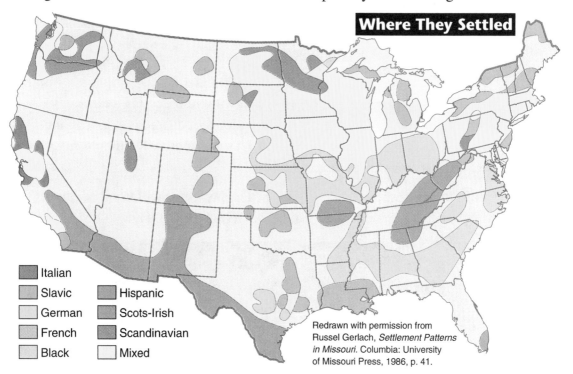

Where They Settled

Italian

Slavic

German

French

Black

Hispanic

Scots-Irish

Scandinavian

Mixed

Redrawn with permission from Russel Gerlach, *Settlement Patterns in Missouri*. Columbia: University of Missouri Press, 1986, p. 41.

Most of the immigrants who came before 1870 went west. During those years the United States grew to cover the land from ocean to ocean. The country needed people to live on that land. As long as land could be found for a good price, immigrants followed their dreams and bought their own farms. Sometimes whole villages in the old country packed up and moved to the American West.

Look at the map. It shows where different groups of immigrants settled. What groups settled west of the Mississippi River? Why do you think so many Scandinavian and Slavic people settled in the West?

The Kvsvick family emigrated from Norway in 1918.

Not every immigrant who went west bought a farm. Nineteen-year-old John Kvsvick worked on a large farm owned by another man. John's brother, who had come from Norway earlier, helped him to find the job. Many immigrants got help finding work from family and friends. John worked hard and saved all his money. After four years John headed home to Norway. Do you think he stayed?

Back in Norway, John married Jennie Thomsen. They had three children, but John was not happy in Norway. It was hard to earn enough money to care for his growing family. And he did not agree with the way God's Word was preached in the church there. John remembered how things had been for him in America. He told his little family, "I must go back to America. I will send money for you as soon as I can."

John went again to Minnesota. But he did not work on a farm this time. Other kinds of work were easier to find now. New western cities

The house that John Kvsvick built in America

needed factory workers. Other immigrants found work on the railroads. This time John worked in a lumber camp. It took a few years, but he finally saved enough money to send for his family.

Little Italy, about 1899

After 1870, many immigrants went no further than the city where their ship had landed. In New York City, three of every four people were immigrants or the children of immigrants. Most were poor people who did not have money to travel any farther. They had spent all they had to get to America.

Others stayed in the cities because they did not want to be farmers. Remember the

A butcher in his shop in Chinatown

Irish immigrants? After their experience with the potato blight, many Irishmen did not want to be farmers ever again. Instead they worked in factories in the cities. Some Irish immigrants did go west but not to farm. They helped to build the railroads and canals.

Often immigrants formed their own communities. German farmers bought land near other farmers from Germany. Italian immigrants found places to live in neighborhoods settled by other Italians. Why would the immigrants want to live near others from their old countries?

tunnpannkakor med lingonsylt:
Swedish thin pancakes with lingonberry sauce

At first, most immigrants felt like strangers in a strange new land. It was comforting to live near people who spoke their language and understood their customs. These *ethnic* communities were small copies of the old country. There the immigrants could buy the foods they had eaten all their lives. They could find newspapers written in their language. Parties and celebrations were just like the ones in the old country. And sermons at the community church were preached in the immigrants' language.

Enoch Malmfeldt and Hattie Hallberg lived in an ethnic community in Kansas City. Both young people had emigrated from Sweden. They met at the Old Swedish Baptist Church in Kansas City and were married there. What language do you think the preacher at the church spoke? In the small Swedish community, many of the people spoke only Swedish.

Enoch worked as a tailor, and Hattie worked as a maid in the home of a wealthy family. They could speak a little English, but at home they spoke Swedish. But that changed when their oldest son went to school. "Papa, the other children make fun of the way I talk. I do not want to go back to school anymore," the young boy told his father. Enoch decided that, for the sake of the children, the family would speak only English from then on. Do you think that was a good idea?

Enoch and Hattie Malmfeldt

An Immigrant Becomes a U.S. Citizen

1. Get Notebook page 13 and a pencil.
2. Read the list of requirements for becoming a *citizen*. (A citizen is a person with all the rights and privileges of someone born in this country.) If you were an immigrant, how many points would keep you from becoming a citizen today?
3. Now read the pledge on your Notebook page. Listen as your teacher explains the pledge. Why do you think the American people wanted the immigrants to agree with the things in the pledge? What things do you think are important for a United States citizen to promise? Write your own citizenship pledge.

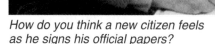

How do you think a new citizen feels as he signs his official papers?

Learning the customs of a new country

After a time, immigrants became more comfortable in their new country. They began to think of home as the United States rather than the old country. No matter where they went, the children of immigrants became "American" more quickly than their parents. In schools and in the streets and playgrounds, children learned the language and ways of their new home.

Life was often not as easy as an immigrant had dreamed it would be. Even when an immigrant's life in America was not all he hoped for, it was better than it might have been in the old country. Few ever went back to their old homes, except to visit. All in all, they were glad they had made the decision to come to the land of liberty.

Ending the Flood

As more and more immigrants poured into the United States, Americans began to get worried. Land for farming was getting hard to find. Cities were crowded. And what if the new immigrants did not become "American"? Shouldn't America be for Americans? Perhaps, some thought, it is time to close the golden door.

People from all over still come to America.

Some Americans wanted to make laws that would keep more immigrants from coming. In 1882, laws were made that said criminals, people with mental handicaps, and anyone who could not take care of himself could not come in. Then people in California complained about the ways of the Chinese immigrants there. Soon a law said that no one could come to America from China. Every few years, a new law kept more people from coming. By 1924, almost no new immigrants were coming to America.

Today immigrants are again coming to America. They come from different places—South America, Mexico, and Asia. But they come for the same reasons that brought the very first immigrants. During the past two hundred years, about fifty million people have come to America. They left 140 different homelands searching for freedom or better opportunity in the New World.

Today's immigrants do not often come by boat. Most come by car or bus or plane. And they do not have to go through immigrant stations like Ellis Island. Instead, Ellis Island is a national monument. Hundreds of people visit Ellis Island each day. They remember their brave family members who came to a new home, a new hope, and a new life.

> *"Now the Lord had said unto Abram,*
> *Get thee out of thy country,*
> *and from thy kindred,*
> *and from thy father's house,*
> *unto a land that I will shew thee."*
>
> **Genesis 12:1**

3

American Voices

People from All Over

Imagine for a moment that you live in a small village in Hungary about one hundred years ago. There are only a dozen houses there, forty cows, a few pigs, and some chickens. The land you live on was your grandfather's; the house you live in has only two rooms.

Then imagine what you think when someone returns to your village from America and tells you that there the trees have grown for a thousand years by the big ocean and have gotten to be one hundred feet around. Think how your heart pounds when he tells about gold mines where men get rich as kings in a single day and how your mind races when he says that Americans in a place called Texas own ranches fifty times bigger than your whole village.

And then imagine your surprise when you hear that in that far-off America one can go up to the president and shake his hand. Incredible! But suddenly you begin to think that perhaps you could go to America too. And once you were there, you could become more than you had ever hoped. The idea gets bigger and bigger in your heart, until one day, you decide you have to go; you have to become an American.

Immigrants arriving at Ellis Island, hoping to start a new life

In many villages, cities, and farms all over the world, men and women, boys and girls had much the same idea. They saved their money, sold their houses, and said good-bye to all that was familiar—customs, family, friends, language, and even food. And they set off for America from Turkey, from China, from Poland, from Russia, from Scotland, from Greece, from France, from Norway, from Mexico, from everywhere. Once they passed through customs at Ellis Island in New York or a few other places, these new-comers found that being in America was not all grandeur and gold.

The first problem was always the language. Few of the immigrants could speak much English. Those who could speak it usually did so with an accent. The way immigrants spoke often made them targets for ridicule and the subjects of jokes. Many times it kept them from getting jobs. What do you think the immigrants did about this serious problem?

Learning English

A boy from Turkey arrived at Ellis Island when he was eleven. His father and mother did not speak English; neither did he. He had not been able to go to school in his homeland because there was a war going on there. Once in America and in school, he began to learn some English words. That is not to say that he had an easy time—older boys teased him, and boys his own age picked fights with him because he dressed differently and because his accent was thick. How do you think you would have treated him?

Immigrant children (and some adults) learned English in schools like this one.

To dislike someone without knowing anything about him is to be *prejudiced.* Many Americans have felt such unjust dislike directed at them. And even some who have felt prejudice from others have been prejudiced themselves. Why do you think some people dislike those whom they do not know?

Some of the other students helped the new boy. At recess, they pointed out objects and repeated the English words for them over and over: *chair, window, shoes, collar, cat.* Soon, because he was bright and because he really tried hard, the Turkish boy learned the language of his new home. His father was learning a little English too at his job as a dishwasher in a big restaurant. But his mother stayed inside the room they rented and did not learn the new speech.

Some schools had special classes for students who knew little English. And there were classes at night for adults who needed help with the new language. But mostly people picked up the American way of talking by being with others in the neighborhood.

Jane Addams and Lillian Wald
(1860-1935) (1867-1940)

Although many Americans were unkind to new immigrants (forgetting that all but Native Americans were immigrants or descendants of immigrants), others tried hard to help.

Jane Addams, a woman with a kind heart and a good mind, decided that it was not only wrong but harmful to everyone for immigrants to be treated badly. She thought that helping them become "Americanized" would make the whole country stronger. How do you think that might be true?

Addams started a center for helping immigrants, Hull House, in Chicago in 1889. Hull House ran nurseries for small children whose mothers worked, offered English classes as well as other classes, pro-

Jane Addams

vided instruction in cleanliness and housekeeping skills, and even gave music and art lessons. Why do you think Hull House had so many services?

Other cities also started *settlement houses,* such as the Henry Street settlement in New York, run by Lillian Wald. All the settlements were staffed by volunteers. But as hard as they worked, they could not do all that was needed. So Jane Addams and others pushed for the government to help. Before long, New Jersey, New York, Massachusetts, and California were providing classes in English, hygiene, and American history.

Hull House

A young man named Leon Surmelian, from Armenia, arrived in New York with little money but much hope. He had been given a train ticket to Kansas, where he was wanting to go to college. On the train he bought a bag of peanuts and a Coca-Cola. He thought the drink had a "peculiar taste," but drinking it made him "feel more American."

Two days later, Surmelian arrived in Kansas and took a taxi to the college campus. He set out to find the vice president. He showed a student the vice president's name on the letter he carried, and the student took him to the right office. Surmelian pretended to know English, but soon had to admit he did not. The man asked Surmelian whether he could speak German. Surmelian said no. But he could speak French. The vice president sent for the French teacher. Now Surmelian could communicate, but the news was not good.

He was too late to get a job to pay for his schooling. He had to live in a basement and sweep floors. He worked hard all that winter, living at first on only bread and cheese and water. The next summer, he went to work on a farm. In a book he wrote much later, after graduating from the University of Kansas, he tells how his desire to be an American came alive again that summer.

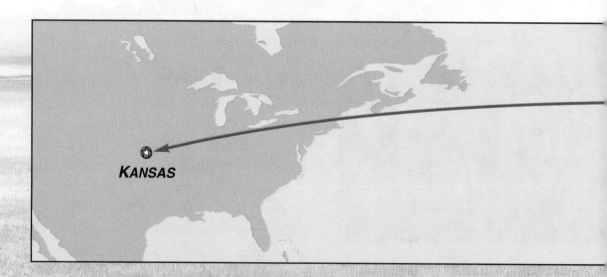

KANSAS

Early the next morning I began my apprenticeship on an American farm, wearing overalls. In them I felt like an American. Harry and I went to the pasture to bring in the cows. It was a golden June morning. The young corn crackled in the breeze, and the orchard was ablaze with ripe sour cherries. I was in secret rapture over those cherry trees.

"Do you know," I said to Harry, who majored in horticulture, "cherries come from a place near my hometown, from Cerasus, or Kerasund, on the Black Sea. That's why they're called cherries."

He was surprised.

"And do you know the scientific name of the apricot?"

"No," he said.

"*Prunus armeniaca.* Armenian prune. Oh, a lot of other fruits from my country! Chestnuts, for example. The English word chestnut is derived from the Armenian word *kaskeni,* which means chestnut tree."

A little brook ran through the pasture, where I saw blackberry and gooseberry bushes. To complete this miraculous picture, a spring flowed from under a rock through a narrow wooden trough, with a leaf dangling from its end! I wondered if I was dreaming. . . .

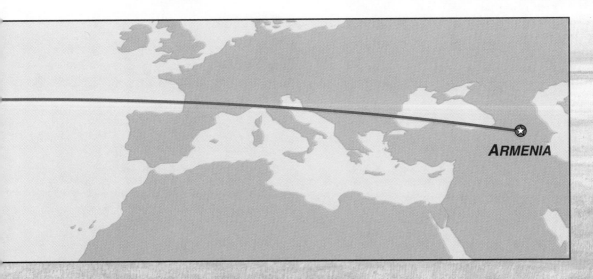

ARMENIA

It was an excellent breakfast they served when we finished milking—grapefruit, bran flakes and cream, home-cured ham and eggs, fresh country butter, homemade bread, good hot coffee. Mr. Schultz said grace, thanking God for His many blessings—the God of America. Yes, America seemed to have a different God, a more generous one. . . .

A field had to be plowed, and I begged Harry to let me do it. What a thing of beauty and precision the modern steel plow was! Harry showed me how to cut furrows of uniform depth and width, turning the surface completely under.

A no less heroic task was pitching hay in the afternoon. This was sheer poetry. True, my hands became blistered, my face, neck, and shoulders sunburned and the blue shirt on my back wringing wet with perspiration. . . . But I exulted in the powerful heat of the earth, in the dust and odor of alfalfa hay.

By nightfall I was dead tired, with a fine fatigue.

Something important had happened to me, but I did not know how to word it, not even to myself. Somehow I felt as if the earth and sun of Kansas flowed through my veins, that I had suddenly become an American. . . .

What is it makes nations? Language, history, traditions, political organizations? These are contributing factors, yes; but fundamentally it is the land . . . with dandelions and moonlight and crickets and the crackling of young corn.

Like Surmelian, many new Americans found that not knowing English gave them a bad start. A French girl was invited to a tea party. She knew only one English word—*yes*. A lady at the party asked her whether her clothes were like what the girls were wearing in France. "Yes," she said. Then the lady asked her what kind of hats they were wearing. "Yes," she said. The lady, puzzled, asked again about the hats, what sort of trims they had on them. "Yes," said the girl. The lady, thinking the girl was being rude, asked her, "Do you think I'm stupid?" The girl, still smiling brightly, said, "Yes." Another woman rescued the girl and told her she must start learning English right away!

Keeping Customs

Like Surmelian, many Americans also wanted familiar things in the new country to comfort them and to make them feel at home.

Most people liked to have some of the food they were used to. Italian settlers brought lasagna and a round, hard bread. The Greeks made pita bread; the Austrians made croissants. Today Americans eat these foods often; but before 1900, the foods from other countries were looked on with as much suspicion as the people.

Breads from many countries are popular in America.

Many American immigrants like to dress as they did in their homelands.

Another thing people liked to bring with them from their old homes was *tradition.* A tradition is a practice or a belief that is handed down from generation to generation. Another word for *tradition* is *custom.* Italian people liked to eat fish on Christmas Eve. Germans liked to put up Christmas trees. The Chinese liked to shoot off fireworks to bring in their new year. Japanese people bowed to each other in greeting. In places like New York City, many different kinds of people lived close together, observing each other. Some traditions began to spread to other people. Can you think of any?

Most immigrants came from places where all the people dressed alike, spoke the same language, and had the same traditions. But in America, immigrants had to learn to get along with others who had different ideas and customs. Sometimes the clash led to new problems; sometimes it helped form a new *culture.* A culture is the way of life of the people who live in a certain place.

America has a *pluralistic culture.* What does that mean? *Plural* means "more than one." So a pluralistic culture is a way of life that has more than one way within it. If Japanese, German, Korean, Bulgarian, Welsh, Australian, and English people all live near each other in, say, California but keep many of their native customs, they form a pluralistic culture. They are all Americans, but they are all different from each other in many ways. How can this arrangement be good for a country? How can it be bad?

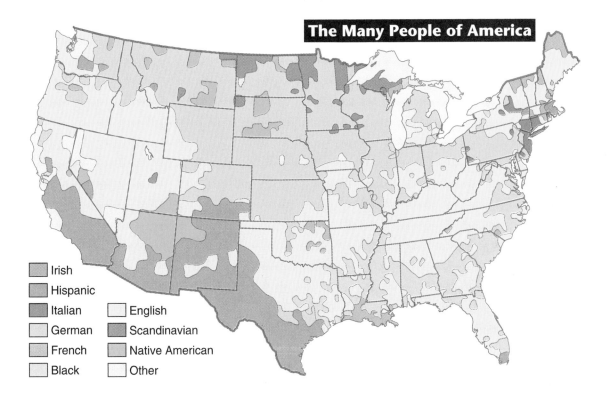

The Many People of America

Irish
Hispanic
Italian   English
German   Scandinavian
French   Native American
Black   Other

Look at this map. What groups settled in your area? What influences do you see from these people? Look in a telephone book for names that represent the group or groups of settlers who came to your area. What street and city names, foods, games, sayings, and traditions may the settlers have contributed?

Borrowing Words

Many words we use every day come from other languages. *Kindergarten,* for example, is German for "child garden." And when you eat a hamburger, you pay tribute to the German city the food came from—Hamburg.

An Old World food, now an American standard

Many of our cities, lakes, and rivers have names that are Native American: Tioga, Omaha, Susquehanna, and Huron, to name only a few. Other places and bodies of water have Spanish names: Colorado, Los Angeles, and Rio Grande.

When you say you want a cookie, you are using a word from Holland. When you point out New Orleans on the map, you find a city name from the French. When you talk about putting horses in a corral, you are using an African-derived word. Having goulash for supper? That is a Hungarian dish.

Spaghetti, a traditional Italian dish, is now a favorite in America.

When you eat spaghetti, thank the Italians for the word as well as the food. Do you like to ski? The Norwegians gave us that activity and the name we call it by. Browse through a dictionary and you will hear "echoes" of people who came before. Even the very name of our country, *America,* is an "echo" of the Italian name *Amerigo.*

Immigrants Came to the United States

1. Prepare a list of questions that you would like to ask an immigrant. Perhaps you would like to ask when the person learned to speak English or when he began to feel "Americanized." You may want to ask what customs from his old home he still keeps. Let your teacher read over your questions.

The Zoltán Gaal family immigrated to America from Hungary.

2. Ask an immigrant to let you interview him. If you do not know an immigrant, ask your teacher or your parents to help you. You may need to write a letter to the person if he lives far away.

3. After you get your answers, remember to write a thank-you note to the person. Then write about the person you met. When you report to the class, be prepared to show on a globe or map the country that was once home to the person you interviewed.

A writer named Walt Whitman once said that our country is "a nation of nations." What do you think he meant? Do you agree? Try to name as many proofs as you can that America is the result of many cultures coming together in one place.

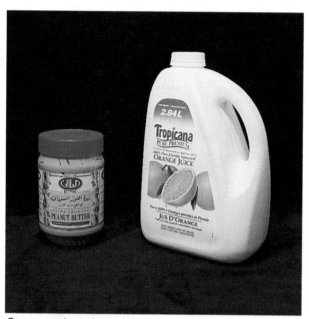

Some products have labels in two languages.

It may also be said, however, that America is entirely one nation. How is that so? It has one Constitution, one central government, and one president. How else are Americans one people? Do most Americans speak English? Do you think they should?

What reasons might some people give for not learning the language of their new home? People who were forced to immigrate—slaves—would resent the language that their captors used. Native Americans often felt that it was wrong to forget the speech that their people had used for centuries, to take up the language used by those who had invaded their lands. Some immigrants perhaps felt they were too old or too slow to learn another tongue. Still others could not learn until someone would teach them. If there were no others kind enough to teach them, they would sometimes give up trying to learn.

Today there is much debate over whether every American should learn to speak English. Some schools offer classes taught in two or more different languages. Many street signs have two or three languages giving the same message. Do you see this as a good or bad method of dealing with the language problem?

Making Their Own Language

Although most immigrants learn the language of their new country and can communicate in it (sometimes with an accent), sometimes people mix the old and new languages, making a third language.

Gullah weaver and baskets

In Pennsylvania, German settlers kept some of their old language, Deutsch, and took some of the new speech they heard from their Pennsylvania neighbors. The way of talking that came from that mixture kept the word order and a few of the old words mingled with English. It is called "Pennsylvania Dutch." Can you see the mixture even in the name?

Along the coasts of South Carolina and Georgia live people descended from people of the Sierra Leone coast of West Africa. Brought as slaves to grow rice in the Sea Islands, these people learned only enough English to speak to their masters. They kept many of their own words and patterns of speech. The people, and their speech, became known as *Gullah.*

Gullah uses more than four thousand words from African languages, mostly from groups such as the Fanti, Bambara, Wolof, Mende, and Krio. Because the Islands were long isolated from modern life, more than one hundred thousand people still speak Gullah and many (perhaps ten thousand) speak only Gullah. Children learn English in schools, but Gullah is now a written language and is studied as a second language in some schools.

SEA ISLANDS

■ Region where Gullah is spoken

Becoming "American"

Why do you think English is the main language of America? Why do you think that one of the Native American languages or French or Chinese or Spanish is not? There are many people from many places here in the United States. Why are there not many languages?

For people to live in one place together, they have to be able to communicate with each other. Early settlers sometimes used sign language to talk with their Native American neighbors. But eventually, both parties had to learn some of the other's words. There were many languages spoken by the Native Americans, too many to find one that all should learn.

The first newcomers who had the most influence were English— they built permanent towns much like the ones in England, set up English laws, and brought English books and traditions. Some English settlers learned Sioux, some Cree, some Algonquian. But all Native Americans who met Englishmen had to know a little English. When other immigrants came to America, they usually came into towns where English was already being spoken and English laws were being obeyed. To fit in, the later immigrants had to adapt to English talk and English ways. Thus English became the language of America.

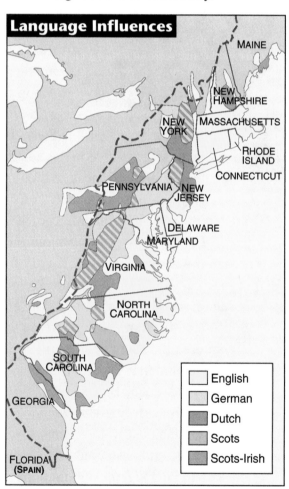

Language Influences

MAINE
NEW HAMPSHIRE
NEW YORK
MASSACHUSETTS
RHODE ISLAND
CONNECTICUT
PENNSYLVANIA
NEW JERSEY
DELAWARE
MARYLAND
VIRGINIA
NORTH CAROLINA
SOUTH CAROLINA
GEORGIA
FLORIDA (SPAIN)

☐ English
☐ German
■ Dutch
☐ Scots
■ Scots-Irish

One Swedish woman who came into an English settlement and could not understand the neighbors said, "It is like standing outside looking in, with the door locked on both the inside and the outside. You cannot go in and they cannot let you in, but I have decided that I shall be one of the neighbors. I am going to learn the American language!"

And she did, trading English lessons for spinning wool for someone. The next spring, she taught English to Danish immigrants. Then later she taught English to some people she would never have believed she would.

One day, Anna saw that a group of Chippewa had camped nearby. She took some bread and yarn that she had made and went to visit. At first, she did not know how to talk to the Chippewa. She wrote in her diary, "There is a strong conviction inside myself: that all human beings . . . have certain rights that no other human beings have the right to violate."

Anna and Mia, a daughter of one of the Chippewa chiefs, became good friends. Soon Anna was welcome in the camp, and Anna looked forward to the time every year when her friends would come back.

After many years, other settlers wanted to run the Chippewa off, to "put them in their place." Anna asked, "What is 'their place' in their own country?"

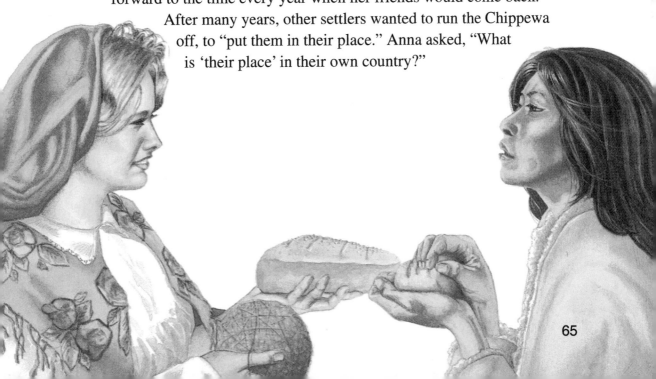

Anna did not see her friends for a long time. Then she got a letter from a preacher rather far away. It said that he had met some Chippewa people who could spin and weave and who talked "the American language with a Swedish accent." Anna smiled. There might be much wrong in the new country; but when people wanted to, they could work together to overcome it.

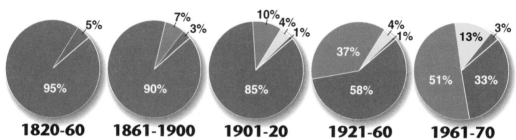

| 1820-60 | 1861-1900 | 1901-20 | 1921-60 | 1961-70 |

Immigration Today

Compare the graphs above. Were the same groups of people coming in 1960 that came in 1860? Can you say what group of immigrants increased most between 1961 and 1985? Is the heritage of your family represented on the charts?

People are still coming to America. Sometimes they come illegally, crossing the borders without proper admittance.

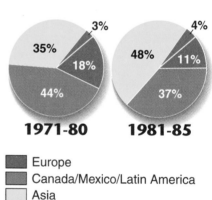

1971-80   **1981-85**

■ Europe
■ Canada/Mexico/Latin America
□ Asia
■ Other

Some come on small, risky boats from Haiti and Cuba; some come on foot from Mexico; some brave the Pacific to come from the Asian coasts. Many come legally, from Haiti, Cuba, Mexico, and all over the world. Wherever they come from, immigrants bring their ways of cooking and talking, thinking and celebrating. And they all enter a culture that has certain expectations of them—and for them.

4

Preaching
the Word

Julia Ward Howe looked out upon the fires that night, dozens and dozens warming the Union soldiers near Washington, D.C. She heard the soldiers singing; she felt the coming of war in her heart, weighing her with sadness and determination. She turned to God for comfort and strength. And the next morning she wrote a poem that told in grand and somber words how many Americans were feeling. The poem became one of America's most famous patriotic songs, "The Battle Hymn of the Republic." This is the second verse:

> I have seen Him in the watchfires of a hundred circling camps;
> They have builded Him an altar in the evening dews and damps;
> I can read His righteous sentence by the dim and flaring lamps;
> His day is marching on.

Men who sat around campfires awaiting the morning, and battle, had much to think about. Death was near for many, and many did not feel ready. Some tried not to think about death too much—they played cards and joked with each other. Others wrote letters, telling their wives not to worry and their children to keep watching for them to come home. But others, many others, started to think about their souls and what would happen if they were killed.

An actor at a reenactment plays a flute as soldiers in the Civil War did.

A scene from the film Sheffey, *showing how a camp meeting would have looked*

There were, among the men in most camps, preachers who knew how to talk to men facing death. Called *chaplains,* these preachers told the soldiers how Christ had already suffered death for them so that when they died—whether tomorrow on the battlefield or at home as old men—they need not fear. They told the men that they had only to believe in Christ. Many soldiers accepted Christ during the war.

After the war, many American soldiers were different. The terrible battles they had seen and the destruction they still saw everywhere kept them thinking about how short life was. Those who had lived through battles and cannon fire often came back determined to live better lives. It had been many years since there was so much interest in godly things.

The revival did not stop on the battlefields and in the camps. It swept across the country, touching almost every city, every village. Songwriters wrote many more hymns and gospel songs. Circuit-riding preachers went out by the hundreds. They traveled on horseback and held camp meetings. Church attendance grew. And in the hearts of Christians in America and other countries was a growing desire to take the gospel to the ends of the earth.

Missions Begins at Home:
Dwight L. Moody (1837-99)

Dwight was tired. Cutting broomcorn was a hard job, and he had been working since morning. But he had almost finished the field, and the eight-year-old knew his mother would be pleased with the money he had earned.

The Moody family lived in Massachusetts. All the Moody children learned to work when they were young. Their father had died when Dwight was only four. Mrs. Moody taught her nine children to trust the Lord for the things they needed, but she also expected them to work.

When Dwight was older, he agreed to work for a neighboring farmer. He received his meals for his pay. But Dwight did not like the way things turned out. "Mother," Dwight said, "I am not going to work for that man any longer."

"Why not, Son? The work isn't too hard for you, is it?" Mrs. Moody was puzzled. Dwight had been pleased to get the job. "Are you getting enough to eat?" she asked.

Dwight answered, "I guess I get enough, Mother. But do you know what I've had for the last nineteen meals? Cornmeal mush and milk. That's all! Meal after meal! I'm tired of it. I'm not going back!"

Mrs. Moody sighed. She knew how he felt. "Dwight, you promised to work all winter. You must keep your promise. You must keep every promise you make, even when it is hard or unpleasant. God expects us to keep our word." Dwight went back to work, but he never learned to like farming.

One day when Dwight was seventeen, an older brother gave him five dollars. Dwight believed that this was his chance. He told his family good-bye and took a train for Boston. Dwight's uncle, Sam Holton, had a shoe store in Boston, but Dwight did not ask him for a job. He wanted to get a job on his own.

For a week the country boy hunted for work, but no one would hire him. He ran out of money, and he was hungry. Finally, he went to his uncle and asked for a job in his shoe store.

Mr. Holton thought it over. He did not like his nephew much because the boy was bold and liked to have things his own way. At last he told Dwight he could have a job if he would make three promises. First, he must do his best. Second, he must ask about things he did not understand. Third, he must go to Sunday school and church every Sunday. Dwight agreed.

Dwight had gone to church almost every Sunday of his life, but he was not a Christian. One day his Sunday school teacher in Boston decided to tell Dwight that he needed to be saved. He went to the shoe store and found the young man in the back, wrapping up shoes. The man reminded Dwight that Christ loved him and that the Lord wanted Dwight to love Him too. He asked Dwight whether he wanted to be saved. And there in the back room of a shoe store, Dwight L. Moody gave his life to Christ.

In those days, the talk was always about going west. Moody listened and thought about it. At last he made up his mind and told his uncle he was leaving. He went to the train station, bought a ticket to Chicago, and got on the train.

Two days after Moody reached Chicago, he found a job in another shoe store. On the first Wednesday night in Chicago, he went to a prayer meeting. He quickly made many friends there.

Moody did not forget that he had given his life to the Lord. He worked as hard for the Lord on Sunday as he did for himself during the week. His special job was bringing children to a mission Sunday school that was held on Sunday afternoons.

One of Moody's Sunday school classes; Moody is in the back row on the left.

Three years passed. By then almost a thousand children were coming to his Sunday school, most of them poor. They all loved Mr. Moody. He understood them because he had been poor too.

One Sunday afternoon Abraham Lincoln visited Moody's class. He heard the songs and prayers. He told the children, "I was once as poor as any boy in this school, but I am now president of the United States. If you will attend to what is taught you here, some of you may yet be president of the United States."

73

Mr. Hibbert, a fellow teacher, became too sick to teach his Sunday school class any more. He asked Moody to visit each of his pupils with him before he died. He wanted to ask each one to become a Christian. Moody wanted to work that day, but he thought he should help his friend. In house after house, Moody watched Mr. Hibbert plead with his students, sincerely grieving over their souls. Almost all the students were saved that day.

Now young Mr. Moody knew what he was going to do. He knew that he would rather see people saved than be the richest man in the world. The next day he quit his job. He chose to work only for God.

In April 1861, Fort Sumter fell. Now Moody had another choice to make. Should he join the army? He agreed with President Lincoln that the Southern states should not be allowed to leave the Union. He thought slavery was wrong. But he did not think he could kill a person. Besides, he had promised God that he would work for Him.

Some friends made a suggestion. Why not take the Word of God to the soldiers? Who needed to hear the gospel more than men who were going into battle or men who were wounded and perhaps dying? His friends promised to raise the money he would need if he would go.

So Moody went to the soldiers. He preached in army camps, in prison camps, in hospitals, on trains, and on boats. He took a trip on a boat down the Tennessee River. Four hundred fifty men were on the boat, many of them badly wounded. Moody made up his mind that he would not let any man on the boat die without hearing of Christ and heaven. And he did not: he went to each one with a drink of water and told him about the Lord.

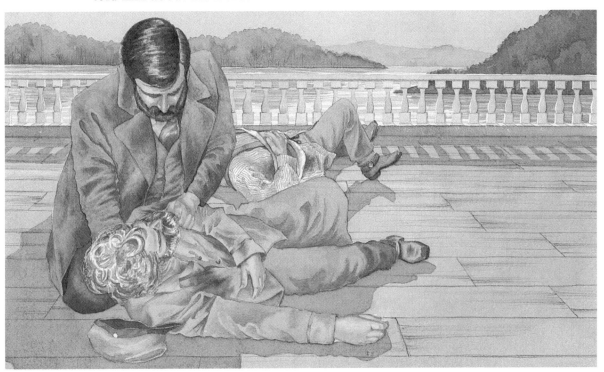

Nine times Moody went to the battlefields. Hundreds, even thousands of times, he knelt beside wounded and weary men and told them of Christ.

"Chaplain, help me die." The soldier wounded in a battle in Tennessee could only whisper. "I've been fighting Christ all my life."

Moody gave him many verses from the Bible, but the man did not understand. Then Moody read the story of Nicodemus in the third chapter of John. He came to verse fifteen: "That whosoever believeth in him should not perish, but have eternal life."

The soldier lifted his hand. "What's that? Is it true? Read it again. That's good! Won't you read it again?"

Moody read the verse three times. The man smiled with understanding now and died a forgiven man.

Moody also went to a camp near Chicago where prisoners from the Southern army were held. Hundreds of these men were saved as they listened to God's Word.

One night Moody heard a preacher say, "The world has yet to see what God can do with one man who is wholly committed to Him." Moody could not get the words out of his mind. Before he went to sleep that night, he told God that he would be that man.

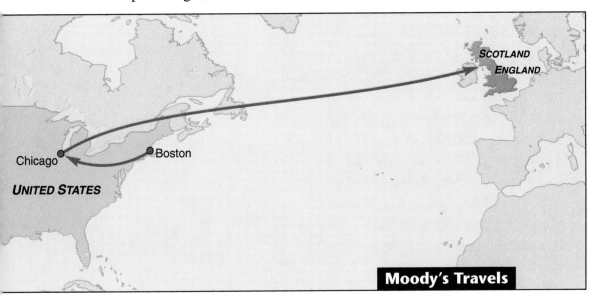

Moody's Travels

Moody met a singer named Ira Sankey and asked him to work with him. Moody, Sankey, and their wives went to England and Scotland to hold gospel meetings. Their American ways were strange to the people there. Dwight spoke as he had back home in the country, and Ira sang solos in the meetings. No one else did that in English churches. Crowds of people—about two million in the London services alone—came to hear the "crazy Americans." Thousands accepted the Lord Jesus as their Savior.

Mr. Moody started a school for girls and then a school for boys in his hometown of Northfield, Massachusetts. In Chicago he started a Bible school to train young men and women to serve God. When he died at age sixty-two, Dwight L. Moody had lived a life that showed the world what God could do through a man who was wholly committed to Him.

SCOTLAND

Pray On:
Mary Slessor (1848-1915)

Mary Slessor was a petite Scottish girl with brilliant blue eyes and curly red hair. She was born into a poor family. Her father drank too much, but she had a godly mother. At the age of eleven, Mary went to work at a spinning mill. She worked twelve hours a day six days a week to help with the family's finances. In her heart, however, she dreamed of going to Africa as a missionary. When she heard that David Livingstone—a famous missionary in Africa—had died, she asked her mother, "Could I become a missionary?" Her mother gave her permission. Mary learned of the customs and living conditions in Calabar, Nigeria, and believed that was the place God wanted her to go.

In September 1876, she sailed for Calabar. She began her work eagerly, wanting to see immediate results. But the Lord taught her to be patient. She was horrified by the custom of killing newborn twins. The people of Calabar believed that twins were the children of demons. Slessor was able to rescue some of these children and raise them as her own.

Calabar

After spending a few years at the mission station on the coast, Slessor felt God wanted her to go up the river to witness to several cannibal tribes. At first the mission was opposed to the idea, but finally she was allowed to go. Taking her children with her, she settled in one of the cannibal villages. Her love for the people was clear: she tended the sick and cared for the unwanted. The people returned her love by giving her the honored title of Ma ("mother").

Mary Slessor

When Calabar was taken over by the British government in 1889, Mary Slessor was made vice consul for the interior of the Niger Coast Protectorate. She was responsible for establishing law and order there. But she remained true to her primary task of winning people to the Lord; she faithfully gave out God's Word. When she moved fifteen years later, she left behind many Christians.

After thirty-nine years of loving service, her frail body could take no more; she went to be with the Lord on January 13, 1915. What was the secret to her successful work for the Lord? Mary Slessor said, "I have no idea how and why God has carried me over so many hard places, and made these hordes submit to me . . . except in answer to prayer at home for me. It is all beyond my comprehension. The only way I can explain it is on the ground that I have been prayed for more than most. Pray on—power lies that way."

To the Uttermost:
J. Hudson Taylor (1832-1905)

J. Hudson Taylor was a man who set himself to do God's will. At the age of five, after hearing his father talk about the need for taking the gospel to China, he declared, "One day I will go to that country." In 1849, at seventeen, he dedicated himself to the Lord's service. In 1853, after receiving a medical degree, he set sail for China.

A Chinese city such as Taylor might have seen

After nearly six months, the twenty-two-year-old Hudson Taylor arrived in Shanghai. In the city streets were men with long pigtails and women with tiny bound feet. Everywhere he heard the Chinese language. Later, he wrote in his journal: "Mingled with thankfulness for deliverance from many dangers and joy at finding myself at last on Chinese soil came a vivid realization of the great distance between me and those I loved, and that I was a stranger in a strange land."

Taylor spent many hours learning to speak and read Chinese. He came to believe that the best way to reach the Chinese was to become as nearly Chinese as possible. After much prayer, Taylor decided to follow Paul in being made all things to all men (I Cor. 9:22). He knew the other missionaries would think he was wrong, even crazy. But Taylor was sure it was God's leading:

"We wish to see . . . men and women truly Christian but truly Chinese in every right sense. We wish to see Churches of such believers presided over by pastors and officers of their own countrymen, worshipping God in their own tongue, in edifices of a thoroughly native style."

To the horror of the other missionaries in China, Taylor had his head shaved except for a section in back. Into those remaining hairs, he had a pigtail woven (eventually he grew his own, which he shaved off when on furlough in England). He purchased Chinese clothing, including a long silk outer gown with full sleeves that marked him as a teacher. He was soon received eagerly by the Chinese, who listened intently to his message. Many were won to the Lord because of his willingness to give up his English appearance and be scorned by his friends.

Missionaries were allowed to teach only near the coasts and the ports of China. Soon after he landed, however, Taylor began thinking about the people living inland. During the next seven years, he made many inland trips. With each visit, he wanted more and more to go to the millions who had not heard the gospel. In 1860 poor health forced him to return to England, yet his desire to help the Chinese grew stronger.

> "But what things were gain to me, those I counted loss for Christ. Yea doubtless, and I count all things but loss for the excellency of the knowledge of Christ Jesus my Lord: for whom I have suffered the loss of all things, and do count them but dung, that I may win Christ."
>
> **Philippians 3:7-8**

Hudson Taylor dressed in Chinese clothes

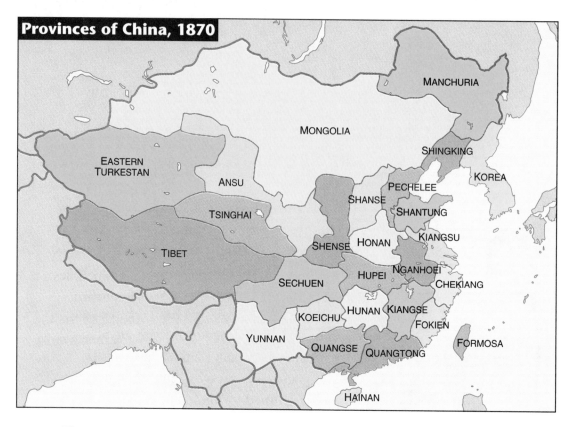

Provinces of China, 1870

Five years went by. Taylor revised the Chinese New Testament, waiting to go where there were "a million a month dying without God." But in the summer of 1865, he prayed that God would send twenty-four workers to inland China. Immediately he felt a peace in his heart and strength in his body. He opened a bank account in the name of the China Inland Mission, an organization dedicated to missionary work in China. He was acting on faith: the account held only ten pounds. God honored his faith. On May 26, 1866, Taylor, his family, and twenty-four dedicated men and women set sail for China.

Hudson Taylor and the other missionaries were often called "foreign devil" or "Western dog." Some Chinese people hated foreigners so much that they spread terrible stories. The worst was that the missionaries kidnapped children to use their eyes and hearts for medicine. Returning good for evil, the missionaries won respect among the people. By the time he died in 1905, Hudson Taylor had seen mission stations set up in every province.

Getting Missionary Support

Most missionaries are supported by money from churches and people in their home country. The missionaries use this money to pay for the things they need: food, clothing, and housing. The money often pays the costs of their ministry too. Because other Christians give money to their work, the missionaries can spend their time spreading the gospel and training Christians.

Missionaries receive money for their work in different ways. Sometimes one church will support just a few missionaries. Sometimes many churches give money to a *mission board.* The mission board uses the money to support missionaries. Most often, missionaries visit many churches and ask each one to give a part of the money they need.

When missionaries go to a field, they usually go with the promise of a certain amount of money to support them each month. If, after they arrive on the field, prices rise faster than expected, the missionaries may have to move to cheaper housing and cut food and clothing expenses. It is important that God's people make themselves aware of missionaries' needs and strive to meet them.

The Randall Studdard family, missionaries in northern Cameroon

To Help Missionaries

1. Get your Notebook, a pen or pencil, and the letter or card your teacher gives you.

A letter from Cameroon

2. Read the letter or card from the missionary your teacher tells you about.

3. Summarize the letter for your classmates.

4. Make suggestions about how your class can help meet missionaries' needs.

Talking about how to be a help to missionaries

Other Missionaries

Francisco Penzotti

In 1864, thirteen-year-old Francisco Penzotti received an amazing offer. One of his relatives was moving from Italy to South America, and he asked Francisco to go with him. The young Italian eagerly agreed, and soon he was living in Montevideo, Uruguay. One day when he was about twenty-five years old, Penzotti attended a church service, and he was converted.

Penzotti began passing out Bibles in Bolivia, Chile, and Peru. While in Peru, Penzotti realized the people needed more than just Bibles. He moved his family to the city of Callao and began a church.

Modern seller of Bibles in area where Penzotti worked

Laws about non-Catholic churches were very strict in Peru. Penzotti carefully obeyed the rules, but in 1890 the authorities arrested him for breaking the religious laws. Protestants and other lovers of freedom all over Latin America rallied to support Penzotti. Newspapers, ministers, and politicians in the United States urged Peru's government to release the preacher. For two years his case dragged through the courts while Penzotti lived in a filthy jail known as "the house that kills." At last the government released Penzotti. He had won not only his own freedom but also the freedom to preach the gospel even more widely throughout Peru.

Pandita Ramabai

Pandita Ramabai was born in India in 1858. Her father, a high-caste Hindu teacher, unlike other Hindu leaders of that time, believed that women should receive the same education as men. He taught Pandita to read and memorize the religious literature of India.

After her parents died in a famine, Pandita married an Indian lawyer. Within two years, her husband

Pandita with the people that she helped

died, leaving her with a small child. A widow in Hinduism had to shave her head, was forced to wear special garments, and could associate with very few people. Pandita began studying English and the Scriptures with a Christian schoolteacher from Great Britain. Pandita became convinced that Christianity was the true religion. She believed the Bible, but she did not personally accept Christ as Savior.

Pandita Ramabai

Pandita began a home for young widows. And she kept reading the Bible. Soon she realized that she needed the Savior. She led her students to Christ as well. Many Hindus who had been giving her money and other help pulled away. With the help of God, however, Pandita continued her home. And the work flourished; as many as nineteen hundred girls lived at the home at one time. By the time of her death in 1922, Pandita Ramabai had taken in and helped over three thousand people.

John Lang

AUSTRALIA

• Sydney

John Dunmore Lang

John Lang moved from Scotland to Sydney, Australia, in 1823 to minister to the Presbyterian settlers there. He soon earned a reputation for being both bold and blunt. He was sometimes a little stubborn and outspoken, but no one could deny his courage and sincerity.

Lang loved his new homeland. He believed Australia had a good future if everyone would work hard to make the land better. He also wanted to bring self-rule to Australia. He hoped that it would become a self-governing republic like the United States. Lang believed it was every Christian's duty to work for the improvement of his nation.

Lang was a Christian first and a statesman second. He preached all over Australia. He spent his own money to bring settlers from Scotland and Germany but not just to help the country economically. One group of Germans, for example, came only to help reach the Australian people with the gospel. Lang began new churches, brought in more pastors, and even built a college—much of this at his own expense. In serving God, Lang contributed to the future of an entire continent.

Andrew Murray

Andrew Murray was born in South Africa, where his parents had moved from Scotland to minister to the Dutch settlers. When Andrew was only ten, his father sent him to Scotland to study. There Murray decided to follow in his father's footsteps and enter the ministry. After graduating from Aberdeen University, Murray went to Holland. Although he had studied the Bible and theology for years, he did not feel sure that he was saved. But while in Holland, young Murray

Andrew Murray, who spent his long life in God's service

trusted the Lord completely. He began to practice his Dutch intensely so that he could teach both British and Dutch settlers in South Africa.

In 1848 Murray returned to his homeland. He pastored several churches and became a leader in the Dutch Reformed Church. Some Dutch Reformed pastors began to teach that Christ was not the Son of God and that His blood could not save people from their sins. Murray and the other Bible-believing pastors did everything they could to stop such preaching in South Africa. Murray followed the Bible's command to "earnestly contend for the faith which was once delivered unto the saints" (Jude 3).

Andrew Murray was both a preacher and a writer. He toured South Africa, preaching in churches all over the country. He also helped start a school for training preachers and another for missionaries. He wrote more than 250 books, in both Dutch and English. He organized missions in other parts of Africa. He, like many other missionaries, found that having compassion for others' souls did indeed make a difference (Jude 22).

SOUTH AFRICA

5

The Fifty States

When you look at a map of the United States, what do you see? Fifty different sections of land, each with its own shape and color. Some of these sections are large, and others are quite small. Each section has its own name, often a beautiful name that rolls off the tongue like a line of poetry. The sections are separated from one another by lines—some straight and some squiggly. And all these sections together make up the country we call the United States.

Come along on a tour of the fifty states without even leaving your chair. See the special things each state has to offer.

Portland
Head Light

Maine

In the Northeast, the nation's easternmost state is Maine. Because of Maine's cool climate, pine trees grow well in its forests. Maine's nickname is "the Pine Tree State," and the white pine is its official state tree.

Maine is well known for its long, rocky coastline. A famous lighthouse called the Portland Head Light stands on Maine's southeast coast. This 101-foot lighthouse has steered ships away from the rocky shore since 1791. Because of their nearness to the sea, many people in Maine like to fish. Lobsters are most often the catch of the day.

New Hampshire

Southwest of Maine is New Hampshire. "The Granite State" gets its nickname from the large granite quarries found there. New Hampshire was the only colony that British soldiers never invaded during the War for Independence. New Hampshire took as its motto "Live Free or Die."

New Hampshire still boasts many buildings and churches built during the Colonial period.

People often visit New Hampshire to see its mountains dressed in their fall colors. One peak in the White Mountains has an interesting rock formation that people call "Old Man of the Mountain." What do you think it looks like? It looks like the head of an old man frozen in stone, looking out across the valley.

Vermont

New Hampshire's neighbor to the west is Vermont, "the Green Mountain State." Can you guess how it got its nickname? If you stand at any given spot in Vermont,

Autumn on a Vermont farm

you can see mountains in at least one direction. Vermont got its name from the French phrase *vert mont* meaning "green mountain."

Do you like to eat maple syrup on pancakes? Vermont is the state to thank for most of the maple syrup produced in this country. In autumn its thousands of maple trees turn to bright oranges and golds. The Bennington Battle Monument, a 306-foot granite tower, was built to honor the men who won a famous battle against the British in 1777.

New York

West of Vermont lies the largest northeastern state, New York. George Washington took his oath of office as our first president in New York. He once said that New York might become the seat of a new empire. New York is nicknamed "the Empire State."

When you think of New York, do you think first of New York City? With its busy streets and tall skyscrapers, the city is a major center of New York life. Have you ever heard of a building so large

New York City

that it took up more than one zip code? The World Trade Center has a separate zip code for each of its two towers. Another attraction is the magnificent Niagara Falls near Buffalo. And what famous lady raises her torch above New York Harbor?

This minuteman statue stands at Lexington Battle Green.

Massachusetts

Massachusetts, New York's neighbor to the east, is one of four states that are known as *commonwealths*. Massachusetts is named for the people who first lived there. Its nickname is "the Bay State" because it used to be the Massachusetts Bay Colony.

Can you remember any important historical events that happened in Massachusetts? At Plymouth Plantation, visitors can see what Pilgrim villages might have looked like in the 1620s. In Boston they can walk the Freedom Trail, visiting sixteen Colonial sites. At Lexington Battle Green they can learn about the first battle of the War for Independence. Cape Cod, the state's southeastern peninsula, offers sandy beaches, quaint houses, and boat rides.

Mark Twain's Victorian home in Rocky Hill

Connecticut

Connecticut is south of Massachusetts. In the Algonquian language, *Connecticut* means "on the long tidal river." The Connecticut River divides the state in two. Do you remember the Great Compromise at the Constitutional Convention of 1787? A man from Connecticut thought of that. Connecticut also had the first written state constitution. Those are two reasons that Connecticut is nicknamed "the Constitution State."

Connecticut has the nation's largest ship museum, called Mystic Seaport. With its tall-masted boats and old buildings, it looks like a whaling village from the 1800s. Since 1701, Connecticut has been the home of Yale University. Many aircraft engines and parts are produced in Connecticut.

Rhode Island

East of Connecticut is Rhode Island, our country's smallest state. Its official nickname is "the Ocean State," but it is often called "Little Rhody." Rhode Island was begun by people who disagreed with the Puritan religion. They named its capital Providence because they wanted to thank God for His care and protection.

Slater Mill

Rhode Island is actually not an island. It is a mainland and thirty-six small islands in Narragansett Bay. Would you like to live in a mansion? The city of Newport has mansions and other historic buildings. Trinity Church in Newport has a specially marked pew where George Washington once sat and prayed. In Pawtucket is Slater Mill, where the American textile industry began. Rhode Island is also a center for jewelry making.

Liberty Bell

Pennsylvania

South of New York is Pennsylvania. Pennsylvania means "Penn's Woods." William Penn started the colony for Quakers. Pennsylvania is nicknamed "the Keystone State" because it was at the center of the arch formed by the first thirteen states.

Do you like chocolate? You would probably enjoy a trip to the world's largest chocolate factory in Hershey, Pennsylvania. Even the streetlamps in Hershey are shaped like chocolate kisses. Pennsylvania Dutch people live in southeast Pennsylvania. They are skilled in cooking, arts, and crafts. Philadelphia, which means "city of brotherly love," displays the Liberty Bell, a famous symbol of American freedom. Two of our nation's most important documents were drawn up in Philadelphia. Can you name them?

Workers harvest cranberries from a bog.

New Jersey

New Jersey, "the Garden State," is east of Pennsylvania. Its nickname comes from its flower gardens, farms, and orchards. New Jersey is the most crowded state; it has more people per square mile than any other state.

Have you ever tasted juice or sauce made from cranberries? Cranberries are often grown in New Jersey's bogs, or swampy areas. At Batsto State Historic Site, visitors can stroll through a Colonial village and watch ironmakers and glassmakers at work. Would you like to know what a fort from the War for Independence looked like? Morristown National Historical Park includes Fort Nonsense, a restored fort that was first built in 1777.

Delaware

Fishing is a popular industry.

South of New Jersey is Delaware. Delaware is nicknamed "the First State" because it was the first of the thirteen colonies to accept the United States Constitution. Because of their brave fighting during the War for Independence, Delaware's troops came to be called the "Blue Hen's Chickens," after a famous breed of fighting gamecock. The blue hen chicken is now the state bird of Delaware.

People from many different European countries have lived in Delaware. At the Zwaanendael Museum in Lewes, visitors can learn about the Dutch colony founded in Delaware in 1631. Swedish and Finnish settlers built America's first log cabins in this state. The Old Swedes Church in Wilmington is our nation's oldest church still in use. In the southwest corner of Delaware live descendants of the Nanticoke people, who hold a special powwow in Millsboro every September.

Chesapeake Bay is dotted with sailboats every summer.

Maryland

We complete our tour of the northeastern states with Maryland. Named for the wife of King Charles I of England, Maryland is nicknamed "the Old Line State." The soldiers in the Maryland line were famous for their courage in the War for Independence.

If you have ever wanted to be a knight, Maryland would be a good place to visit. Maryland's state sport is jousting, or fighting with lances on horseback. Jousting contests are held there each year. Maryland is also the home of Fort McHenry. The British attacked this fort in 1814, but its soldiers held their ground. Francis Scott Key wrote "The Star-Spangled Banner" as he watched the American flag flying over Fort McHenry the next morning.

Virginia

Virginia is our first stop in the South-east region of the United States. Virginia, a commonwealth, was named after Elizabeth I of England, the "Virgin Queen." It is nicknamed "Old Dominion" because of its loyalty to the British crown in the 1600s. Virginia is often called "Mother of Presidents." Eight presidents were born there. Can you name any of them?

Mount Vernon mansion

Two famous homes are located in Virginia. One is Mount Vernon, George Washington's home. Another is Monticello, the mansion Thomas Jefferson designed for himself. Would you like to see what a Colonial wigmaker's or candlemaker's shop looked like? Williamsburg has these and many other shops. It also has The College of William and Mary, the second-oldest college in the United States. In Arlington National Cemetery, visitors can see memorials to Robert E. Lee and John F. Kennedy as well as the tombs of honored military heroes.

The Washington Monument and the Capitol Building

Washington, D.C.

Located between Virginia and Maryland is our nation's capital, Washington, D.C. *D.C.* stands for "District of Columbia." The city of Washington takes up the entire District of Columbia. Washington, D.C., is not a state. It is a section of land owned by the United States government.

West Virginia

West Virginia is northwest of Virginia. It is nicknamed "the Mountain State" because of its rugged land. The mountains and hills of the Appalachian Range nearly cover the state. West Virginia was once part of Virginia. When Virginia joined the Confederacy, the northwestern part of the state broke away and formed its own government, remaining loyal to the Union. West Virginia has as its motto "Mountaineers Are Always Free."

West Virginia is rich with an important resource. Over half of its land has coal buried beneath it. Coal mining is one of West Virginia's primary industries, along with pottery and glassmaking. Have you ever played with glass marbles? West Virginia makes most of the nation's glass marbles at factories in Parkersburg. The historic town of Harpers Ferry, on the northern boundary of the state, has been restored to the way it was when John Brown seized its armory just before the Civil War.

Perhaps you have played with West Virginia's famous product?

Kentucky

Kentucky borders West Virginia on the northeast and Virginia on the east. Kentucky, a commonwealth, is nicknamed "the Bluegrass State." Kentucky's bluegrass actually looks green, but during the spring it blossoms with tiny blue flowers.

A horse farm in Kentucky's Bluegrass region

Have you ever watched the Kentucky Derby? It is the oldest horse race still being run each year in the United States. The first running was in 1875. The Bluegrass region of Kentucky, around Lexington, is an ideal place for raising Thoroughbred racehorses. Does the thought of buried treasure excite you? Most of the gold owned by the United States—worth more than six billion dollars—is stored in Fort Knox's underground vaults.

Lookout Mountain

Tennessee

Tennessee is Kentucky's neighbor to the south. It got its name from a Cherokee village in that region called *Tanasie*. Tennessee is nicknamed "the Volunteer State" because its people were known for being willing to volunteer for military service.

The Great Smoky Mountains are located in eastern Tennessee. On a peak called Lookout Mountain, an important battle was fought in the War Between the States. Visitors to this battleground can see parts of five different states on a clear day. Another popular place to see is the Hermitage, Andrew Jackson's home near Nashville. Tennessee has another nickname: "the Big Bend State." The Tennessee River has a large bend in it, and it flows through the state twice.

Wright Brothers National Memorial

North Carolina

East of Tennessee is North Carolina. North Carolina's nickname is "the Tar Heel State." Most people think this name goes back to the Civil War. Soldiers from North Carolina offered to "tar the heels" of some other Confederate soldiers who had fled from a battle and left them to fight on their own.

Cape Hatteras, at the tip of an island off North Carolina's coast, is known as "the Graveyard of the Atlantic." Many ships have been wrecked there, as well as on the other islands and reefs offshore. North Carolina contains parts of the Great Smoky Mountains and the Blue Ridge Mountains. Why do you think this state is often called "First in Flight"? In Kitty Hawk, the Wright brothers made the first successful flight in a powered aircraft.

South Carolina

South Carolina is North Carolina's neighbor to the south. It is nicknamed "the Palmetto State" after its state tree.

South Carolina played a key role in the American Civil War. It was the first state to secede from the Union. The first shot of the war was fired at Fort Sumter, on an island

The gardens of Middleton Plantation in Charleston

off South Carolina's coast. Visitors can still view the remains of this fort in Charleston Harbor. Charleston also has many stately houses from before the war. Have you ever been inside a fabric store? There is a good chance that some of the fabrics you see were produced in South Carolina. Making textiles is its biggest industry.

Stone Mountain

Georgia

Georgia is southwest of South Carolina. Georgia is famous for the large, sweet peaches it grows. It is nick-named "the Peach State." Another nickname is "the Empire State of the South" because it is the largest southern state. It has more land than any other state east of the Mississippi River.

Near Atlanta is Stone Mountain, which displays a huge sculpture of three Confederate leaders on horses. Which three men do you think these are? They are Jefferson Davis, Robert E. Lee, and Stonewall Jackson. Underneath Georgia are large deposits of marble. Georgia marble was used to build the Lincoln Memorial. Do you like peanuts? Georgia produces more of them than any other state.

Florida

Orange groves

South of Georgia is Florida, one of the states people visit most often. Florida's nick-name is "the Sunshine State" because of its warm, mild climate. The Spanish explorer Juan Ponce de León first claimed this land for Spain in 1513. He saw all of the flowers there and named it Florida, or *flowery* in Spanish.

Florida contains the oldest city in the United States. St. Augustine was founded in 1565, and in this city is the oldest house in the nation, built in the late 1500s. Florida offers many beautiful beaches and palm trees. It is also the home of Walt Disney World. The southern tip of Florida lies near the island of Cuba. Many Cuban people have come to live in Florida. Did you drink orange juice with your breakfast this morning? Florida produces almost all of the nation's orange juice.

Rocket Park in Huntsville

Alabama

Georgia's western neighbor is the state of Alabama. Alabama's nickname is "the Yellowhammer State," after the state bird, which has yellow spots beneath its wings. During the Civil War, some of the Alabama soldiers, also called *yellowhammers,* wore uniforms trimmed with bright yellow cloth.

The city of Huntsville has been called *Rocket City, U.S.A.* It is the home of Redstone Arsenal and the George C. Marshall Space Flight Center, where scientists develop rockets and other space flight equipment. In Mobile Bay, visitors can see the U.S.S. *Alabama,* a famous battleship preserved from World War II. Do you remember the man who discovered over three hundred uses for the peanut? George Washington Carver taught at Tuskegee Institute in Alabama, a college for African Americans. Today the college houses a museum in his honor.

Mississippi

West of Alabama is Mississippi. Mississippi takes its name from the river that borders it on the west. The name means "Great Water." Mississippi is nicknamed "the Magnolia State."

Natchez, the oldest town along the Mississippi River, is a good place to find old plantation homes and colorful flowers. Do you remember which battle was a turning point in the American Civil War? Vicksburg National Military Park is a memorial of the battle of Vicksburg, which ended in victory for the Union. Biloxi, on the southern coast of Mississippi, is often called "the Shrimp Capital" of the United States because its bay is well supplied with shrimp. Mississippi is also known for its wooded, swampy areas like Cypress Swamp near Jackson.

Shrimp is the catch of the day for these boats.

101

Waterfalls on a river in the Ozarks

Arkansas

Arkansas is northwest of Mississippi. Arkansas was once nicknamed "the Land of Opportunity." What opportunities does Arkansas offer? It has beautiful mountains and valleys, good farmland, rich mines, and busy factories. Arkansas means "land of downstream people."

Now Arkansas is "the Natural State." Hot Springs, Arkansas, is the only city in the United States that has almost an entire national park within it. People believe the park's natural hot springs relieve pain from arthritis and other diseases. How would you like to search for diamonds? Arkansas also has a public diamond mine near Murfreesboro. Visitors who find diamonds there are allowed to keep them. The people of Arkansas, especially those in the Ozark region, are skilled in music and crafts such as woodcarving.

Egrets are a common sight on Avery Island.

Louisiana

South of Arkansas is Louisiana. Louisiana was named in 1682 by the explorer La Salle in honor of the king of France, Louis XIV. Louisiana is nicknamed "the Pelican State." Brown pelicans live along its coast. It is also often called "Sportsman's Paradise."

Louisiana is well known for its bayous. A bayou is a marshy, slow-moving body of water that flows into a lake or river. Many of Louisiana's people are descendants of its French and Spanish settlers. They are called Creoles. Others, known as *Cajuns,* descended from French settlers in Canada. Both groups have their own special types of spicy food. Visitors often stop in New Orleans to see the French and Spanish parts of the city. In the French Quarter are old buildings with fancy iron balconies and a large open marketplace called the French Market.

Ohio

In the Middle West region of the United States, our first stop is Ohio, "the Buckeye State." A buckeye is a type of tree that once grew in the state, but most are gone now because settlers used them to build their cabins. *Ohio* means "something great" in the Iroquois language.

Ohio was the first part of the Northwest Territory to become a state. In 1833, Oberlin College opened for both men and women to attend. Before that time, only men could go to college. Much of Ohio is farmland. Its two major crops are corn and soybeans. In Hillsboro is the Great Serpent Mound, a hill in the shape of a snake built by Native Americans. The Pro Football Hall of Fame is in Canton. In its museum, visitors can see uniforms and equipment worn by famous players.

The Great Serpent Mound contains seven deep curves and extends for more than a quarter of a mile.

Michigan

Mackinac Bridge

North of Ohio is Michigan, which consists of two separate land areas, the Upper Peninsula and the Lower Peninsula. Can you find these two sections on a map? Michigan's nickname is "the Wolverine State" because its wolverine pelts were once valuable items for trade.

Michigan's two peninsulas are connected by the five-mile-long Mackinac Bridge. The shoreline of Michigan touches four of the five great lakes, so water sports and fishing are popular there. Michigan produces more automobiles than any other state. Two men who built some of the first automobiles came from Detroit: Henry Ford and Ransom Olds. Battle Creek, Michigan, is known as the "Cereal Bowl of America." It is the world's leading cereal producer.

Quick teamwork during pit stops helped Gordon Johncock win this Indianapolis 500 by only 0.160 seconds.

Indiana

Indiana, west of Ohio, is called "the Hoosier State." Most people think *Hoosier* was once a slang word used as a greeting, meaning "Who's here?" Indiana is smaller than all the states west of it, except Hawaii.

Indiana is part of a wide section of the Middle West states called the Corn Belt. Its broad, flat plains make good farmland for corn, its main crop. Do you like car races? The nation's most famous automobile race, the Indianapolis 500, has taken place in Indiana each year since 1911. In the 1820s, people in New Harmony, Indiana, tried an experiment. They began teaching boys and girls together in their school. Most other American schools soon adopted their idea. Would you like to have attended the first professional baseball game? It was played in Fort Wayne, Indiana, in 1871.

The Sears Tower dominates the Chicago skyline.

Illinois

Illinois is west of Indiana. The rolling plains that produce one-sixth of all our nation's corn gave Illinois its nickname, "the Prairie State." Another nickname for the state is "the Land of Lincoln" because it was Abraham Lincoln's home for most of his life.

Illinois's most famous city is Chicago, on the coast of Lake Michigan. Almost half of the people in Illinois live in or near Chicago. The city is the home of the Sears Tower, one of the tallest buildings in the world. It is also famous for its industries, museums, and works of art. The first Ferris wheel was put into use at the World's Fair in Chicago in 1883. In Springfield, visitors can see where Lincoln lived before he went to Washington, D.C., as president. His gravesite is there also.

St. Louis arch

Missouri

Missouri, southwest of Illinois, has been given the nickname "the Show Me State." In a speech, a Missouri congressman said that he must be shown something, not just told it, to believe it. The name *Missouri* comes from an Indian word that means "town of the large canoes."

The Mississippi River borders Missouri on the east, and the Missouri River flows across the state. These two waterways, once a major center for transportation, make the land fertile for farming soybeans and corn, especially in the southern Boot Heel region. Can you see from the map how this region got its name? The two largest cities are Kansas City and St. Louis. People often call the tall arch in St. Louis the "Gateway to the West."

Iowa

North of Missouri is Iowa. Iowa is nicknamed "the Hawkeye State" in honor of Chief Black Hawk, whose people once owned some of Iowa's land. Sometimes Iowa is called "the Corn State" or "the land where the tall corn grows." It produces more corn than any other state.

Many of Iowa's farms also produce hogs and dairy cattle. Over 90 percent of Iowa is farmland. But only about 10 percent of Iowa's people are farmers. Most live in cities and small towns. Do you like popcorn? The largest popcorn factory is in Sioux City. In Elk Horn, Iowa, is a Danish windmill that was brought from Denmark piece by piece and rebuilt. In the Amana Colonies, founded by Germans, visitors can see how a woolen mill weaves sweaters and blankets.

The land where the tall corn grows

105

Some Holsteins in the Dells

Wisconsin

Wisconsin is east of Iowa and north of Illinois. In the 1820s, lead miners worked in Wisconsin and lived in caves they dug in the hillsides. They were called *badgers.* Wisconsin is nicknamed "the Badger State."

Black-and-white Holstein dairy cows dot Wisconsin's green pastures. It is often called "America's Dairyland" because it produces more milk than any other state. It also produces one-third of America's cheese and one-fourth of its butter. Two of the Great Lakes—Michigan and Superior—touch Wisconsin. Wisconsin Dells has interesting rock formations carved out of its sandstone cliffs and offers boat rides and water sports. Every year in Oshkosh, Wisconsin, airplanes fly in from around the world for a large experimental aircraft convention.

Minnesota

Wisconsin's neighbor to the west is Minnesota. *Minnesota* means "sky-tinted waters" in the Sioux language. Its nickname is "the Gopher State," but it is also known as "the Bread-and-Butter State," "the North Star State," "Land of Sky-Blue Waters," and "Land of 10,000 Lakes."

Have you eaten any bread or butter today? Minnesota produces more butter than any other state and is also well-known

Minnehaha Falls in Minneapolis

for its flour mills. Two of the state's largest cities, Minneapolis and St. Paul, are so close together that they are called the Twin Cities. Minnesota has very long, cold winters. At the St. Paul Winter Carnival, people make beautiful ice sculptures and compete in sports like ice-skating and ski-jumping. Duluth, on Minnesota's northeastern coast, is the busiest freshwater port in the nation.

A farm on North Dakota's Red River

North Dakota

West of Minnesota is North Dakota. North Dakota is nicknamed "the Flickertail State" because so many flickertail ground squirrels live there. *Dakota* is a Sioux word meaning "allies" or "friends."

Nearly all of North Dakota is covered with farms and ranches. Grains like winter wheat and durum wheat are its chief crops. Visitors to North Dakota may see oil wells at work on the prairies. Some of the state's soft-coal beds burn constantly with a soft glow that can be seen for miles at night. The Badlands in the southwest part of the state are a beautiful stretch of natural sandstone rock formations. At the Canadian border is the International Peace Garden, a park built in honor of the long-time friendship between the United States and Canada.

South Dakota

South Dakota is North Dakota's southern neighbor. How do you think the two states are alike? Both contain the Badlands, grow wheat as their main crop, and have many ranches. South Dakota's nickname is "the Coyote State." Why do you think that is?

Mount Rushmore

South Dakota is also different from North Dakota in several ways. Southwestern South Dakota contains the Black Hills region. These low, rocky mountains are covered with pine trees that look black when seen from the plains. South Dakota also has the Mount Rushmore National Memorial. Four presidents' heads are carved into the top of a 6,000-foot cliff. Can you name these presidents? The Corn Palace in Mitchell, South Dakota, has wall murals made of different colors of corn and other grains.

Nebraska

Chimney Rock was an important landmark to pioneers heading west.

Nebraska is south of South Dakota. "The Cornhusker State" is one of America's chief farming states. The nickname comes from the cornhusking contests once held there. *Nebraska* comes from an Oto word meaning "flat water."

About 95 percent of Nebraska is farmland. Wheat, corn, and cattle are its main products. Pioneers drove their wagons westward through Nebraska on the Oregon Trail. Some of their wagon ruts can still be seen now, more than a century later. Chimney Rock, shaped like a tall spire, is one site that marked the Oregon Trail. Nebraska's government is unique. Its legislature is unicameral, having one house instead of two.

Kansas

Windmill on a Kansas plain

Kansas, south of Nebraska, is nicknamed "the Sunflower State," after its state flower. The fighting between proslavery and antislavery groups centered in Kansas before the American Civil War. Kansas settlers took as their motto "To the Stars Through Difficulties." What do you think this means?

If you drove across Kansas in late summer, you would see fields and fields of golden, waving wheat. Kansas, often called the "Breadbasket of America," produces more wheat than any other state. Another of its nicknames is "Midway, U.S.A." The exact center of North America is in Osborne County, Kansas. In Dodge City, called "the Cowboy Capital of the World," visitors can see Front Street as it was in the days of the Wild West.

To Use an Atlas

1. You will need a road atlas, Notebook page 46, and a pencil.

2. Find the page in the road atlas that has a map of your state. Find the boundary line around your state. Can you name the other states that border yours?

3. Choose two large cities within your state. Can you find a major highway that connects them? Write the number of the highway on your Notebook page.

4. Turn to the page that has a map of the entire United States, probably at the beginning of your atlas. Find your state on this map. With your partner, choose another state that you would like to visit. In what direction would you travel to get to this state?

Native Americans in traditional dress

Oklahoma

Oklahoma, south of Kansas, is our first stop in the Southwest region of the United States. *Oklahoma* comes from two Choctaw words that mean "red people." Oklahoma's nickname is "the Sooner State" because some of its settlers arrived in the land before it officially opened.

What do you think the state of Oklahoma is shaped like? Many people think it looks like a long-handled pan. The long thin section is called the Panhandle. Wheat fields and oil wells are common sights on Oklahoma's plains. It is also a leading producer of natural gas. People from more than sixty different Native American tribes live in Oklahoma. Indian City, U.S.A., and the Cherokee Heritage Center are two places in which visitors can experience Plains Indian and Cherokee culture.

Texas

South of Oklahoma is Texas, nicknamed "the Lone Star State" after the single white star on its flag. Texas is the only state allowed to fly its flag as high as the American flag because it was once an independent republic.

At a rodeo, people can demonstrate their skills in riding and roping.

Texas is the second largest state. It contains more farmland and produces more cattle and sheep than any other state. As you might expect, rodeos are popular events in Texas. Do you remember any of the history behind the statehood of Texas? The Alamo chapel in San Antonio is all that is left of the fort where the Texas soldiers defended themselves against the Mexican army in 1836. Near Houston is the San Jacinto Monument, a tribute to theTexans who fought in the battle that won Texas independence.

New Mexico

West of Texas is New Mexico. Its beautiful scenery has earned it the nickname "the Land of Enchantment." It has rugged mountains, deserts with colorful rocks, and a beautiful river, the Rio Grande.

Would you like to ride on a four-hundred-year-old highway? *El Camino Real,* meaning "the Royal Highway," is the oldest road used by Europeans in America. New Mexico's capital, Santa Fe, is the oldest place of government in the United States. The Palace of Governors houses a museum about the Spanish government that ruled there in the early 1600s.

White Sands, a rugged New Mexico scene

Have you ever seen a bat? At Carlsbad Caverns, a group of caves in southeastern New Mexico, you will see hundreds of thousands of bats. Every evening at dusk, the sky is filled with flapping wings as the bats fly out of the caves.

Arizona

Arizona, the last of the Southwestern states, is west of New Mexico. Its nickname, "the Grand Canyon State," comes from its most well-known feature. The Grand Canyon, located in northern Arizona along the Colorado River, is the largest canyon in the world.

The Grand Canyon

When Arizona was first given to the United States after the Mexican War, many people called it a worthless stretch of desert. But it contains some of our country's most beautiful scenery. The Painted Desert is made up of sand of many different colors. The Petrified Forest and Monument Valley are filled with unusual rock formations. The cactus grows well in Arizona's climate. Would you like to stand in four states at one time? At Four Corners, the borders of Arizona, Colorado, New Mexico, and Utah meet.

Montana

Montana comes from the Spanish word for "mountainous." Does Montana's nickname, "the Treasure State," give you a clue as to what might be there?

A view of the Rockies in Glacier National Park

When gold and silver were discovered in Montana's mountains, settlers rushed to the territory to set up mining camps. Many of the gold-mining camps, like Virginia City, near Dillon, have been restored. Another state nickname is "Big Sky Country" because of the wide, flat plains in eastern Montana. One landmark on the plains is Pompey's Pillar, a two-hundred-foot rock on the bank of the Yellowstone River. In the Rocky Mountains of northwestern Montana is Glacier National Park.

Wyoming

South of Montana is Wyoming. *Wyoming* in the Delaware language means "upon the great plain." Wyoming's nickname is "the Equality State" because women in Wyoming were the first in our nation to vote, serve on juries, and hold public office.

Although Wyoming has the lowest population of all the states, it attracts many visitors. Our country's first and largest national park is in Wyoming. Millions of people come to Yellowstone National Park

Grand Teton National Park

each year to hike, camp, and view its geysers, canyons, and waterfalls. Grand Teton National Park, with its beautiful rocky mountain peaks, is nearby. Do you know what a *butte* is? Wyoming's low areas have many of these tall, rocky towers. Devils Tower, a volcanic tower in northeastern Wyoming, has become a national monument.

Pikes Peak

Colorado

South of Wyoming is Colorado. *Colorado* is a Spanish word meaning "colored red." Spaniards first gave this name to the river that flowed through canyons of red-tinted stone. Colorado's nickname is "the Centennial State" because it joined the Union one hundred years after the United States declared its independence.

The beautiful Rocky Mountains draw skiers, hikers, and nature lovers to Colorado every year. Pikes Peak is the most well known peak in the Rockies. Katherine Lee Bates wrote the words to "America the Beautiful" after she enjoyed a view from the top of Pikes Peak. The world's highest suspension bridge crosses the Royal Gorge, a huge chasm between two mountains near Canon City.

Utah

Sandstone rocks in Bryce Canyon National Park

Colorado's neighbor to the west is Utah, "the Beehive State." Utah's nickname comes from the days when Mormons settled that region. They called their state *Deseret,* meaning "honey bee." The bee symbolized hard work and industry.

Deserts, canyons, and natural rock formations cover much of Utah. Bryce Canyon National Park is filled with red sandstone rocks that have towering spires like those on a church. Utah's Great Salt Lake is saltier than ocean water. Even people who do not swim can easily float in the lake. About 70 percent of Utah's people are Mormons. America's first continental railroad was completed in Utah at Promontory. The Golden Spike National Historic Site now marks the spot where the Union Pacific and Central Pacific railroads were joined.

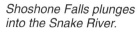
Shoshone Falls plunges into the Snake River.

Idaho

Northwest of Utah is Idaho. Some people say the word *Idaho* was the name of a Native American people meaning "gem of the mountains." Others say *Idaho* is a made-up word. In any case, Idaho took "the Gem State" as its nickname.

Have you eaten mashed potatoes, French fries, or potato chips lately? Idaho is the leading producer of potatoes in the United States. Idaho also has fascinating scenery. National forests, including canyons, waterfalls, lakes, and mountains, cover much of its land. Hells Canyon, the deepest canyon in North America, is near Lewiston, Idaho. Cut out by the Snake River, it is about a mile and a half deep at one point. What do you think a frozen waterfall might look like? Idaho has one in its Crystal Ice Cave.

Nevada

Hoover Dam

Nevada, the last Rocky Mountain state, is southwest of Idaho. *Nevada* comes from the Spanish word for "snow-clad." Nevada has not only snowcapped mountains but also barren deserts. Nevada is nicknamed "the Silver State" because large amounts of silver were once found in its mines.

Nevada receives the least amount of rainfall of any state. Its farmers must use special forms of irrigation to grow their crops. Nevada's Hoover Dam is one of the largest concrete dams in the world. It has a power plant that provides electricity for Arizona, California, and Nevada. Would you like to see a rock shaped like an elephant? This and other red rock formations can be found in Nevada's Valley of Fire State Park.

Washington

Mount Rainier

Finally we come to the Pacific region of the United States, where Washington is our first stop. Washington's nickname is "the Evergreen State" because of all its evergreen trees. Do you know for whom the state of Washington was named? It is the only state named after a president.

What would you expect to find in a city named George? The city of George, Washington, has different types of cherries, such as Bing and Maraschino, for its street names. With its snowcapped mountains, Washington is a popular state for skiers. Rainier Paradise Ranger Station on Mount Rainier holds the North American record for the most snow in one season. Mount Saint Helens is famous for its volcanic eruption in 1980. More apples come from Washington than from any other state.

Oregon

South of Washington is Oregon. Its nickname is "the Beaver State." Beaver skins were the most common item of trade there in its early days. The name *Oregon* probably comes from the French word for the Columbia River. It means "hurricane."

Oregon is a state of great natural beauty. Its snow-covered mountains, green forests, and rocky coastline have earned it the title

Phantom Ship, a rock formation in Crater Lake

of "Pacific Wonderland." Oregon has the deepest lake in the United States. Crater Lake, which fills an extinct volcano in the Cascade Mountains, is 1,932 feet deep—more than a third of a mile! In the 1840s and 1850s, many people braved a rugged journey across America to settle in Oregon. The area where they settled, Willamette Valley, is now the center of industrial life in Oregon.

California

California is south of Oregon. Its nickname is "the Golden State." California was the site of a famous gold rush in 1849. It is also known for its golden sunshine and fair weather nearly all the year around.

The Golden Gate Bridge spans San Francisco Bay.

Do you know anyone who lives in California? Chances are that you do, because more people live in California than in any other state. Four of the nation's largest cities are in California. How many of them can you name? Death Valley, on California's eastern border, is the lowest point in the Western Hemisphere. In 1913, this area had the hottest temperature ever recorded in the United States—134°F. California's long Pacific coastline is a popular place for water sports. California's redwood trees are the tallest and oldest trees in the world.

Alaska

In summer, fireweed adds color to Alaska's mountain scenery.

Alaska, the northernmost state, is nicknamed "the Last Frontier" because much of its land has not yet been settled. William Seward, the secretary of state under President Andrew Johnson, bought Alaska from Russia in 1867. At the time, Americans called it things such as "Seward's Folly," "Icebergia," and "Johnson's Polar Bear Garden."

Do you think buying Alaska was a foolish decision? Alaska is rich in natural resources like fish, minerals, timber, and oil. Mount McKinley, the tallest peak in the United States, is located there. Alaska is the largest state. Its coastline is longer than those of all the other states put together. Although it is very big, it has the second fewest people in the nation.

Hawaii

Hawaii, a state made up of islands in the Pacific, is our nation's youngest state. It joined the Union in 1959. Hawaii is nicknamed "the Aloha State" because of its friendliness toward visitors. *Aloha*

is the Hawaiian word for "love," "greetings," "welcome," or "farewell."

Hawaii is made up of more than one hundred islands. There are eight main islands: Hawaii, Maui, Kahoolawe, Molokai, Lanai, Oahu, Kauai, and Niihau. But people live on only seven of them. Sparkling waterfalls, volcanic mountains, beaches made of black lava particles, and colorful flowers make

One of Hawaii's dramatic tropical landscapes

Hawaii beautiful. If you were to visit the islands, you would probably be greeted with the word *aloha,* and someone would place a *lei,* a wreath of flowers, around your neck. Do you like pineapple? That is one of Hawaii's most famous products.

Other U.S. Lands

In addition to the fifty states, the United States owns other lands, called *territories.* The U.S. Virgin Islands are located in the Caribbean Sea, about a thousand miles east of the tip of Florida. The United States bought them from Denmark. Guam, an island in the Pacific Ocean, is nearly four thousand miles west of Hawaii. An important American naval base during the Spanish-American War, Guam was later ceded to the United States by Spain. American Samoa, in the south-central Pacific Ocean, is another island territory that our navy once used as a coaling station. Other

Charlotte Amalie, on the island of St. Thomas, is the capital city of the Virgin Islands.

small Pacific islands like Wake Island, the Midway Islands, and most of Micronesia are United States territories also.

Puerto Rico's coastline

Two other United States territories have become commonwealths. Puerto Rico lies between the Atlantic Ocean and the Caribbean Sea. Its Spanish name means "rich harbor," and it was ceded to the United States following the Spanish-American War. The Northern Mariana Islands in Micronesia, just north of Guam, became a United States commonwealth in 1986.

"But the land, whither ye go to possess it, is a land of hills and valleys, and drinketh water of the rain of heaven: A land which the Lord thy God careth for: the eyes of the Lord thy God are always upon it, from the beginning of the year even unto the end of the year."

Deuteronomy 11:11-12

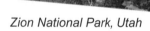
Zion National Park, Utah

Next time you look at a map of the United States, think about all the different places and people that make up this country. If you could visit any of the fifty states, which one would you choose?

6

Newfangled Ideas

Have you ever seen anything quite like this device before? In 1882, a man named Samuel Applegate had an idea for getting people up on time each day. Can you figure out how his contraption works?

We call Samuel Applegate's idea an *invention*. Do you know what an invention is? An invention might be a new object, or it might be an old object made better. An invention might make a difficult job easier. It could help make a long process quicker. In some way, an invention helps to make life better for the people who use it. Any new idea or way of doing something can be called an invention. Can you think of other things that were invented?

Look around your classroom. Almost everything you see—from the knobs and hinges on the classroom door to the lead pencils and crayons in your desk—was invented by someone. Someone, somewhere, thought of each thing. He worked to make his idea into something real and usable. Bulletin boards, window screens, Thermos bottles, screws, and computers are the creations of *inventors*.

When the inventor's work is done, it is easy to see whether his idea was a good one. Maybe you have said, "That seems like a simple gadget. I should have thought of it." What makes one person think of an invention before anyone else? Where do inventors get their ideas?

An invention might happen by accident. One afternoon in 1849, Walter Hunt sat in his workshop twisting a piece of wire. Mr. Hunt was trying to invent a better rifle. He needed to make a wire clasp that would open and close without breaking. Do you think he succeeded? Instead of making the rifle clasp, he discovered a way to make a pin that opened and closed. He called his pin a *safety pin*. Have you ever used Walter Hunt's little invention?

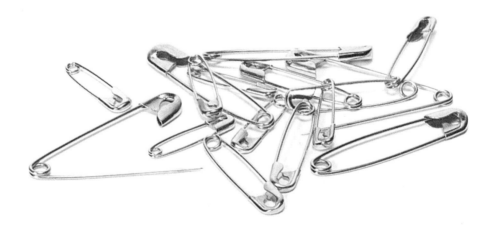

At other times, inventors invent things they think someone needs. Remember Mr. Applegate's invention? He knew that to get to work on time, a person needed to get out of bed in the morning. His invention was a device for waking someone from sleep. Samuel Applegate took sixty small pieces of cork. He fastened each piece of cork to a length of string. The corks were attached to a clock by a cord and then hung together over the head of a sleeping person. When it was time to wake up, the clock would let go of the cord and drop the corks. Do you think the corks would wake up the sleeper? Would you rather be awakened by Mr. Applegate's invention or by the alarm clock you used this morning?

Still other inventors take an old thing and find a new or better way to use it. Before 1884, some writing pens were made from feathers. Some pens were made with wooden handles and metal tips. But all pens had to be dipped in a well of ink to write just a few words. Then Lewis Waterman made a writing pen with a hollow handle. Inside the handle, he put ink. The *fountain pen,* as he called it, had to be filled with ink from time to time, but not after every few words like the old pens.

In 1820, a visitor to the United States said, "The moment an American hears the word invention, he pricks up his ears." Why did Americans want to know about new inventions? Almost every invention made life easier for a few people. And some made a difference to almost everyone. If you were asked to make a list of the most important inventions, which ones would you choose?

A New Engine

One invention that changed life for many people in America was built in England in 1712. There an inventor heated water until it became steam and then cooled it quickly to make the engine run. At first the steam engine could only pump water from the bottom of deep mines.

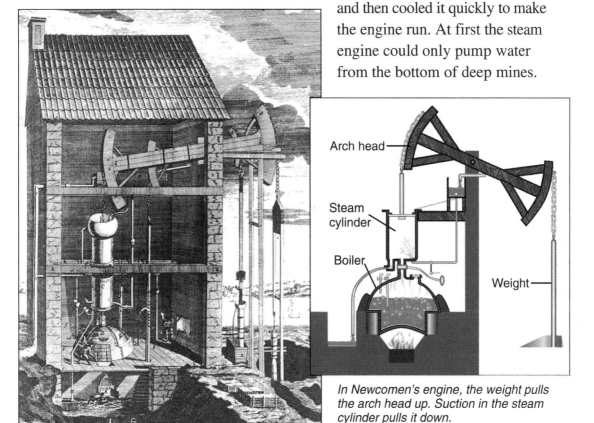

In Newcomen's engine, the weight pulls the arch head up. Suction in the steam cylinder pulls it down.

Left: A later "atmospheric engine" in Sweden in 1734, based on Newcomen's

A steamboat in use around 1860

More than fifty years after the steam engine was first used, twenty-seven-year-old James Watt was busy in his shop. A steam engine had broken down, and Watt had been asked to fix it. The engine broke often. When it did work, it lost steam quickly. And it took huge amounts of coal to keep the engine hot. "There must be a way to make this engine work better," Watt thought.

Encouraged by his family and friends, Watt began work on a better steam engine. He found a way to save steam and coal by cooling the steam in a separate tube, or *cylinder.* After ten years of hard work, James Watt's better steam engine was ready to use. In five more years, Watt built almost three hundred new steam engines.

Throughout the rest of his life, James Watt thought of new ways to make his steam engine better. When he died in 1819, the steam engine was an important tool for many businesses in England. Before this invention, men had used their own muscle power or the power of animals, wind, or water to get work done. Now one steam engine could do the work of one hundred horses.

Soon people in other countries heard about the steam engine and the things it could do. Do you think they wanted to use the new steam engine?

The Cotton Gin and Interchangeable Parts

Eli Whitney

While James Watt worked on his steam engine in England, another inventor was growing up on a farm in Massachusetts: Eli Whitney. Eli was about ten years old when the War for Independence began. Eli's parents thought he would want to take over the farm when he was older. But Eli wanted to go to college.

After college, Whitney planned to teach the children of a rich Georgia planter. But he never made it to the plantation. On the way, Whitney saw the cotton plant for the first time. He heard how hard it was to remove the seeds from the sticky cotton. And he learned that the people of the South could become rich from selling cotton if only someone could find an easy way to remove the seeds.

Whitney decided to build a machine that would remove the seeds from cotton. It took six months of constant work. But by early 1793, he

Slaves worked this cotton gin by turning the crank.

had a machine that could clean as much cotton as one thousand slaves could. The machine could be worked by a man, a team of oxen, or a water wheel. Later, the *cotton gin* would be run by another machine. Can you guess which one?

The Eli Whitney Gun Factory *by William Giles Munson, painted 1826-28*

We remember Eli Whitney most for his cotton gin. But the cotton gin was not his only invention. His next invention was not an object but a new way of doing things. This idea was even more important than his cotton gin.

In Whitney's day, all the parts for machines and tools were made by hand. No two parts were quite the same. And no two finished tools were exactly alike. Replacing parts and fixing broken equipment was very difficult.

Whitney began making muskets for the new United States army in 1798. In his factory, Whitney built machines for making each part of the musket. The machines made each part exactly alike. Now each trigger was just like all the other triggers. And each trigger would fit any one of Whitney's muskets. Suddenly, making the muskets was quicker. Fixing broken muskets was easier too because the parts were *interchangeable*. How do you think Whitney's idea helped other inventors?

An Inventor Works

1. You will need a pencil, some paper, and materials to build your invention.

2. Think about things you use that could work better or problems you would like to solve. Make a list of as many things as you can think of. Then reread each idea. Is it really new? Would other people think it was a good idea? How easy would the thing be to make?

3. Choose one of your ideas and try to draw a picture that shows how it would work. Do you need more information to make your invention? Where can you find the information?

4. Try to put your invention together. Does it work? Do you need more information? Can you do something another way? Show your working invention to your classmates. Is your invention something they can use?

127

Cyrus McCormick's Reaper

Ripe wheat must be gathered quickly. But harvesting the grain with a scythe was slow and difficult work. A good worker would spend a whole day cutting just two acres of wheat. For years people tried to make a machine that would reap, or harvest, wheat. How would such a machine help farmers?

Robert McCormick was one of many who tried to build a reaping machine. When he gave up, his oldest son, Cyrus, decided to try. Cyrus McCormick and his helper, a slave named Jo Anderson, were ready to test their invention.

McCormick tests his reaper in Virginia

McCormick set up his reaper in one of his father's fields. People came from across the Virginia countryside to watch. A horse pulled the reaper slowly across the field, and the cut wheat stalks fell neatly behind the machine. It worked! How do you think the crowd of farmers felt as they watched the machine?

Cyrus McCormick

McCormick spent more time making his machine work even better. But when he was ready to sell his reaper, the farmers in the East were not ready to buy it. Most thought they did not need such a contraption on their small, hilly farms. But McCormick would not give up.

On a visit to the Midwest, McCormick saw stretches of flat land ready for planting with wheat. When some farmers in the Midwest bought his reaper, McCormick made a decision. He moved to Chicago, Illinois. There he built a factory for making his reapers. How might moving nearer to his customers help McCormick to sell more of his reapers?

In his factory, Cyrus McCormick made his reapers from interchangeable parts. If a part broke on a reaper, the farmer simply sent for a new part to replace it. When the part came in the mail, the farmer could fix the reaper himself. What other inventor had thought of the idea of interchangeable parts?

"Honour the Lord with thy substance, and with the firstfruits of all thine increase: So shall thy barns be filled with plenty, and thy presses shall burst out with new wine."

Proverbs 3:9-10

Soon McCormick was a very rich man. He had earned more than a million dollars by selling his reapers. He gave money to build schools and churches. He gave money to the evangelist D. L. Moody. And he printed two Christian magazines. As long as Cyrus McCormick lived, he used his money to help in the Lord's work.

Obtaining a Patent

All the inventors you will read about in this chapter have one thing in common: each applied for and received a *patent* from the United States government. Obtaining a patent is an important way to make an invention known to other people. But what is a patent?

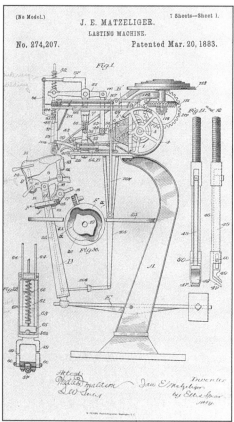

Jan Matzeliger's patent application for a machine that would last shoes

A patent is an agreement. The inventor agrees to explain all the details of his invention to anyone who wants to know. Then the U.S. government agrees to protect the rights of the inventor. A patent says that only the inventor may make or sell his invention for seventeen years. Why would an inventor want to make this agreement?

It is not easy to qualify for a patent. An invention must be a new idea, and it must work. The inventor needs to write a description of his invention. If he can, he should include a drawing of the invention, inside and out. The drawing helps the people at the Patent and Trademark Office understand how the invention works.

A worker at the Patent and Trademark Office looks over the description and drawings. If there is no other invention like his, the inventor is granted a patent. The Massachusetts Colony granted the first American patent to Joseph Jenks. He had made a better *scythe,* a tool for cutting wheat. Today more than one hundred thousand patents are given to inventors each year.

Elias Howe and His Sewing Machine

Elias Howe could not help overhearing his boss talking to a friend. "Someone needs to invent a machine that can take the place of sewing by hand," he said. "That person would make a fortune." What would you have done if you had heard that?

In 1841 Howe worked in a shop making different kinds of machines. The more he thought about what he had heard, the more he felt sure that he could build a machine for sewing. So Howe quit his job at the machine shop. And he spent all his time working on his idea.

For five years Howe worked on his sewing machine. For five years his family made do with only a little bit of money. But things would be better when Howe finished his machine. When he finally made a sewing machine that worked, he received a patent and made plans to sell his wonderful invention.

Howe patented his sewing machine in 1846.

Elias Howe

The sewing machine saved hours of work on every garment made.

What do you think happened then? It was not what Howe had expected. The tailors and seamstresses did not like his machine! They thought that the sewing machine could not do the fine work as well as they could. And they feared that it would take away their jobs. Besides, the machine cost too much to make. Even if someone wanted to buy a sewing machine, no one had enough money to spend on such nonsense.

Howe tried to sell his machine in the United States. He left his home and sailed for England to try selling the sewing machine there. Finally he gave up. No one seemed to be interested in Howe's invention. Had his old boss been wrong?

Discouraged, Elias Howe came home to the United States. And what do you think he found? People everywhere were using his sewing machine! But they had not bought the machines from Howe. Other men had used Howe's ideas to make and sell sewing machines.

Howe had done a smart thing. Do you remember what he had done? He had gotten a patent on his invention. Now all the people who were selling his sewing machine had to pay money to Howe. Soon Elias Howe was a millionaire. But he never forgot how hard it had been to be poor. He used his money to help other people get the things they needed.

A shoe-making factory
Lynn, Massachusetts
May 29, 1885

After it was invented in 1846, Elias Howe's sewing machine was used to sew parts of a shoe together. But one part of the work could not be done with a sewing machine—the *lasting*.

Preparing to sew a shoe upper to a sole by hand

Lasting meant sewing the upper of a shoe to the sole. Lasting had to be done by hand. The lasters believed that a machine could never do such difficult work.

Jan Matzeliger was an immigrant who worked in a shoe factory. He studied the way the lasters did their work.

Jan Matzeliger

Matzeliger began building a machine in a room over the old West Lynn Mission. His machine copied the way a laster's hands worked. On this day, Matzeliger's machine lasted seventy-five pairs of ladies' shoes perfectly.

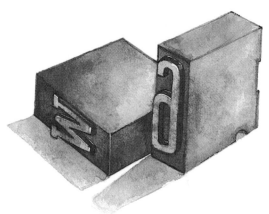

A Machine for the Office

Do you know someone who works in an office? He may use Christopher Sholes's invention. Since 1872, it has made the job of many office workers easier. Christopher called his machine a *Type-Writer.*

Christopher grew up around printing presses and cases of type. His older brother owned a printing shop. When Christopher was fourteen years old, he became a printer's apprentice. He learned his job quickly. When he was eighteen, he went to work for his brother's newspaper.

During the next twenty years, Sholes worked in many printing shops. In the last of these shops, Sholes printed a newspaper. He also made sure that blank books, tickets, and other small items were printed. Each thing the shop

Before a machine could set type in 1886, a compositor picked each letter from a type case.

printed needed to be stamped with a number. It was slow work, and it was easy to make mistakes. Sholes and a friend decided to make a machine to print the numbers.

Samuel Clemens (Mark Twain) was the first author to type his manuscript. The book was Life on the Mississippi. *He used a machine similar to the one shown below.*

When Sholes finished his numbering machine, it worked just as he had planned. He showed his invention to a friend. "Chris," he said, "if you can make a machine to print numbers, why can't you make one to print letters and words too?" Sholes thought it was a good idea. So he set to work on a second invention.

Look at one of Sholes's typewriters. What do you think it looks like? The machine printed only capital letters. But people liked the clear, neat pages the typewriter printed. Sholes kept working.

He found a friend who was willing to try the typewriter in his office. Whenever he found a problem with the machine, he brought it back to Sholes. Each time, Sholes fixed the problem by making a new and better typewriter. He made more than fifty typewriters before he had a machine that worked perfectly.

Before Christopher Sholes built his typewriter, the office was a man's place. Letters and notes and forms were slowly written by hand. With the typewriter came big changes. Letters were written quickly and neatly. And ladies were hired to work the new machine. Today there are as many women as men who work in offices. Some still use a machine like Christopher Sholes's.

William Burt made an attempt at a typewriter in 1829. But Sholes and his friends Carlos Glidden and Samuel Soulé developed the model that is considered standard. The three sold out to the Remington Company, which manufactured guns and sewing machines before making the first commercial typewriter.

135

With the Flip of a Switch

A room for invention at Menlo Park

No American inventor patented more new ideas than Thomas Alva Edison. When he died at the age of eighty-four, he had patents for more than one thousand inventions. After he opened his workshop in Menlo Park, New Jersey, he promised to build a little invention every ten days. And he promised a big invention every six months. Do you think he kept his promise?

Al Edison was the youngest of seven children. Since Mrs. Edison had been a schoolteacher, she decided to teach her youngest son at home. Al learned to read the Bible. Before long, he would read almost any book his mother could find.

When he was nine, Al's parents gave him a book on science experiments. Soon he was spending all his time trying out the experiments. The basement of his home became his first laboratory, or workshop.

At first, Al's parents did not mind. But soon the experiments made the house smell funny. And the things Al needed to make the experiments work cost too much money. Do you think he gave up his experimenting?

Edison and his phonograph

He did not. Al found a job selling newspapers and sandwiches on a train. He set up a new laboratory in one of the train cars.

Between the ages of twelve and twenty-two, Edison had many different jobs. Each new job gave him just a bit more money to spend on his experiments. And his experiments gave him ideas for new inventions. Soon he began building and trying out his ideas.

The *phonograph,* or record player, finished in 1877, was one of Edison's first inventions. Two years later he invented the electric light bulb, and later he found a way to bring electricity into people's homes. Soon other inventors were finding ways to use electricity too. How many things that need electricity have you used today?

Edison often worked more than one hundred hours a week on his inventions. About how many hours did he work each day? Edison did not work hard so that he would become rich. He wanted to be the best inventor and to make the most inventions. Did he reach his goal?

Edison and his movie camera

To Construct a Time Line

1. You will need a ruler, a pencil, a large piece of paper, some scrap paper, crayons, and some books about inventions.

2. Draw a straight line across the middle of your large piece of paper. Use the ruler to divide the line into small sections. Will each section on your time line stand for one year, five years, or ten years? Beginning with 1750, mark the years on your time line.

3. Look through your textbook to find inventions. Write the name of the inventors and the names and years of the inventions on your scrap paper. Then add the inventions to your time line. If you like, draw a picture for each invention.

4. Find out about other important or unusual inventions. Add them to your time line. How many different things were invented during the years your time line shows? Why are time lines useful?

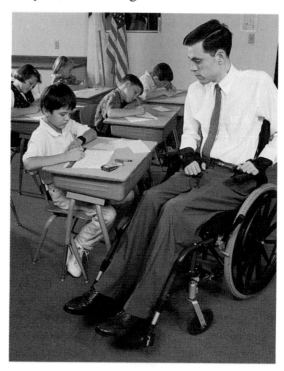

Few inventions work perfectly the first time. Do you think this one will?

What Makes a Good Inventor?

Many inventors are adults. But children can be inventors too. Thomas Alva Edison built his first invention when he was just sixteen years old. And George Washington Carver began working with plants before he was ten. People of all ages have received patents for their ideas. Young or old, a good inventor needs to have four things. Do any of the words describe you?

Inventors have *curiosity*. When they do not understand how or why something works, they ask questions. They study and experiment until they figure it out. Do you like to figure out how things work?

Good inventors should have *confidence*. A person who has confidence is sure of himself and his ideas. He does not give up when people tell him his invention will not work. He keeps looking for someone who likes his idea. Did any of the famous inventors you have read about need confidence?

George Washington Carver
About 1864-1943

No one knows for sure exactly when George Washington Carver was born. His mother was a slave. When she was kidnapped near the end of the Civil War, her owners took the baby George and raised him as their son.

Young George was not a healthy child. He could not help with the hard jobs on the farm. But he loved to care for plants, and he learned to tell sick plants from strong ones. He also learned what things would make a plant stronger. Soon neighbors called George the "plant doctor."

George wanted to learn more. To learn, he needed to go to school. So when he was twelve, he left his home with the Carvers. He worked hard at his studies. And he worked hard to earn money to pay for the

George Washington Carver

things he needed. It took many years for George to finish school. When he did, he knew he wanted to share the things he had learned.

George Carver began teaching at the Tuskegee Institute, a school for African Americans. While teaching the southern farmers about plants, Carver found out that the cotton plant was ruining the soil. He tried to get the farmers to grow other plants. But other plants would not bring as much money to the farmers as cotton could.

So Carver began experimenting. He invented 325 ways to use the peanut, from peanut butter to pickles to ink. He found 118 uses for the sweet potato. And he found many ways to use cowpeas as well. Soon farmers were planting peanuts, sweet potatoes, and cowpeas. And they were selling them and making money. Even today these crops are important to southern farmers.

An inventor needs *imagination* too. It takes an imaginative inventor to think of new ways of doing things. Sometimes an inventor's imagination helps him to think of a new use for something old. Do you know anyone who uses his imagination?

The most important thing an inventor needs is *persistence.* Most times it takes more than one try to solve a problem. An inventor cannot give up if his first idea does not work. He must keep trying until he finds the best solution to his problem. Thomas Edison tried 9,990 different experiments before he made an electric light bulb that worked well. He said, "Genius is 99 percent perspiration and 1 percent inspiration." What do you think he meant?

Edison's largest experimental light bulb

Some of Edison's nearly 10,000 attempts at a good light bulb

Look at the two houses below. One shows how a house would have looked in colonial times. Can you tell which one? The other picture shows a house in 1900. How many new inventions can you see in the 1900 house? Can you think of anything in your house today that you do not see in either of these houses?

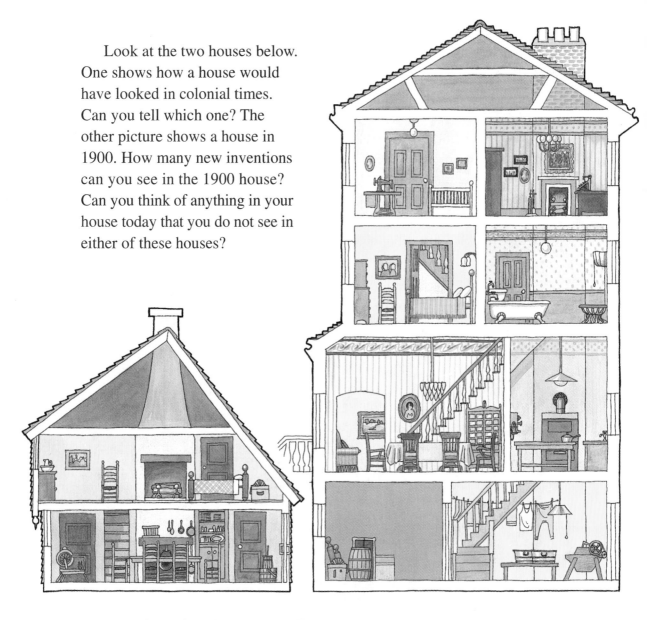

Many inventions have been built during the last two hundred years. Everyday, you use inventions that your great-grandparents could not have imagined. What inventions might your grandchildren and great-grandchildren be using seventy-five years from now? How many of those new things will have been invented by you?

In the Market

Do you know how to play the game Monopoly? Players buy property and try to improve it, collecting money from renters and paying taxes. The game teaches, among other things, that you have to pay more taxes when you own more land and that it is easy to be ruined by overspending.

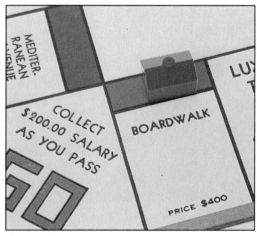

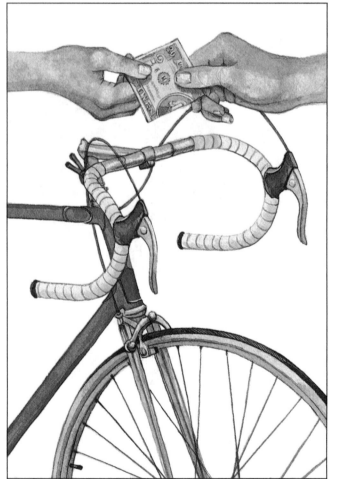

The game of Monopoly is something like the real business of buying and selling. People buy property they think will be valuable. They sell property when they need money or when they can make a *profit*. A profit is an amount that is more than the original cost of something. For example, if you buy a used bicycle for ten dollars and spend five dollars to fix it up and then sell it for twenty dollars, you make a profit of five dollars.

Buying a bicycle

In the United States much buying and selling goes on every day. Citizens buy and sell within the country, and the United States government buys from and sells to other governments. The way a country handles its money and resources is called its *economy*. Perhaps you have heard adults talking about "the state of the economy." They are referring to the way the government uses money and goods.

Goods being loaded onto a ship for foreign export

Inventing Games

The game that became Monopoly was probably invented by Elizabeth Magie Phillips, a woman who wanted to teach children that it was wrong to try to own everything. She called her game The Landlord's Game and had it patented in 1904.

But since The Landlord's Game was never packaged for sale, people in the area who played the game began to make up their own rules and to change some of the names of the places. And they called it Monopoly. Then others, especially college students going home on breaks, took the game to other states. Dan Layman took his new pastime to Indiana. There he made many changes and called the game Finance.

Many Monopoly games have markers that are miniatures of hats, cars, ships, and other objects.

An Indiana woman took the game of Finance to New Jersey, where she and her friends named places on the board after places in Atlantic City—places such as Boardwalk and Marvin Gardens. Then the game came into the hands of Philadelphian Charles Darrow, who made his own board and rules and sold the package to Parker Brothers, a large manufacturer of games and toys.

But the game was not Darrow's invention; it was a folk game that had grown out of Mrs. Phillips's idea. When Parker Brothers discovered Darrow's lie, the company was already making a lot of money on the game. So the owners decided to buy out all other claims to Monopoly, including the original one. Mrs. Phillips got five hundred dollars for her rights to the game that became the world's most popular board game.

What do you think Mrs. Phillips would say of her idea now?

147

A diamond has many qualities that make it valuable.

What's It Worth?

Suppose you have a button and a diamond. Which do you think would bring more money? You probably said the diamond. And you might be right. Diamonds have great *value,* or worth in money. Why do you think they do? For one thing, they are beautiful, and many people want them for their beauty. A good rhinestone can look as lovely, yet rhinestones are not nearly as expensive as diamonds. Why is that?

Rhinestones may look like diamonds, but they are worth far less.

148

Mining for diamonds

Diamonds are hard to get. They are not at all plentiful. Rhinestones, on the other hand, can be made easily, by the millions. Because real diamonds are scarce, they have more value. Can you think of other things that are valuable because they are rare?

Pretend again that you have a button and a diamond. The diamond, though real, is quite small and has a flaw in it. But the button is rather old. In fact, it is one of the buttons from George Washington's military uniform. Now which item do you think might bring more money? Why?

George Washington in military attire— how much for a collar button?

One man's junk is another man's treasure!

When people decide they want to buy or sell something, they think about the value of the item going up for sale. Some items have value because of what they are. Gold, for instance, is rare, useful, and hard to get. Therefore, it has value in itself. But there are other ways of deciding value too.

Suppose you were in a foreign country and could not get home. There is one airplane ticket to the United States left, but you do not have any money to pay for it. However, you have a gold necklace worth two thousand American dollars. The plane ticket costs only six hundred American dollars. The person who owns the ticket is willing to trade it for your necklace. At that time, the gold chain may not seem as valuable as the last ticket out of the country. How have the values changed?

Because many things can change the value of items, prices do not stay the same. A six-hundred-dollar ticket can become worth two thousand dollars. A button that once cost a penny is now worth one thousand dollars. So how do stores and other businesses set prices?

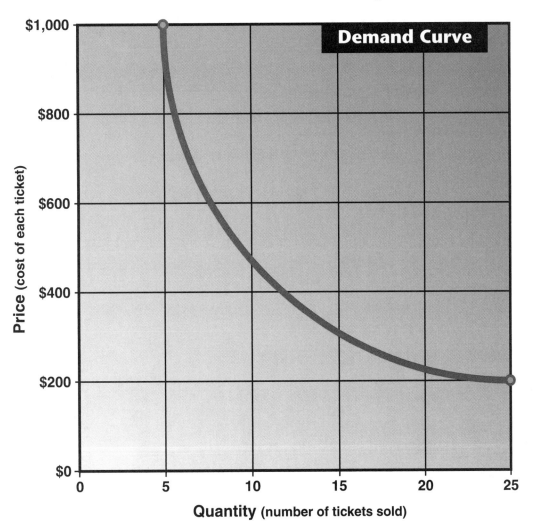

Supply and Demand

Prices are numerical ways of saying how much value an item has. If something costs five dollars, it is worth five times as much as something that costs one dollar. Or at least that is what the seller thinks. Suppose the buyer tells the seller that he will give three dollars for the higher-priced item, and the seller agrees. Now what is the value of the item?

Suppose now that the seller, who has many of the same item priced at five dollars, lowers the price to three dollars. What do you think will happen? People who were interested in the item but thought it was too highly priced may buy it. If you were the seller, what would you think was better: to sell a few items for five dollars or to sell more for three dollars? If you choose to sell more at a lower price, you are responding to the laws of *supply and demand.*

A price tag tells what the seller believes his item is worth.
How does a buyer indicate what he thinks?

For people to pay a high price, they must believe the product is especially good or scarce.

If there is a large supply of an item, the price usually must be lower. People think they can get the item anywhere and will try to get the best price. Sellers who keep the price high will not sell as many as those who lower the price. As long as the supply remains, the demand will keep the price low.

If many stores have the same product, the prices will usually stay lower.

Can you think of an item that would not be in great supply, that could not be made easily, and that people would want a great deal? Paintings are such items. An artist who is no longer living cannot make any more paintings. The supply of paintings is limited. What do you think will happen to the prices? They will probably go up. Why do you think sellers can raise the prices?

How does supply effect price in this case? What else may affect the price? If the artist is not a good artist, no one may want to buy his work no matter how scarce it is. What does that tell you about the laws of supply and demand?

Art museums are full of paintings upon which people have placed a high value.

If you are a seller, you want to find a price that will not only get people to buy but will also let you make a profit. Why do you think stores sometimes put things "on sale"?

To Read a Demand Curve

1. Get Notebook page 64 and a colored pencil or pen.

2. Listen as your teacher explains the demand curve pictured on the graph.

3. Answer the questions on the page.

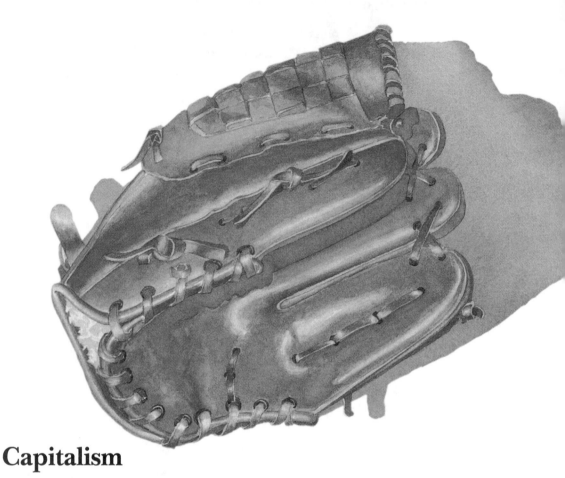

Capitalism

In the United States, businesses and individual sellers can choose to raise or lower prices for their goods and services. For example, if a toy store has many of a certain kind of toy, the manager could decide to lower the price so that more people would buy it. Why is having a choice important?

In the United States, the government does not own the businesses or the goods. Individual people and groups of people do. They choose what to make and sell and what to offer as services. They choose how they will market the goods or provide the services. A country that allows the people this ownership and the freedom to make choices is called *capitalistic. Capital* is wealth that is owned and used by one person or a group of people working together. Do you see where capitalism gets its name?

In America, store owners, not the government, decide how much an item will cost.

Waiting in long lines is common in some countries.

In some countries, there is no such choice. The government owns the factories and stores, sets prices, decides who will be allowed to work and where, and selects who gets the profits. Such countries are called *socialistic*. The word *social* comes from a Latin word that means "partner." Do you think socialism is a fitting name?

According to capitalism, the best way to run business is to let profits cause people to make decisions. For example, if a toy is popular, many companies will want to make it. The company that makes it best and sells it for the best price will be the one that makes the profits. How is such competition between the companies good for the people who buy toys?

How would things be different in a socialist country in which the price of the toy must be the same in every store? Why is this kind of pricing not good for the consumer? Can you think of any other reasons this system would not be good?

In socialist countries in which everyone has to have a job, businesses do not improve rapidly. If a machine could do the work of ten people more economically, the capitalist country would use it. But the socialist country would not, unless jobs could be found for the ten people who would be put out of work. Which country, then, would likely make more progress?

A shoe factory in a socialist country

A modern textile factory in Adana, Turkey

A car factory in the United States

Capitalism Works

1. Get your Notebook, a pencil, and a pair of scissors.

2. Cut out the coupons from Notebook page 65.

3. Listen to your teacher for explanations about what you will sell and buy.

4. Answer the questions on Notebook page 66 to compare capitalism and socialism.

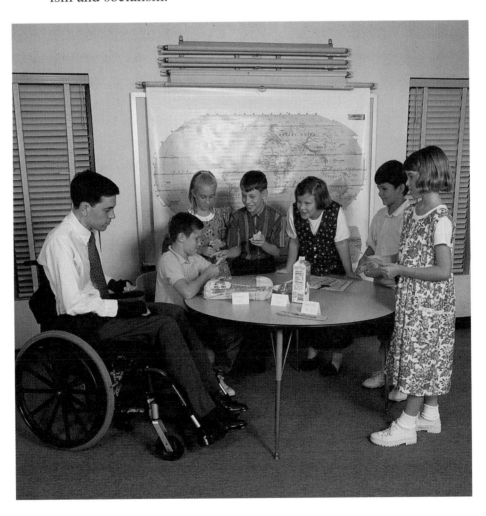

Needs and Wants

When you are thinking of buying something, what must you consider? Certainly the price is important. You should have enough money before you make a purchase.

But money may not be what you should think of first. You might ask yourself whether the item is something you *need* or you just *want*.

Businesses try to meet the needs and wants of people who buy. Businesses that sell things, or *goods,* and businesses that do work, or provide *services,* sometimes try to make people think they *need* what they really only *want*. For example, if a commercial tells about a new toy that "everyone is getting," you may think you have to get one. But the truth is that you only *want* one.

The Christian can trust in God to meet his needs. And he can know that his reward is eternal. He can believe that God, like a loving father, will give him "the desires of his heart." No Christian needs to fear the future or worry about the present. He need not entangle himself in the affairs of this world. His God will provide for him, no matter what governments and economies are doing.

> *"For what is a man profited, if he shall gain the whole world, and lose his own soul? or what shall a man give in exchange for his soul?"*
>
> **Matthew 16:26**

God has promised to meet the needs of His children.

8

Steam Engines and Smokestacks

Today people can buy all kinds of clothes readymade.

Making Things

Before there were stores to buy clothes and food and tools and shoes in, before there were factories and big mills and plants for producing goods, people made their own goods—even toys and wagons and hats.

By Hand

If you had to make all of your clothes yourself, what would you do first? Go buy fabric? What if you had to make the cloth before you could sew the clothes? What would you do?

You could get a *loom,* a large frame used to make cloth from yarn or thread. You could weave cloth to make clothes. But where would you get the thread or yarn? Before there were yarn shops, people had to spin their own yarn and thread.

From what would you make your yarn or thread? You might choose wool or cotton. But first you would have to shear the sheep or pick the

cotton. And before that, you would have had to raise the sheep or plant the cotton. Do you think you would have as many clothes as you do right now if you had to go through this process every time you needed a new piece of clothing?

Many people knit clothing, but few spin their own yarn first.

Shearing sheep

When the Separatists came to the New World on the *Mayflower,* they brought only a few extra clothes with them. But clothes wear out after a while. Where do you think they got new ones? Some ships from England brought more, including shoes. But the Separatists also made clothes.

Most women at that time knew how to make yarn, how to weave it into cloth, and how to make clothes from the cloth. It could take weeks or months to get a jacket or a skirt ready to wear. Why do you think it took so long?

Families often raised their own sheep. One of the children's jobs was to look after the flock. Why was this an important job? When the sheep's wool grew long, the farmer cut it off; he *sheared* the sheep.

Carding wool

After a sheep is sheared, the wool has to be combed, or *carded,* to smooth it out for spinning. *Spinning,* making a long yarn from the sheep's wool, requires a spinning wheel and someone to run the wheel. The person in this picture is making wool yarn. Then the wool is dyed. How much yarn do you think it takes to make a yard of cloth?

Spinning yarn

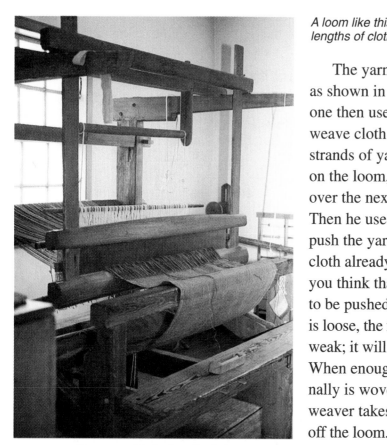

A loom like this can produce wide lengths of cloth fairly quickly.

The yarn is put on a loom, as shown in the picture. Someone then uses more yarn to weave cloth. The weaver puts strands of yarn across the yarn on the loom, under one and over the next, again and again. Then he uses a *beater bar* to push the yarn tight against the cloth already woven. Why do you think that the yarns have to be pushed tight? If the yarn is loose, the fabric will be weak; it will be easily torn. When enough cloth finally is woven, the weaver takes it off the loom.

Do you think the cloth is now ready to be used for clothing? Not yet. First it has to be washed and shrunk so that it will be sturdy. Making the cloth tighter by shrinking and pressing it is called *fulling*. If the weaver wants the cloth a different color, he must *dye* it by boiling it in water tinted with color. Then the cloth has to be dried and stretched before it can at last be used to make clothes.

Dyeing the cloth

Often whole families were involved in the weaving business.

After the colonists had lived in the New World for a few years and had cleared large farms, they began to make more cloth than their own families needed. What do you think they did with the extra cloth? They traded it to other people for things they needed.

More and more people came to live in the New World. Soon some people who liked to weave began to make much cloth to sell. *Weavers* worked so many hours at their looms that they did not have time to make other things for themselves, such as shoes and tools. What do you think happened then?

The weavers traded their cloth for shoes, tools, and other items. They traded with people who mainly made shoes or tools. Soon, instead of families making all the things they needed for themselves, people were concentrating on making one product and trading for the rest. People began to *specialize*. What does that mean?

Suppose you were a weaver and you had more orders for cloth than you could fill. What could you do? You could hire people to help you; you would have to buy another loom and more yarn. But what if the spinners could not make enough yarn to keep your looms running?

By Machine

When the demands got bigger than people could meet, something had to change. A man named James Hargreaves had an idea. He made a machine called a *spinning jenny* that helped a spinner make twenty times as much yarn or thread in a day. Hargreaves lived in England, and he wanted to keep his idea just for the English. But the idea spread to other places. Why do you think he wanted to keep the idea in England? How do you think ideas get from one country to another?

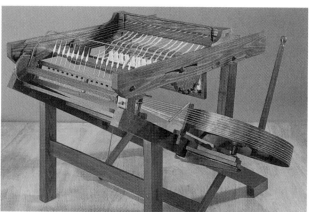

Hargreaves's spinning jenny

Then Samuel Crompton, another Englishman, made an even better machine. It ran on steam power; it made two or three hundred times more yarn in a day. Now spinners could supply all the yarn needed.

In fact, the spinners made far more yarn than the weavers could use up. For a while, the weavers worked faster and faster. But at last the weavers saw that they could not keep up. Then what do you think happened? The weaving business had to make some changes. A new weaving machine had to be invented.

Yards of thread spun by hand

Yards of thread spun by spinning jenny

Yards of thread spun by steam-powered machine

Amount of Spinning in One Day by One Person

Hand Weavers Employed Between 1770 and 1850

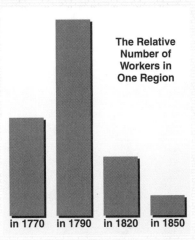

The Relative Number of Workers in One Region

in 1770   in 1790   in 1820   in 1850

And soon it was. A large engine-driven loom changed forever how weaving was done. No longer did someone sit at a small loom and make a yard or two of fabric a day. Now one person could run a big machine that made that much or more in an hour. If such a machine could do the weaving of a dozen people, what do you think happened to the weavers who used the old looms? They soon had no work. How do you think those people felt about the new machines?

Some people who lost their work hated the new inventions. A few even broke into shops at night and smashed the machines. Others tried to get laws passed that would keep machines out of their towns. But the speed and power of the machines made them too useful to be ignored. Owners of businesses saw that with the faster methods they could make a lot of money. They did not want to worry about the craftsmen who were "going out of style."

Running a spinning mule, based on Crompton's design

When the weavers and spinners began to work much faster, what do you think happened to the cotton growers? They soon found that people wanted far more cotton from them than they could get ready. Although they could grow enough, they couldn't get the seeds out of it fast enough. Do you remember who invented a machine to take care of that problem?

Compare the graphs. By how much did the cotton gin increase the amount of cotton cleaned in a day? How did the gin affect cotton growing?

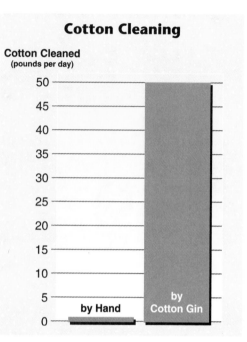

Cotton Cleaning

Cotton Cleaned
(pounds per day)

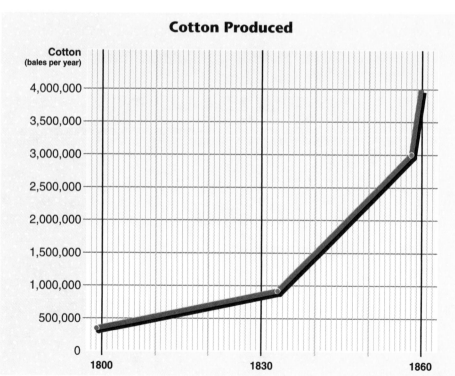

Cotton Produced

Cotton
(bales per year)

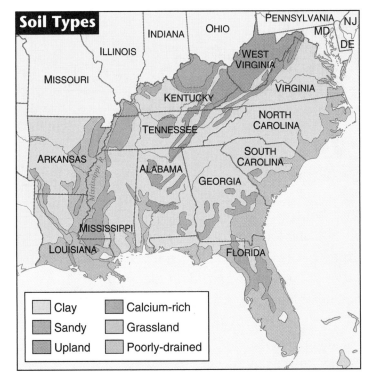

Soil Types

Legend:
- Clay
- Sandy
- Upland
- Calcium-rich
- Grassland
- Poorly-drained

There are two kinds of cotton—long-strand and short-strand. The short-strand grows easily, but the seeds are hard to take out. The long-strand cotton needs a certain climate to grow well, but the seeds come out with less trouble. Mississippi, Alabama, and Louisiana grew the most short-strand cotton. The coasts of South Carolina and Georgia grew much long-strand.

Look at the soil and growing season maps. What kinds of soils and growing seasons do you think the two kinds needed?

Growing Seasons

Legend:
- 120–150 days
- 150–180 days
- 180–210 days
- 210–240 days
- Over 240 days

Sawyers using a two-man saw

Machines were changing other work as well. Before steam power, loggers and lumbermen worked hard and long to get wood from the forest and to make boards from it. A *hewer* cut down the trees with an axe. *Sawyers* cut the trees into logs and trimmed off the branches with two-man saws and other big saws. A *logging wagon driver* pulled the logs out in big loads with a sled and horses. Then other lumbermen cut the logs into boards with big saws. After a while, mills using a water wheel sawed boards faster.

Still it took far too long to cut logs and boards in this way for all the people who were building houses and shops. Some lumbermen built bigger mills and hired more workers. But even then the demand for lumber was greater than they could handle. When the steam engine was invented, it changed the lumber mills as it had the cloth-making business.

Do you think the new machines put the hewers and sawyers out of work? No, they didn't. In fact, more of these workers were needed in the woods. For a while the lumber business *boomed*. What do you think a *boom* in business is?

A logging wagon driver

170

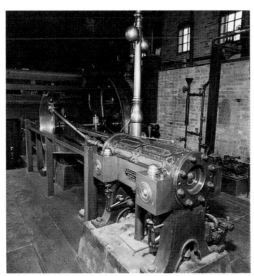

This steam engine powered a grist mill.

Hardly a business was untouched by the new steam-powered machines. Sheep shearers now had steam-powered clippers that could quickly cut the wool from ewes. Farmers began to use reapers and threshers run by steam engines.

Horses and carriages were replaced by trains running on steam. How do you think these changes made life different for everyone?

One change was in prices—

Thomas Edison used this steam engine to power tools in his laboratory at Menlo Park.

they went down on many items. Now more people could afford to buy clothes and tools rather than make them for themselves. Another change was in the places people lived. Before the machines, most people lived on small farms. As mills and shops became bigger, more people began to move to the towns and cities to live and to work at jobs other than farming. Life was quite different in the city for people used to living in the country.

Names

Although the new machines caused many jobs to disappear, some of the names still "echo" in our times. Just the meanings have changed. For example, someone who spun thread was called a *spinster.* Often this

Being a crossing guard is a big responsibility.

person was a woman who stayed with her parents to take care of the spinning, weaving, and other household work. The word has since come to mean any unmarried woman past the usual age for marrying.

A *vendor* was once (and still is in some of the larger cities) a person who sold goods from a small street cart. Oystermen, muffin men, peanut girls, gingerbread ladies, and fish sellers were vendors on streets long ago. Today the word *vendor* usually means a person or a company that provides a service or goods.

Teamster used to refer to someone who drove a wagon and horses. Today the word *teamster* is used in a more general way. The Teamsters' Union includes truck drivers and warehousemen and others, but none of them work with horses.

Once a *crossing guard* stopped people from crossing tracks when a train was coming. What does the modern crossing guard do?

This vendor carts apples through the streets, calling, "Apples, fresh apples!"

It Was Called a Revolution

Revolution usually means a big change which comes suddenly and often with violence. Do you think the change from handwork to machines should be called a revolution? In America, the change was not as dramatic as the word *revolution* might make it sound.

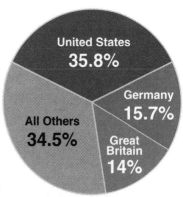

World Manufacturing in 1913

Money Spent on Running Factories in the U.S.

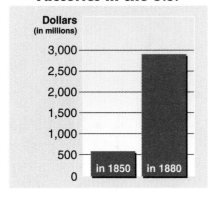

Number of People Working in Factories in the U.S.

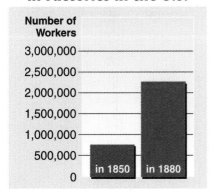

Although the change took many years, it made life in the United States completely different after the American Civil War. Many families now saw each other only when they were not working at a factory. Towns and cities grew fast; the nation became more "city" than "country."

In England, using more machines and factories was called the *Industrial Revolution*. *Industry* comes from an old word meaning "skill." *Factory,* a place where industry goes on, comes from an old word that means "a place for makers." The word *manufacture* comes from words meaning "to make by hand." How did the Industrial Revolution change the definition for that word?

Look at the graphs. What changes occurred in thirty years? How much money was being spent on factories by 1880? Where could you learn how much is being spent today? What country was first in manufacturing by 1913? Which country was second?

The American Industrial Revolution

Americans had their reasons for not using machines and setting up factories as soon as other countries did. For one, the land in America was vast and unsettled. People who came from the crowded cities in other countries wanted to spend their money buying land. They did not want to stay in the towns. Even factory owners who paid good wages could not compete with the American desire to own land.

Early Railroads

Chicago
Philadelphia
St. Joseph
Richmond

Water Power

Grain hopper
Grindstones
Gears
Water wheel

The "revolution" was slow in America also because it was a land with thousands of streams and rivers. Why, said the mill owners, should steam engines be used where the water power is easy to get and free? Although it was free, water did have its drawbacks: it sometimes froze in winter and dried up in summer. Then the mills and workshops had to close down and wait for better weather.

Perhaps the biggest problem for American business was the terrible condition of most of the roads. Many were still just paths through the wilderness. A factory owner could have steam-powered machines and good workers to run them but not have a way to get products to market. One thing that most helped solve this problem was the railroad.

To Use Distribution Maps

1. Get some colored pencils or crayons and Notebook page 70.

2. Color the map and key as your teacher tells you.

3. Then read the map and answer the questions.

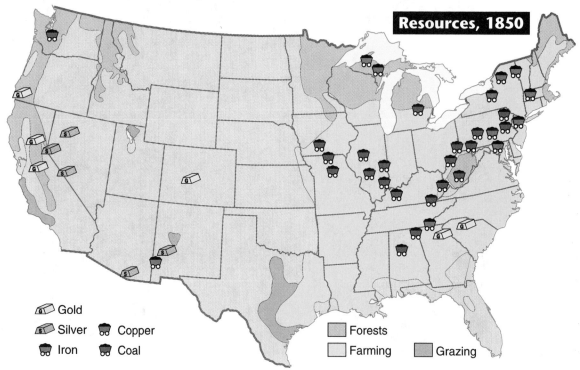

Bangor
Portland
Albany
Boston
Buffalo
Detroit
Newburg
Newark
New York
Brooklyn
Lancaster
Philadelphia
Pittsburgh
Wilmington
Cincinnati
Washington
Baltimore
St. Louis
Richmond
Louisville
Petersburg
Charleston
Savannah
Mobile

When the Union and the Confederacy went to war, industries sprang up almost overnight. Suddenly armies needed clothes, food, guns, tents, and other supplies—more than handworkers toiling night and day could get made in time. Machines were the only answer.

Most factories burned coal to make steam to run the engines. Compare the two maps on this page. Where were the best deposits of coal and metal ore? Why do you think the population was so much larger in some areas than others? Compare these maps with the railroad map on page 174. Why did the railroad companies build the tracks where they did?

Resources, 1850

Gold
Silver   Copper
Iron   Coal

Forests
Farming   Grazing

The Workers

David was eight years old when his father decided to move the family to town. A cotton mill there had a job for him. He could make more money there than he could on the farm. And with five children, he needed to. David hated to leave his big garden and the woods where he played sometimes. But he knew his father wanted to do the best for them.

The house that David's family moved into was much smaller than the one they had had in the country. His mother made it look like home when she put the rocking chair by the window and set the cradle by the chair. David's little brother Joshua lay in the cradle and held up his hand to a beam of light.

Man working in a textile mill

David's father went to the mill right away. He worked until late at night. He left early every morning. David rarely saw him until Sundays. If David got up before the sun came up, he could talk to his father as he was eating or making a fire in the stove. But mostly, David had to wait until Sunday afternoon. It had never been that way on the farm. There his father had always been around somewhere.

One day, just before David turned nine, his father came home earlier than usual. He said he wanted to ask David a question.

"What is it, Papa? Did I do something wrong?"

His father smiled and shook his head. "No, Son. Not at all. Down at the mill—" He paused. "Down at the mill, they have a job for a boy. Running errands for Mr. Shapp, the owner. What would you say to working at the mill with me?"

David felt his heart pounding. "Me? I could go to work?"

"I need you to, Son."

"Yes, Papa. Tell them yes!"

David's father nodded and looked away. He did not smile or say any more. David wondered why his father was not as happy as he was. He could hardly wait to be earning money. It would be like being all grown up. He was bursting to tell his younger brothers and sisters.

There were no rules then about how old someone had to be before he could go to work. Sometimes children as young as six or seven had to help support the family. To David, the job seemed like an adventure. To his father, it was the end of a too-short childhood for David.

Children sometimes worked in mills at machinery such as this.

Child Labor

David worked for Mr. Shapp, a kind man, who asked him to run with messages to different parts of the mill. Sometimes he sent David with a letter to the post office. Other times David waited for the train and directed businessmen to the mill. Although David worked from seven in the morning until six at night, others his age had harder jobs.

Girls aged 6, 8, and 10 returning from a day of work shucking oysters

Some children worked in coal mines, staying in the dampness and the dark for fourteen hours a day. They could come up into the sunshine for lunch—always for less than an hour. Sometimes miners would scare them with stories of monsters in the tunnels. Many children got sick, but they had to work anyway. How was this child labor different from the apprenticeships of Benjamin Franklin's time?

Other children had to help run the noisy, dangerous machines. And because they worked such long hours, they often fell asleep at the job. What do you think happened then? At best, they would be rapped with a stick and told to wake up and get back to work. At worst, they would fall into the machine and get badly hurt.

179

A few factory owners took good care of the children who worked for them. They made sure they were schooled and had plenty to eat and did not work where it was dangerous. But far more owners cared more about their machines than they did for the boys and girls who worked them. Many factory children could not write their own names, and they often worked fourteen or fifteen hours a day. Their wages were only pennies a day.

Women worked as long and hard as men in factories.

The Men and Women Who Worked

Many women also began to work away from home. They became seamstresses in factories, ran machines that made thread and cloth, and did other jobs that women had never done before. How do you think that changed life at home?

Men had to learn new jobs too. Think of the weavers who lost their work when machines were invented to do weaving faster. What do you think those people did? Some of them learned to run the new machines. Others went into different work. And others moved to towns where hand-weavers could still make a living. What would you have done?

Many of the machines were open; that is, they had no covers over the chains and gears. There were many bad accidents before owners of factories put rails and shields around machinery that could hurt people. The faster way to work had many prices—many of which no one foresaw. It cost children their childhood, many people their jobs, some people their homes, and even a few people their lives.

Protest signs and riots sometimes accompanied strikes.

Some people tried to make the owners of factories help the workers more. These people, mostly the workers themselves, asked for shorter hours. They said ten hours a day would be better. How many hours a day do most people now work?

The workers wanted safer machines. When the owners ignored the workers' requests, the workers decided to band together and demand what they felt were their rights. They formed *unions,* groups of workers who join together, or unite, to help each other.

The unions asked the owners to listen to them. Many owners did. Although the workers did not get everything they wanted, they did get a ten-hour day and attention to the needs of the children.

Later, when unions were bigger, the members refused to work if their requests were not answered. They called the time when they would not work a *strike.* Have you heard of any strikes today? What do you think happened when workers went on strike? Sometimes the owners met the demands right away. Sometimes they fired the workers. Sometimes the workers and the owners went to court.

Most of the time, the judges decided that the workers were wrong to strike, and the workers had to return to their jobs—usually losing pay for when they did not work. Workers had been hired by agreement— so much work for so much pay. When they went on strike, they broke a contract. How else might they have made their needs known to the owners? They could have gone to court.

Big Business

When America was a brand new country, its biggest business was farming. In 1925, President Calvin Coolidge said, "The business of America is business." What do you think he meant? And what had happened in one hundred ten years to change our country from a country of farms to a country of businesses? Look at the time line.

In 1815, England shipped many goods to the United States at low prices. The prices were so low, in fact, that the English were selling them at a loss. Why do you think the English were willing to do that? What else is happening on the time line right then? The United States is just beginning to build factories. England is already running big factories. How would selling English goods cheaply keep factories out of America?

How would a new patent law, making inventions easier to protect and easier to sell, help the Industrial Revolution? It encouraged people to come up with new ideas for faster and better machines. Americans have always been known for improving inventions and thinking up new ways of doing things.

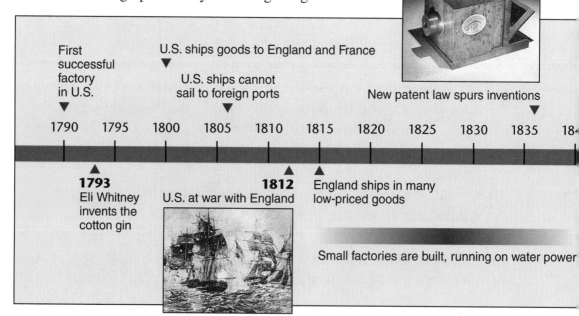

First successful factory in U.S. ▼

U.S. ships goods to England and France ▼

U.S. ships cannot sail to foreign ports ▼

New patent law spurs inventions ▼

| 1790 | 1795 | 1800 | 1805 | 1810 | 1815 | 1820 | 1825 | 1830 | 1835 | 18- |

▲ **1793** Eli Whitney invents the cotton gin

▲ **1812** U.S. at war with England

▲ England ships in many low-priced goods

Small factories are built, running on water power

In little more than ten years' time, the Industrial Revolution turned cities like Wichita, Kansas, from small cattle towns into prospering industrial centers.

Although there were problems that came with new industry, there were many advantages too. Lower- and middle-class people had more money; they lived longer; they had better houses and furniture; they had some time for leisure. Life improved for nearly everyone, not just the rich.

Can you name some reasons that people came to the United States after 1840? How would suddenly having many more people help the Industrial Revolution? There were now plenty of workers for the factories.

It was because of the thousands of people who were willing to work hard at unpleasant jobs that the United States got its railroads built, its roads paved, and its industries growing. The work they accomplished actually made more jobs; as the nation got richer and more powerful, it needed more and more work done. Although at first it seemed the many newcomers would destroy America's big business, they indeed ensured its success.

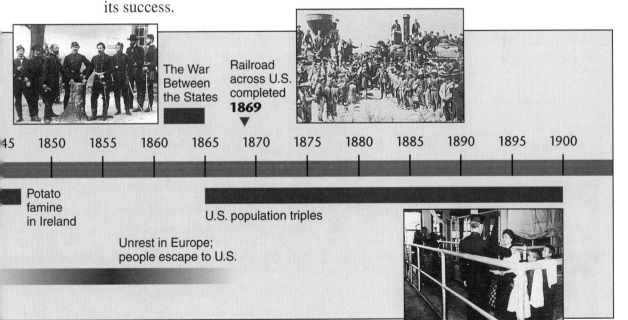

The War Between the States

Railroad across U.S. completed **1869** ▼

45   1850   1855   1860   1865   1870   1875   1880   1885   1890   1895   1900

Potato famine in Ireland

U.S. population triples

Unrest in Europe; people escape to U.S.

Andrew Carnegie
(1835-1919)

A weaver who lost his job in Scotland moved to America in 1848. His thirteen-year-old son, Andrew, became a bobbin boy in a cotton mill; he worked twelve hours a day six days a week and made $1.20 a week. How much was that an hour?

Do you think Andrew Carnegie ever regretted the hard work he had done as a teenager?

Andrew later worked as a messenger boy for a telegraph office for $2.50 a week. He went early every day to learn how to send telegrams. When he was seventeen, he was so skillful that a superintendent of the Pennsylvania Railroad hired him to send his messages. Andrew learned about the train business and, seven years later, became vice president.

As he always had, Carnegie saved all his money. When he had enough, he invested it in oil, a grain elevator, and an iron business. From then on, the more money he made, the more businesses he bought. After the American Civil War, when other businesses failed, Carnegie's prospered. By age sixty, he was one of the wealthiest men in the world.

> *"Seest thou a man diligent in his business? he shall stand before kings; he shall not stand before mean men."*
>
> **Proverbs 22:29**

But his last ambition was to die poor. Andrew Carnegie gave money to build over three thousand libraries; he built schools and gave millions of dollars to universities (because he had been able to go to school so little himself). And he bought beautiful organs and furniture for churches. Despite his goal to become poor, he died still having $22,000,000!

9

Stoking
the Fires

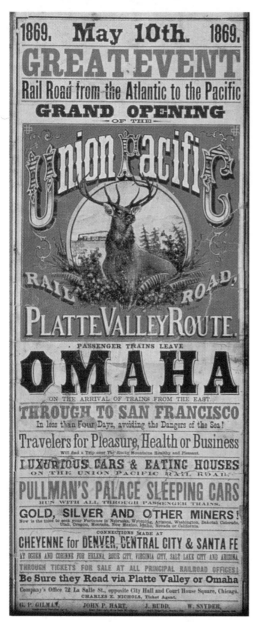

Poster announcing coast-to-coast travel

America was getting richer and stronger all the time. Its machines and inventions, its immigrants and settlers, its resources and vast lands made it the envy of the world. But what seemed growth and light to some was destruction and darkness to others.

Railroad Ties

The railroads made travel easier and faster than many could ever have imagined just a few years before. The steam engines sped people and goods from one side of the country to the other. In many ways, the railroads united the people of America. But the builders of the rails found out how hard it is for different people to get along, to understand each other, and to work together.

When the transcontinental railroad was being built, many more workers were needed than was originally thought. Many men wanted to go west to look for gold rather than to labor on the endless rails. So the man in charge of the railroad builders, Charlie Crocker, decided to send to California for Chinese workers. Many of the men already working for the railroad were Irish; they did not like the idea of Chinese men working on the railroad. Why do you think that was?

186

Building a railroad was exhausting labor; these men looked forward to rest.

Other leaders in the railroad business thought Crocker had a bad idea. But Crocker said that the Chinese people had built the Great Wall of China and they certainly would be able to help with a railroad. They proved him right: the Chinese were efficient, diligent, and quick to learn the work. And they were often given the hardest and most dangerous jobs.

There were many reasons that people did not get along. For one thing, the Irish ate beef, bread, potatoes, and coffee; and they could not understand why the Chinese ate fish, seaweed, pork, and tea. They did not like the woven hats the Chinese wore, and they did not like it that the Chinese behaved differently from them.

The Irish workers talked and sang as they worked. The Chinese rarely made any noise, except for the thud of their picks and the chug and swish of their shovels. When the Irish shouted names at them, they expected the Chinese to return the insults. But the Chinese, who did not understand what was said or pretended not to understand, kept on working in silence.

The silence was a far greater insult to the Irish than any reply could have been. Some of the Irish picked up clods of dirt and threw them at the Chinese. Still they worked on quietly. The Irish were furious by then. Some of them took the heads off their picks and attacked the Chinese with the wooden handles. Since the Irish were almost a foot taller than most of the Chinese workers, they thought it would be a quick and easy fight. They were wrong.

The Chinese at last fought back. They came at the Irishmen by twos, one throwing himself at an Irishman's legs, the other grabbing his shoulders and throwing him off balance. Pick handles were of little use to a man lying on his back with the opposition on top of him. In a short while, the Irish went back to their work. But the trouble was not over.

Some of the non-Chinese workers made hand bombs from the explosives meant for blasting rock. Most that they threw at the Chinese never went off. But a few of these bombs actually worked. Many Chinese workers were seriously hurt. Charlie Crocker tried to stop the fighting. Other leaders of the railroad work demanded that it stop. But it took more than their words to get results. It took a terrible accident.

An explosion, possibly meant to injure more Chinese, caused an instantaneous and huge avalanche. Rocks and earth crashed down into a hollow where many Irish workers were. Many, many men died suddenly, with no hope and no warning. All the men, Chinese and Irish and others, were stunned. After that, neither side made any moves against the other.

About 60,000 Chinese workers helped build the transcontinental railroad. Chinese workers hold the record for laying the most track in one day: ten miles.

189

The Blizzards of 1866-67 and 1886-87

The weather could prove a worse enemy to railroad builders and ranchers and others than almost any other threat. The winter of 1866 blew in cold and sudden. Few people in the Sierra Nevada had any idea what lay ahead.

The railroad builders, most of them Chinese, worked through deep snow in November, December, and January. Thousands of men did nothing but shovel snow to keep the way clear for those who tried to lay the track. Others built snow sheds, shelters for the workers. Then in February, there came a blizzard like none had seen before. It raged for twelve days and nights. Drifts over sixty feet high made going on almost impossible. Shelters collapsed; people froze to death. If one

The golden spike is hammered in; it was a moment workers had dreamed of for years.

man was more than a yard from the next, he could neither see nor hear his companion, so loud was the wind, so thick was the snow.

Some men died in avalanches; a few were found encased in ice, standing, still holding their pickaxes, nearly three months later. Little progress was made on the tracks over the mountains that month. The miracle is that any track was laid at all. But by the end of the summer, the worst part of the mountains was behind the workers. The driving of the golden spike was less than two years away.

As bad as that blizzard was, it may have seemed small to the survivors of the winters between 1885 and 1900. Those winters, terrible storms raged over the West. In 1885, some ranchers lost more than half their cattle to cold and snow. During the winter of 1886-87, the temperature was often forty degrees Fahrenheit below zero or colder; the winds howled for days at a time. In the spring, men had the ugly job of finding all the carcasses of their cattle.

Some years before, ranchers had put up fences on the open range. The cattle were used to roaming wide spaces to find food and to stay ahead of storms. When the storms came, the cattle tried to walk out of them. But they were caught at the fences and froze or starved to death. Many ranchers went out of business: some because the losses were too much, some because they did not want to own animals they could not care for in terrible weather.

In the eastern part of the country, where blizzards are far more rare, a storm hit that is still talked about. In March 1888, the snow and the cold and the wind roared over states from Maryland to

West 11th Street in New York City

Maine. The temperature fell to nearly zero degrees Fahrenheit; the wind whipped at more than thirty miles an hour; and almost two feet of snow came down in sand-sized, biting grains. Although storms since have rivaled that blizzard, it became one of the most famous in American history.

Part of the reason for its fame is the stories that came from it. Although more than three hundred people died, most of the survivors remembered the heroes the storm created. One hero was twelve-year-old Milton Daub. He made himself a pair of snowshoes from barrel hoops and twine and went out to get milk for his family. When other people saw that he was getting along on the top of the snow, they asked him to help get them food and medicine. So Milton served others all day and never charged them more than the goods had cost him to get. But the grateful people gave him many tips. At night he crawled back into his house through a window with bread and milk and went to sleep—for twelve hours. When his mother and father counted the money he had given them, they found he had made more than sixty-seven dollars. Today that would be like making more than eight hundred dollars.

Words of the Chiefs

Geronimo, an Apache warrior, led many raids on settlers and soldiers.

When the railroads and the telegraph lines were finished, there was almost no hope for the Sioux and other peoples who had lived in the lands that were now the United States to regain their old way of life. Some chiefs wanted to keep fighting, to try to hold back the tide of people they saw as invaders. Others began to realize that the fight was useless.

The Apaches had lived peaceably with white settlers for many years. After the War Between the States, though, the Apaches began to defend their homes and to raid white settlements. At last, the United States government demanded that the Apaches move to a reservation in New Mexico. An Apache chief, Cochise, made a speech then. The general who was sent to make the Apaches move was so impressed by the speech that he asked the government to let the people stay. Here is part of Chief Cochise's speech:

> When I was young I walked all over this country, east and west, and I saw no other people but Apaches. After many summers I walked again and found another race of people had come to take it. How is it? Why is it that the Apaches wait to die—that they carry their lives on their fingernails? They roam over the hills and plains and want the heavens to fall on them. The Apaches were once a great nation. They are now only a few.

What do you think Chief Cochise meant when he said that his people carried their lives on their fingernails? Why do you think that the Apaches wanted the heavens to fall on them? What reasons can you give for the Apache nation's becoming small?

Chief Ten Bears, speaking for the Comanches, tried to hold on to the buffalo lands his people had always hunted on:

Viewing a vanishing way of life

Two years ago, I came upon this road, following the buffalo, that my wives and children might have their cheeks plump and their bodies warm. But the soldiers fired on us. And since that time there has been a noise like thunder, and we have not known which way to go. . . .

I was born on the prairie, where the wind blew free and there was nothing to break the light of the sun. I was born where there were no fences and everything drew a free breath. . . . I know every stream and every woods between the Rio Grande and the Arkansas. I have hunted and lived over that country. I live like my fathers before me and, like them, I live happily.

When I was at Washington the Great Father told me that all the Comanche land was ours, and that nobody should stop us from living on it. So why do you ask us to leave the rivers, and the sun, and the wind?

Chief Joseph

Another chief, Chief Joseph, also made a speech about the plight of his people, the Nez Perce. President Grant had declared that the people would never have to leave their homes. They lived in the rich and beautiful valley of the Clearwater River, now in Washington State. But the land there was so good that soon the other settlers wanted it; they did not care what the president had promised. What do you think happened?

Soon the president's order was taken back and the Nez Perce were told to leave the valley. They were told to go to a reservation within thirty days. Chief Joseph asked for more time because he had many women, children, horses, and goods to move. But the general in charge, the same one who had helped Cochise, said no. Chief Joseph told his people to get ready to move. The Snake River was flooded; it would be hard to cross. But the Nez Perce had no choice.

They made the crossing, but it was dangerous and tiring. While they were crossing, some white people came and stole some of their cattle. A few of the young Nez Perce men wanted revenge; they killed some white people. Then the war was on.

Chief Joseph led his people toward Canada to escape the army that wanted to capture him and his people. He outwitted and outfought a force twice the size of his own many times. But at last he and his people, weary and despairing, gave up. Chief Joseph appealed to his captors:

> I know that my race must change. We cannot hold our own with the white men as we are. We ask only an even chance to live as other men live. We ask to be recognized as men. We ask that the same law work alike on all men. If the Indian breaks the law, punish him by the law. If the white man breaks the law, punish him also.
>
> Let me be a free man—free to travel, free to stop, free to work, free to trade where I choose, free to choose my own teachers, free to follow the religion of my fathers, free to think and act and talk for myself—and I will obey every law, or submit to the penalty.
>
> Whenever the white man treats the Indian as they treat each other, then we will have no more wars.

What do you think of Chief Joseph's requests? Check his requests against the first nine amendments of the Constitution of the United States. Which of his requests did the writers of that document consider important too?

Like many other Native Americans, Chief Joseph was heartsick at "all the broken promises."

196

Chief speaking at a council meeting

What do you think happened? Some of Chief Joseph's people were allowed to go back to their homes. But Chief Joseph and others were not. They had to go to a reservation far from their beloved river valley. Chief Joseph died there. The doctor at the reservation said in his official report that the chief had died of "a broken heart."

Why do you think that the leaders of the Nez Perce and the Apaches and other peoples were such good speakers? One reason is that the ability to speak well was considered a great art—greater than painting or carving. Since decisions in most of the nations were made by the whole group, not by just a few leaders, speakers needed to be able to persuade others to agree with them. Those who could speak most movingly became leaders.

Few words of the great chiefs and poets and singers exist today. The poems and speeches and songs were spoken or sung but not written down. How do you think we have any of the words? Some were written down by white translators. But these translators sometimes added their own ideas to the speeches; sometimes they did not translate correctly at all. At the ceremony in which the Union Pacific and Central Pacific Railroads were joined with the golden spike, for example, a Native American made a speech. He said that his people and many others had been cheated by the railroad. But the translator told the crowd that the man had said he was happy that the rails had crossed the land.

Help That Did Not Help

Not all white people wanted to harm the Native Americans. But sometimes they did not know what to do to help. By 1887, people who thought that what was happening to the Apaches and others was wrong demanded that the government help. The Congress passed the Dawes Act to try to make the situation better.

George Catlin, Bull Dance, Mandan Okipa Ceremony, National Collection of Fine Arts, Washington, D.C.

The act said that because the Native Americans' ways of living would no longer work, the Native Americans would have to learn white ways. The people could no longer live in large groups as they always had, with grandparents, aunts, uncles, father, mother, and children all working together. Each father was given up to 160 acres of land and told to become a farmer.

Many of the western peoples were hunters and traders. How do you think they liked being told to become farmers? How do you think they liked being told that they could no longer live in large family groups? Some tried to do as they were told. But the land they were given was usually dry, poor land that the white men did not want. On 160 acres of such ground, few could grow enough for a family to eat.

> *"Providing for honest things, not only in the sight of the Lord, but also in the sight of men."*
>
> **II Corinthians 8:21**

Do you think the Dawes Act made life any better for those who had lost much already? It actually made things worse. The people who had always lived on the open plains were not used to owning land. When dishonest settlers or gold seekers offered to buy the land, they easily cheated the new owners.

Indian Lands

Prior to 1784

1784–1810

1811–1850

1851–1870

Today

Why do you think the white people wanted the Native American people to be like them? Some thought that the white man's ways were the best ways. They thought the white man's houses were better, the white man's clothes were better, and the white man's rules were better. Some even thought that all Native Americans were like small children who needed to be taken care of.

Many believed that it was kindness to make the Native Americans live on *reservations,* special lands set apart for them, and to let the government provide their food and clothing. But was it? When the Cheyenne, for example, could no longer hunt their own food and make the beaded leather clothes they used to wear, they became unhappy; they had nothing to do, nothing to live for. White people who saw them said they were lazy and glum. The white people then tried harder to make the Cheyenne change.

The Native Americans had heroes and criminals among them, just as the white people did. They had good ways and bad ways, just as the white people did. But because they were fewer and because they did not have one leader, like a president, they did not have the power to keep their way of life. And as white hunters killed off the buffalo, more and more Native Americans had to live on reservations and look to the government for food, clothing, and shelter.

A bustling midwestern town

Ghost Towns and Boom Towns

Not everyone benefited from the railroad. Can you tell how the railroads helped take more land from the Native Americans? Can you think of others who might have lost their homes or wealth because of the rails? Some towns had bustled before because they were located on stagecoach roads. But if these towns were too far from the new tracks, people left them to go to towns where railroad stations brought in lots of money.

Some towns just got smaller; a few people stayed, keeping the towns alive. Other towns were deserted altogether. The buildings began to fall apart; the streets blew full of dust and tumbleweeds; the roads grew up with brambles. The towns became *ghost towns.* Why do you think people called them that?

A ghost town in Montana

To Find a Ghost Town

1. Get a good atlas and Notebook pages 75-76.

2. Choose a western state.

3. Look at the chart of populations. Select a town with a population of less than fifty. Write down the name of the town and the county it is in. Write down the name of the state and the capital city.

4. Write to the highway department of that state to ask for a free map. Some maps show ghost towns in special print. Or write to the address your teacher helps you find. Local historical societies can give you information.

Montana

Some towns died out; others sprang into existence. People built many towns in a hurry. The gold rush created towns; the camps that men lived in sometimes turned into places like Red Dog and Rich Bar, California. Silver mining also generated towns: Aspen, Colorado, started as one man's small staked claim. Other towns built up around work like logging. Look at the chart that shows the stages of getting a tree from the forest to the sawmill to the carpenters. At which stages do you think a town might develop? Towns that grow quickly because a big business begins are called *boom towns*. What might the name suggest about these towns?

What businesses do you think came first to boom towns? Blacksmithing and storekeeping were needed right away. But no matter how many smithies and shops a place had, it could not be officially called a town until it had a United States post office. Aspen, for example, was just a claim on the Roaring Fork River. The man who owned the claim went to Washington, D.C., to ask for a post office; he planned to name the town Ute City. When he got back, someone had stolen his land and named the place Aspen.

Lumber Making

1. Trees are cut, trimmed, and pulled to the river.

2. Logs floating toward the mills are moved by men with poles to prevent log jams.

3. Logs, stripped of bark, are "buzzed" into boards.

The Children Too

Sometimes it seems that only adults had adventures and important work to do. But in almost every job, except in building railroads, children were working right along with the adults. Even in the sawmills, children oiled the machinery and swept sawdust from under the saws.

A one-room school in Kansas

They helped look after the horses. If they did not keep to their work, all work slowed down. There was time to play, however. In the summer, the mill pond was good for fishing and swimming; in the winter it was good for skating.

For many years, children did not have to go to school regularly. It was more important that they help get work done. Farmers' children, for example, could go to school only when there was not planting or harvesting to be done. When did they go to school? Some children in cities never went at all. Because children's wages were less, they were given jobs that adults usually did. By 1900, however, every state had laws that said all children had to go to school for at least a few years. Why do you think those laws were made? Partly it was to get some of the children's jobs back for the adults.

Schools today have grades, like the fourth grade. But in the 1800s, schools were not always separated into grades. In the big city schools, where there were more children than places for them, teachers began to put students of the same age together: eight grades in elementary, four in high school. In smaller schools and in country schools, many students were put together in one room, taller and older students in the back and younger and smaller ones in the front. Students in such schools were often grouped by ability rather than by age. Which school would you have liked better?

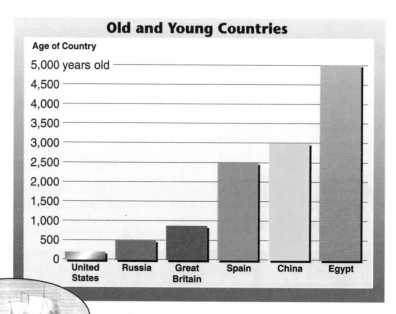

Old and Young Countries

Age of Country

Country	Age
United States	(small)
Russia	~450
Great Britain	~850
Spain	~2,450
China	~2,950
Egypt	~5,000

The Spanish-American War

America was still a young nation—especially in the eyes of the old countries in Europe. Many Americans wanted to prove that their nation was a world power. How do you think countries become important powers among other countries?

One way is to be wealthy. Having a lot of money to spend makes a country seem important. Another way is to have a strong army and navy that command respect. Although America had won independence from England in 1776 and had held its own in the War of 1812, the young nation was not yet considered a military power.

Spain was an old country with a long history of exploring, conquering, and settling. Other countries viewed Spain as powerful and important. Americans knew that their country was not feared as Spain was. Some Americans wanted to change that view; they wanted to gain more land and make a great army and navy. Others wanted America to mind her own business.

The Monroe Doctrine

In 1823, President James Monroe told the countries of Europe that the United States did not want them to make any more colonies in the New World. He said that the United States was establishing a democracy and that governments holding colonies were "dangerous to our peace and safety." What do you think he meant?

Do you think President Monroe could make his declaration work? What would he need if some country refused to go along with his statement? He needed a strong army and navy to enforce his new rule. But America's navy was small.

England had the strongest navy in the world then. England agreed to help America make other countries obey the Monroe Doctrine. But

England did not help out just to be neighborly. English leaders wanted to trade with South American countries, and they did not want Spain to take back its South American colonies. America was happy to have English help, whatever the reason.

By the time Cuba, a Spanish colony, tried to get out of Spain's control in 1895, Americans had built a powerful navy. Some people tried to get the United States government to help Cuba, claiming that the Monroe Doctrine demanded such action. But did it?

The doctrine said only that new colonies should not be made; it said nothing about removing existing ones. Nonetheless, the Monroe Doctrine "echoed" wherever there was a debate over Cuba.

Rumblings of Trouble

How do you think a war gets started? Wars have started for many reasons—most of them seemingly small reasons. Some wars have started by accident—neither side meant to begin the fighting. The Spanish-American War had several causes.

Early in the war, American papers mocked the Spanish view that America was weak.

"Notice of funeral hereafter."

For one thing, two newspapermen were trying to outdo each other in sales. They each tried to get the biggest news first and put it in their newspapers. Sometimes, when the news was not exciting enough, these men would "spice it up" a little. Do you think that is right? William Randolph Hearst and Joseph Pulitzer said that they had a right to print what they wanted.

In 1898, Hearst and Pulitzer were looking for some really big news to print. But, for the moment, there were no big troubles in the world. There were only the usual stories—such as President McKinley's un-popularity because some people thought he was not using the Monroe Doctrine in the right way. What could Hearst and Pulitzer put in their newspapers to make people buy them? They decided to check into the trouble in Cuba.

Clara Barton
(1821-1912)

As a girl Clara Barton had traveled with her father when he fought with the Indians out West. Then, as a young woman, she served as a nurse in the Civil War. She spent her own money to find missing soldiers and to get help for the badly hurt. The group called the American Red Cross came to be because Clara Barton believed that such a group was needed. Perhaps you have seen a truck or a building with the red cross on it.

In 1898, Clara, then seventy-seven years old, heard that people in Cuba were suffering under the Spanish rulers. She could never hear of suffering without trying to help. She went to President McKinley and

asked whether she could take some food and medicine to the Cuban people. He told her she could.

When she got there, Miss Barton saw people starving and beaten. She saw little children with no food or clothes. She was horrified and grieved. She wrote a book, *The Red Cross,* to tell what life was like for some in Cuba.

Miss Barton had no idea how her book would be used. She had no idea how large and important the American Red Cross group would become. She only knew she had to live her life to help others.

Clara Barton

Theodore Roosevelt (in glasses beside flag) with the "Rough Riders"

Hearst and Pulitzer read about the trouble in Cuba. They decided to send writers there. Soon many reports were printed in the newspapers, telling the Americans that the Spanish were cruel and wicked, that the Cubans were dying only because the Spanish treated them so badly. Americans were angry. Those Spanish had to be stopped! The newspapers were not telling *all* the story. However, Americans did not seem to want to hear any more; they wanted action.

President McKinley said that America's army was not ready to go to war. He wanted to talk to the Spanish. And he did. The Spanish did not want a war either; they were too far from home to take on the United States in battle. To show that they did not want to fight, the Spanish sent one of their generals back to Spain. He was the general that the papers in the United States had been calling a "butcher." What do you think the Americans thought of this action?

Many Americans were somewhat calmed when the Spanish sent their general home. A few still wanted to make the Spanish do more. One of these was a man named Theodore Roosevelt. Roosevelt was in charge of a group of men called the "Rough Riders." What do you think the name tells about the group? Roosevelt wanted a war, and he wanted to be ready for it.

A Mysterious Explosion

The Americans sent a ship, the *Maine,* to Cuba to show that they could back up their demands. The Spanish did not like to see the ship come, but they were polite; they gave the Americans gifts and treated them with respect. Everyone began to believe that a war would not happen.

Then one night, as the sailors slept, a huge explosion lifted the great ship out of the water. She immediately began to take on water and to sink. The captain could not save his ship. By morning, with the help of a nearby Spanish ship, the captain had rescued 102 of his men. But more than 250 had died.

No one knew exactly what had caused the ship to explode. President McKinley sent men to find out, but they could not say for sure. Many experts thought it was an accident. But the newspapers in America printed headlines like these: "*Maine* Blown Up by Enemy," and "Split in Two by Enemy's Secret Infernal Machine." What do you think headlines like that did to the Americans' desire for war?

The Spanish did not want war. They quickly did everything that the United States wanted—and more. But it was not enough. America declared war on Spain.

An artist's version of the wreck of the Maine

A Short War

The American navy sent more ships to fire on Spanish forts in Cuba. Then the American army went on land to fight the Spanish soldiers. Teddy Roosevelt's Rough Riders were among the first to go in. They were in-

deed a rough group who did not always see the need to obey rules. But they were brave in a fight, and they liked Roosevelt enough to do as he said under fire.

The Americans thought that the Cubans they were rescuing would help with the fighting. But the Cubans were not prepared to fight; they had little training and few weapons. So the war that was supposed to be almost bloodless began to cost many American lives.

Soon the Americans had control of the whole island. The American generals, some of whom had fought in the American Civil War, demanded that the Spanish surrender. At first the Spanish said no. Then the United States offered to take all the Spanish soldiers home to Spain on American ships. The Spanish quickly surrendered. The Spanish flag that had flown over Cuba for almost four hundred years came down. The Stars and Stripes went up.

Back in the United States, everyone was celebrating. America had gone to war against an important country and had won. Now America had new lands—the island of Cuba and other islands.

10
Getting
the Message

Did You Hear?

A drumming of hooves and then a shout brought a man out from the pony express station. He ran to the barn to get the fresh horse—it had been saddled and waiting for two hours.

The rider galloped in, pulled up his horse, and leaped off. "Morning," he said to the man holding the fresh horse by the reins. He snatched the *mochila* from the back of the winded horse and threw it onto the new mount. The letters inside the leather pouch shifted.

"Coffee?" said the man still holding the horse.

"Can't," said the rider. "Late." He rolled his shoulders and stretched. Then he hauled himself into the saddle. He nodded to the station man and then pressed his heels into the horse's side. The horse sprang away. Not even a minute had passed since the rider had come in.

Why do you think the rider was in such a hurry? He had just come twenty-five miles, and he had another twenty-five miles to go. He was in a hurry because his job was important: to deliver the mail safely and quickly. But how quick is quick?

A mochila

When the mail was carried on stagecoaches, it took at least three and a half weeks for a letter to get from New York to San Francisco. The pony express could get it there in as little as ten days.

How fast can you get a message to some distant place now? A few minutes? Even seconds? What inventions have made such communication possible?

Newspapers

Once, there were few ways to get news from one place to another. Long ago, most news traveled slowly; usually one person told another and he told another and so on. People who traveled from one town to another carried the news with them. Letters, too, spread information. The Separatists sent letters back to England, telling of their new life in the New World. Much of what we know about earlier times comes from these old letters.

After the printing press was developed, someone in England got another idea about getting the news out. The new idea was called the *London Gazette*. It was a printed paper that told the news. *Gazette* used to mean "official publication."

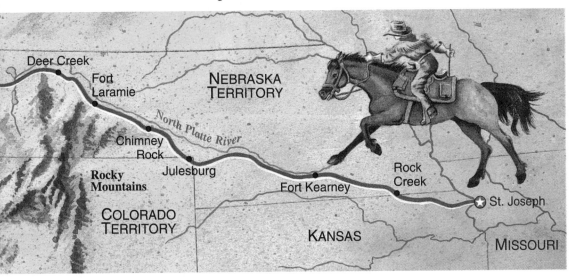

A few years later the word *newspaper* became the name for such publications as the *London Gazette*. In America, the first paper that stayed in business and made money was the *Boston News-Letter*. It did not look like a newspaper today; it was about as big as a sheet of notebook paper. How much news do you think could fit on both sides of one sheet of notebook paper?

Newspapers in those days might better have been called "oldspapers." The "news" in them was sometimes months old by the time the readers got them. They were not published every day either. Why do you think that was?

In 1833, the *New York Sun* changed the way papers were published. The *New York Sun* was bigger—nearly like today's papers. It cost only a penny, and it was published every day. It was the first paper to do other things too. It printed advertisements; it was the first to be delivered to houses; and it was the first to be sold on the street.

Newspapers changed the way people got their news. More people could know about events more quickly. How do you think newspapers changed the way people lived?

Even so, news traveled slowly by modern standards. When George Washington died in 1799, it was an event of world importance. But people in Massachusetts did not read about it until two weeks later. And people in Ohio saw the news in their papers almost three weeks after the funeral.

The 1704 Boston News-Letter

The Telegraph

America was becoming a big country. Newspapers and pony express mail kept the news traveling, but some people had been looking for faster ways to communicate. One of them was a famous painter named Samuel Morse.

Morse had been in France and was coming home by ship. During the long trip, he heard men talking about electricity. Since Benjamin Franklin's ex-

Samuel F. B. Morse

periment with the kite and lightning, people had been fascinated by the possibilities of this energy.

"It's called an electromagnet," one man said. "Looks like a big horseshoe with wire wrapped around it. I saw it back in New York."

"What's the purpose of it?" said another.

"See," said the first man, "when electricity is passed through the wire, the horseshoe becomes magnetic. Works like a giant magnet, it does."

"Really!" said the other. "Does it matter how much wire is used? Does the current slow if the wire is long?"

"No, not at all. Electricity passes instantly from one end to the other no matter how long the wire is."

"Then," said Morse, speaking up for the first time, "I think that wire and electricity might be used to send messages over long distances."

The others talked on, hardly noticing that a painter of portraits had gotten an idea that would soon change the world.

Morse worked on his idea for years, but he had to keep painting and teaching to make a living. In 1837, Morse had his message machine ready to test. He hung seventeen hundred feet of wire around the walls of his classroom in New York University. At one end he attached a device connected by a wire to a battery. The device had a base and a metal arm that could be pressed down. At the end of the arm was a funnel-shaped *key*. When that key was pressed down to touch a similar key on the base, electricity from the battery passed through the device and all the way to the end of the wire strung about the room.

"It works!" said one of his students.

"Now to prove it to the rest of the world," said Morse.

"What will you call it?" said the students.

"A *telegraph machine,*" Morse said, "because *tele-* means 'far off,' and *-graph* means 'writing.' "

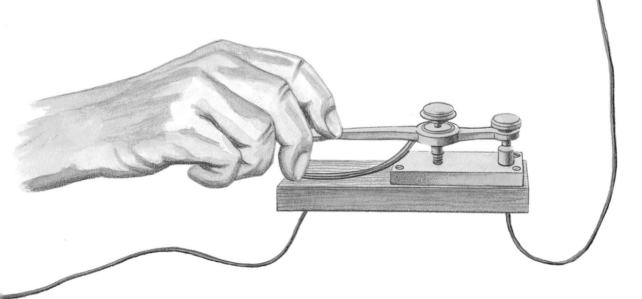

International Morse Code

A ·—	J ·———	S ···
B —···	K —·—	T —
C —·—·	L ·—··	U ··—
D —··	M ——	V ···—
E ·	N —·	W ·——
F ··—·	O ———	X —··—
G ——·	P ·——·	Y —·——
H ····	Q ——·—	Z ——··
I ··	R ·—·	

1 ·————	6 —····
2 ··———	7 ——···
3 ···——	8 ———··
4 ····—	9 ————·
5 ·····	0 —————

For the telegraph to "write far off," two people were needed: one to send the message and one to receive it. The sender would press down the key in two ways. If he pressed the key down quickly and let it up, a short pulse of electricity flashed through the wire. If he held the key down a bit longer, a longer burst of electricity passed through. The short pulses were called *dots,* and the longer ones were called *dashes.*

At the receiving end, Morse used an electro-magnet, much like the one he had heard about on the ship that day in 1832. When the electricity came through the wire wrapped around a metal bar, the bar became magnetized and drew up to the metal base. When it touched the base it made a click. If a • came through, it made a short click; a ━ made a longer sound.

The receiver listened to the clicks and translated them into letters. Look at the chart of letters. How long do you think it would take to send your name with Morse code?

◆ LEARNING HOW ◆

To Use Morse Code

1. Get a pencil and Notebook page 84.

2. Use Morse code to decode the messages on the Notebook page.

3. Make up a code message. Give it to another student to decode.

Inventions such as the telegraph created opportunities for women to have jobs in offices.

Morse took his invention to President Martin Van Buren and his cabinet. He strung ten miles of wire around a room in the Capitol. He sent signals just as he had in his classroom in New York. He stepped back expecting everyone to be amazed and pleased. Do you think they were? Most of the people there said it was all nonsense and a waste of time. Morse was vastly disappointed.

But Morse did not give up. Six years later he went back to Congress with an improved telegraph. He put up wires between rooms in the Capitol and sent messages. Still the people laughed at Morse's "talking

wires." When he asked the Congress for money to run a telegraph wire over the forty miles between Washington, D.C., and Baltimore, Maryland, the congressmen made jokes.

But finally Morse was granted the money, and he built the telegraph. On May 24, 1844, a small group of people sat in a Capitol room waiting to receive the first formal telegraph message. Annie Ellsworth, the daughter of one of Morse's friends, leaned over and told Morse the message she had chosen to send. He sent it, clicking the key in a steady rhythm. In just a few seconds, the receiver at Baltimore sent the same words back: *What hath God wrought!*

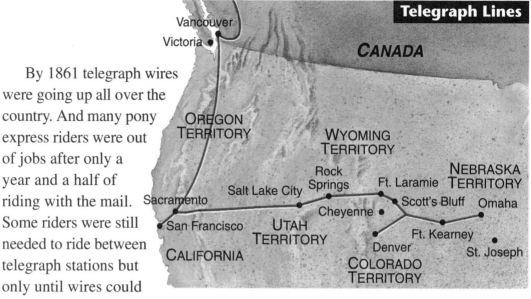

Telegraph Lines

By 1861 telegraph wires were going up all over the country. And many pony express riders were out of jobs after only a year and a half of riding with the mail. Some riders were still needed to ride between telegraph stations but only until wires could be connected coast to coast. There were many new jobs now: telegraph receivers, who took and sent messages; linemen, who put up the lines and looked after them; lumbermen, who cut the poles.

Everywhere a new telegraph station was built, there was much celebration. Why do you think people were happy to have a station in their town? The speedy telegraph made them feel close to cities that only the day before had been days or weeks away. Some people said that the wires on the poles were shrinking the country. What do you think they meant?

The telegraph companies expected to have trouble from storms, the Civil War, and perhaps thieves. But some of the worst trouble came from an unexpected source—the bison. The great, shaggy beasts discovered that the telegraph poles made wonderful rubbing posts. Several would gather at a pole and scratch their backs on it. And soon the pole would wobble and tip over. Sometimes the poles would splinter in two. Then linemen had plenty of work to keep them busy.

Railroads began to use the telegraph to monitor train routes. Reporters during the Civil War used it to send news. Even military leaders used the telegraph to send messages. How do you think the telegraph changed the way people lived? How do you think having such fast communication changed the people themselves?

The Telephone

Fast as the telegraph was, it was not fast enough. People were still looking for better ways to communicate over long distances. One of them was Alexander Bell, a teacher of deaf students.

Bell taught all day and then worked late into the nights trying to improve on the telegraph. He had a helper, Thomas Watson, who could build almost anything and build it quickly. Together they tried and tested many variations on the telegraph.

"You know," said Bell to a friend one day, "I have read somewhere that the tension in a wire changes the way electricity passes through it. If that is so, I wonder—" He stopped and looked thoughtfully away.

"What is it, Bell? What are you thinking?"

Bell brought his gaze back to his friend. "I was wondering whether there is a way to make electricity and wire transmit the sounds of the human voice."

The friend, Joseph Henry, an old man and himself a great inventor, turned a wondering look on Bell. "This," he said, "is the germ of a great invention. Stop all you are doing and work on this alone!"

Alexander Graham Bell later in his career

Bell said, "I'm not sure I have enough knowledge of electricity."

The old man said, "Get it!"

Bell took the old inventor's advice and began to work on a machine that would send the human voice along a wire to the ear of a listener on the other end. Only Watson thought the idea could be made to work. Other people, who had been encouraging Bell before, now told him that he was doing the wrong thing. The father of the girl he wanted to marry told him to get back to the telegraph or he would not let him see the girl again.

What do you think Bell did? He went on with his work harder than ever. For months he tried many different models. He would come with a new idea, and Watson would build a machine. They would try it out. Nothing worked. But Bell was so sure he would be able to find the answer that he applied for a patent on his still unproven ideas. He applied for and received the patent in 1876. It proved to be one of the most valuable patents ever issued.

Bell's description of sound transmission in his patent application of February 14, 1876

Boston, Massachusetts
Friday, March 10, 1876

Evening

Bell and Watson were setting up to test their newest model.

Bell accidentally spilled some acid on his clothes.

He called out, "Mr. Watson, come here. I want you."

In another room, Watson heard the words clearly over the new device.

Bell had proved that his wild idea was not so wild after all.

What do you think is important about that first message? It represents what Bell wanted his invention to do: help people. It is fitting that the first words over the wire, although not planned, should be a call for help.

Bell named his device the *telephone,* which means "far-off sound." He took his new machine to Philadelphia, where there was a huge celebration going on: the United States was one hundred years old. People came from all over the country to the Centennial Exposition, a display of inventions, machinery, and other exhibitions showing the greatness of the country.

Everyone who listened on one end of the wire was amazed to hear a voice, another human being, speaking to him. At last, Bell had support. People wanted to start using his invention.

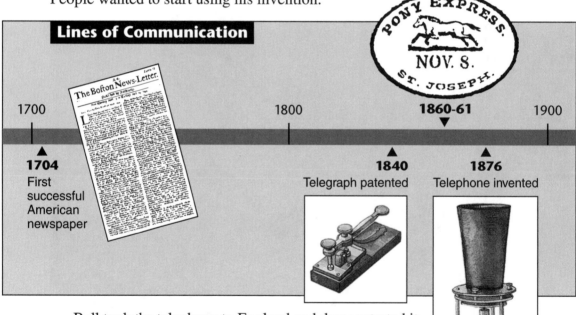

Lines of Communication

PONY EXPRESS.
NOV. 8.
ST. JOSEPH.

| 1700 | 1800 | 1860-61 | 1900 |

1704
First successful American newspaper

The Boston News-Letter.

1840
Telegraph patented

1876
Telephone invented

Bell took the telephone to England and demonstrated it for Queen Victoria. She listened quietly to words coming through the receiver. "Most extraordinary," she said. Bell could not have known how his telephone would extraordinarily change not only the United States but the whole world in just a few years.

Bell married the girl whose father had so opposed his work, and her father put money into the first telephone company. After a few years, Bell lost interest in the telephone and began experimenting with other inventions—some of which are only today being used. One was a system to send sound over a beam of light. Today we call that sort of transmission fiber optics.

Bell's invention has helped save an untold number of lives.

Bell wanted the telephone to make life better and safer for everyone. The cost of owning a telephone was not high, about the same as the cost of heating a house with gas. Soon many businesses and homes had telephones. Today there are millions and millions of telephones in the United States.

Using a telephone is no longer a remarkable event.

Can you count how many telephones you see in a week?

Do you think the telephone put the telegraph companies out of business? No, it did not. Telegraph companies still run today. People send telegrams on special occasions and to places that do not have telephones.

When you use a telephone, you do many things that the first users did not know to do. You probably say "Hello" when you answer the telephone. Most people did not know what to say at first. Bell wanted everyone to say "Hoy, hoy" when picking up the receiver. He was disappointed when the word *hello* became the most popular greeting.

Often people using the telephone would talk at the same time and then complain to the telephone company that the device did not work right! Part of the problem was that with the early telephones, the caller had to speak into and listen to the same part of the telephone. After speaking, he had to quickly move the piece to his ear. If the person on the other end started talking too soon, the caller missed some of the message.

The 1879 wall-mounted telephone used a microphone and receiver designed by Thomas Edison.

The brass desk set was invented in 1897.

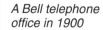

A Bell telephone office in 1900

Another thing happened to those first telephone owners that probably never happens to you. They picked up the receiver and suddenly got "stage fright." They could not think of anything to say. It took years before telephone manners developed to everyone's satisfaction.

Still, not all wanted to use the new invention. Some people thought it was just a toy that would go out of style. Others thought it was evil, a thing to be shunned. And others thought it was all a trick. Why do you think people had such notions?

The Changes in Every Way

Letters and important papers can be transmitted through a fax machine.

Headsets allow people to keep their hands free while talking on the phone.

For good and for bad, the new inventions were here to stay. Inventors like Bell thought only that the new devices would make communication easier, which they did. But they also changed many other things.

Businesses

Before the telegraph and telephone, businesses in cities were built close together. Why do you think that was? People had to walk from one place to another or send messengers if they wanted to communicate with each other. The closer the buildings were, the faster people could communicate.

Today, businesses across the country from each other can do business over the telephone and with a newer invention, the *fax* machine. What do you think Alexander Bell would say about that?

The telephone also made business move faster; more work could be done more quickly. That swiftness caused more money to be made and spent by more people. And the more money that changed hands, the better businesses did. A country needs strong business to keep growing.

The Bell Telephone Company itself—started by Bell, his father-in-law, and Watson—changed American business. It eventually became the largest company in the world, employing thousands and thousands of people directly and making available thousands of other jobs, such as in plastics.

Lifestyles

Before telephones, people presented cards when they came to visit. If you did not want to see a person, you did not let him in. But when someone answered the telephone, he could not know who would be on the other end of the line. The rules separating upper and lower classes had to change because almost everyone could use a telephone.

Ideas about the world changed too. Everything seemed much closer together, much easier to keep up with. Towns no longer were places unto themselves; they were influenced immediately by changes and events in places far away. America was no longer the slowly growing country it had been. It was on its way to becoming the richest, most powerful country in the world.

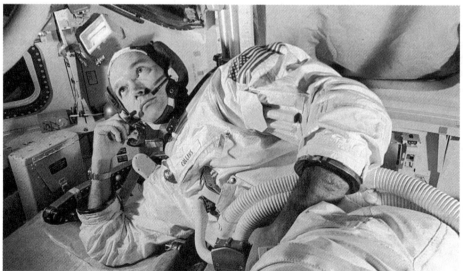

Communication reaches farther now than even Bell might have dreamed it would.

11
Struggles Far Away

At Gettysburg, one of the bloodiest battles of the American Civil War was fought.

What do you think is worth fighting a war for? Some wars have been fought over land, some over money or gold, some over ideas. Do you remember why the American Civil War happened?

Both sides in that war, the North and the South, believed in different ways of living. Many in the North lived in cities and worked in factories; their Southern neighbors preferred a more rural life and farming. More importantly, the two sides disagreed about what laws the states should be allowed to make for themselves. The South said that slavery should be left up to the states; the North said it should not.

In another country, about thirty years later, slavery helped to cause another war. But that war was also about gold and land and the right of people to govern themselves. It was called the *Boer War.*

The Boer War

The Boer people of Africa had come long ago from the Netherlands. Can you find the Netherlands on the map on pages 316-17? A business in the Netherlands, the Dutch East India Company, began a town in Africa. It was on the Cape of Good Hope. Can you find that place on the map on this page? Is it in northern or southern Africa?

The Dutch people who settled on the cape were proud and independent. They believed in God and the Bible, but they thought that only specially chosen people could be saved from sin. And they believed that there was nothing wrong with owning slaves.

When Great Britain conquered and bought much of the land around the cape from the Netherlands, the Boers refused to bow to English rule. They especially did not want to give up their slaves. So they packed up their goods into wagons and moved northeast. They went to lands not owned by the British to set up new countries of their own. They called the move the *Great Trek*.

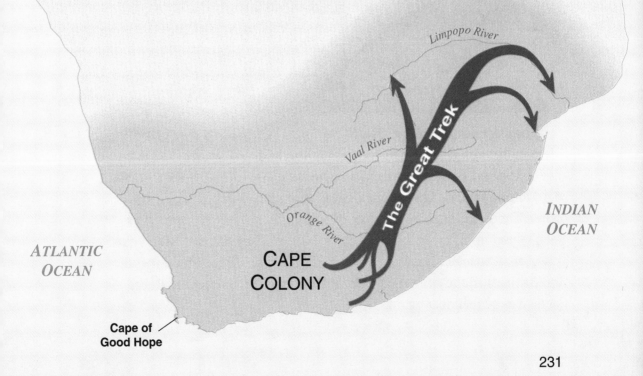

Some Boers stopped in a grassy flatland. Others went on farther north. From these two groups, two states grew. For a while, the Boers were free to wander on the open land, farming and keeping their traditional ways. What does the picture tell you about the Boer life?

But the Boers in the two states could not get along with each other. Their governments could not control the people. When money became hard to get, the two groups began to fight each other. The British decided to take over the states.

These Boer travelers have stopped for the night. After supper, some will sleep in the wagon and some under it, guns always ready.

Do you think the Boers liked British rule? They did not. After four years, they attacked British soldiers in several cities. Taken by surprise, the British lost the skirmishes. Great Britain decided to let the Boer states be independent again.

Then an unexpected thing happened: someone found gold, much gold, on Boer land. How do you think that changed history? Men from all over began to go there looking for gold. The whole Boer area got rich; in fact, it became the richest place in Africa.

Since gold had not been discovered while the British had been in charge, the Boers claimed that God meant the gold only for the Boers. They were not about to share it.

The Boer leaders began to think that they could run the British out of more places in Africa. They thought that the Boers should rule the whole southern tip of Africa. Why do you think they thought they could beat the British?

General Piet Cronje sent a message to the British: "I shall not surrender alive."

President Paul Kruger, a puzzle to his enemies

One reason was that the Boers had beaten the British before. They did not stop to think, though, that the British had not been ready or serious. Also, with all their new wealth, the Boers had been buying weapons from other countries—the biggest, most modern guns they could get. And finally, the Boers believed that God was on their side.

A Boer scout with his cartridge belt, rifle, water bottle, and bedroll

Boer soldiers were excellent horsemen. They were used to sleeping on the ground and getting along on little food. And they were not just paid to fight, as their enemies were; they fought for their families and their farms. They wanted to win, and they wanted to live to go home. Why do you think this attitude made them soldiers to be feared?

Great Britain has never liked to look as though she started a war. So the government has always tried to talk over a problem with the enemy, to see whether terms could be worked out. Why do you think Great Britain wanted to talk first and to appear as though she were pushed into war?

British soldiers retreating to Ladysmith

The Boer leaders agreed to talk. They may have wanted to get their way without war. But they were also waiting for good weather on the plains. The rains had to come so that there would be grass for their war-horses. What do you think happened?

The peace talk went nowhere. The British were not going to meet the Boer terms, and the Boers were not going to meet the British terms. Soon the summer rains began to fall. Now there would be plenty of grass for the horses. The Boers were ready for war.

The British soldiers were not prepared for fighting in the south of Africa. Nor did they understand the enemy. They believed what leaders in the area said: "It will all be over in two weeks."

In the first battle of the war, the British made the Boer soldiers retreat. But at the next battle—and the next and the one after that—the Boers outsmarted and beat the British. The defeats were a terrible embarrassment to the British, with their history of being great in war.

The British used observation balloons to try to find the Boer trenches.

The war went on for three years. The Boers' skill in riding and shooting made them tough enemies. But the British had more men and more money, and in 1902 they finally won. The Boer soldiers had fought long and hard and bravely. They had to give in, but they still carried their heads high and sang their songs. They were a proud people who had fought an enemy that outnumbered them ten times.

The British let the Boers take part in the new government. And England spent much money and gave many goods and animals to help the Boer country rebuild. Many Boer soldiers refused to believe that England ruled them at all. They held on to their old ways and their own language. Some Boers thought it best to get along with the British, but they kept a love for their old country in their hearts. Do you think the British really won? Most British did not think so.

The Boers still wanted the British to leave them alone. They rebelled again twelve years later, but the British soldiers held them back. Then they began to think: most of the leaders were Boer, and few British lived in their lands. They decided to wait, to use their heads instead of their guns. In 1960, only fifty-eight years after the war, the children and grandchildren of the Boer soldiers were allowed to vote themselves free of Britain. The Republic of South Africa became its own country.

South Africa today is rich and powerful. But it has many problems. The people who settled the area—Dutch, Bantu, British—often had conflicts. Although the Dutch and British made up only one-fifth of the population, they built the big cities and farms. They controlled the government. To protect their control, they lived by *apartheid,* a rule that kept blacks from voting and from living and working wherever they wanted.

Why do you think the blacks wanted change? Why do you think the whites did not? Other nations began to condemn South Africa's racist policies, isolating the country by refusing to buy or sell certain goods to it. The South African government began to change. Under President F. W. de Klerk, the government abolished many apartheid laws. In 1990 the president released a prisoner named Nelson Mandela,

Modern Johannesburg, the largest city in South Africa, resulted from the discovery of gold in 1886.

a black man who had served twenty-six years for violence against the government. In 1994, Mandela ran for president—and won. How do you think South Africa has changed?

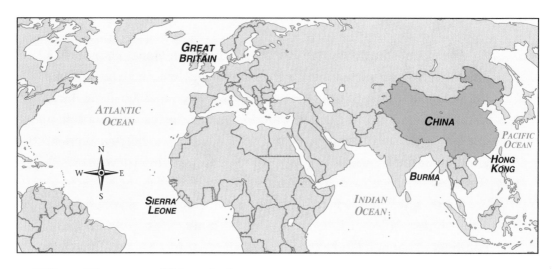

The Boxer Uprising

Do you remember reading about the missionaries to China? Find China on the map. What continent is it on? What direction is it from England? Many Christian workers went to China, and many Chinese people became Christians and left their old religion. The old religion required the people to worship their ancestors. Some missionaries made enemies by trying to change the customs and to interfere with the government in cities. Others stirred up bad feelings by treating the Chinese people as servants or inferiors.

Many Chinese said that Christians did not show respect to the ancestors; they said that Christianity was ruining the Chinese way. Soon groups of people who wanted to keep the old ways began to burn the Christians' property and sometimes attack the Christians themselves. The groups hated the missionaries, but they hated the Chinese Christians more.

One group was bigger and more powerful than any other. They did exercises to make their bodies strong for fighting. Since the exercises looked like the exercises boxers did, the group became known as the *Boxers*. The Boxers wore red to show who they were. Although the Boxers hated all foreigners, they blamed the troubles of China on the Christians. If the Christians were killed, they said, all foreigners would leave and China would again be happy.

But China's troubles were not caused by Christians. Many of the problems began in the court of the old empress, Cixi. She wanted power more than anything else. She made sure her son would be the emperor by having the three highest officials killed. When her son died young, she made everyone agree to let her nephew become the next emperor. She schemed her whole life to get things the way she wanted them. And she thought everything was working out just right.

The Empress Dowager, Cixi

Her nephew, although he said he was grateful to the empress, really disliked her running his life. Even when he was a grown man and the emperor of all China, he had to ask the old empress about everything he did—what trips he took, which people could work for him. The empress declared that she loved him dearly, but secretly she was afraid he would take her power and so had him watched all the time. With all the scheming going on, no one was taking care of China.

The emperor wanted to let China learn from the English and others who came to his land. He thought some of their new ideas were good. But the empress hated all new thinking; she thought it was disloyal to the ancestors—and a threat to her control. What do you think she did? She had the emperor taken to an island and held prisoner. Then she ruled China by herself.

The palace in the Forbidden City can now be visited by anyone.

The empress wanted the Boxers to hurt the foreigners and to destroy their property. She thought such treatment would make the foreigners go home. So no matter what the Boxers did or how many laws they broke, she did nothing to stop them. When the foreigners saw that the empress was not going to help them, they asked their own governments to send soldiers. Soon soldiers from England, Russia, Japan, Austria, Germany, Italy, and the United States were in China. Do you think the trouble stopped?

The Boxers believed that no foreigner's gun and no foreigner's sword could hurt them. They believed their chants would protect them. They were completely unafraid of fighting anyone of another race. Soon the missionaries and the Chinese Christians in Beijing (spelled Peking on older maps) decided to leave their houses and stay together in a mission. It was easier to defend. They began to put barbed wire around the outside of the mission.

Beijing, the capital, was where the empress lived. Her part of Beijing was walled off from the rest of the city; she lived in the Forbidden City. What does the name tell you about the place?

Do you think the foreigners were safe now? No, the Boxers burned down the mission and several other churches. The foreigners moved to another place. The soldiers from the other countries were trying to get to Beijing. Can you follow their route on the map? The soldiers had to fight the Boxers all along the way. They took the city of Tientsin from the Boxers first. About eight hundred foreign soldiers had died and almost five thousand Chinese soldiers and Boxers.

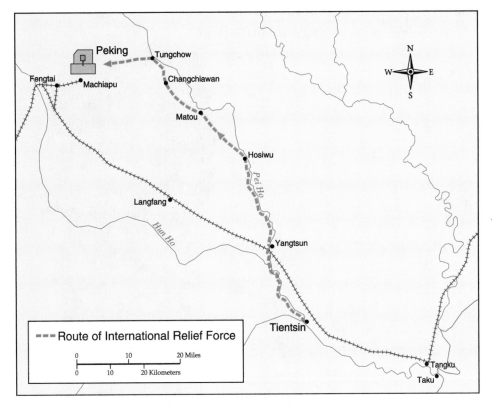

In Beijing the fighting got worse. And more than two thousand Chinese students and Christians went to the foreigners for help. The Boxers (more than 150,000 were in Beijing) had begun to rob anyone, even a Chinese governor. The empress was becoming disgusted; the Boxers were turning into thieves. They were not the brave patriots she had thought.

Ho-I (*Hē′·ē*) was one of the Chinese Christians the Boxers hated. He was a friend of the missionary Jonathan Goforth. When the Boxers threatened the Goforths' mission, Ho-I told the others to run to safety and that he would guard their place.

> *"Blessed are they which are persecuted for righteousness' sake: for theirs is the kingdom of heaven."*
>
> **Matthew 5:10**

The Boxers came soon after the others had left. They beat Ho-I terribly and dragged him through the streets. Some of the Boxers may even have known Ho-I because he had been an idol maker before he became a Christian. He had often been arrested then, for he lived an evil life.

Then the Boxers tied up Ho-I and took him to the court. There they told the official that they wanted him killed for being a Christian. The official looked at Ho-I a moment and then asked him to speak. What do you think Ho-I said?

Ho-I said that he was not ashamed of his Lord. He told the official how he had been saved and how his life had changed. The Boxers waited to carry him outside. But the official was so amazed at what Ho-I said that he let him go. Ho-I went home and lived to serve God another thirty years.

American, Japanese, and British troops storm the palace at Beijing.

The foreigners held off the Boxers for many weeks until the armies from their countries got to Beijing. Then the fighting was bitter and swift. Foreign soldiers pushed into the city. At last, the empress and her court had to flee. They traveled miles from Beijing and hid. After some time, the foreign soldiers broke down the last defenses and walked into the Forbidden City, a place no foreigner had ever been.

The Boxers also fled. They began to realize that foreign bullets and swords could indeed kill them. The foreign soldiers looted the city, taking anything they wanted—furs, silver, dishes, silk. With almost a third of the city burning and the rest being smashed, the empress finally agreed to talk peace.

For more than a year, the peace talks went on. At last, the empress signed a paper that changed many things in China. Many of the old leaders were put to death. It became a law that no one was allowed to join an antiforeign group. And China had to pay the winning countries millions of dollars.

How do you think events might have been different if the empress and other leaders had accepted new ideas earlier?

To Read Double Bar Graphs

1. Get a pencil and Notebook page 89.

2. Read the directions on the page and fill in the answers.

3. Show comparisons on a double bar graph.

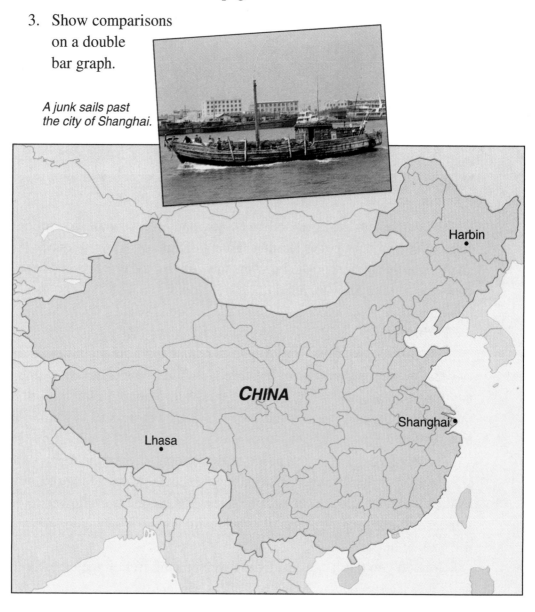

A junk sails past the city of Shanghai.

CHINA

Harbin

Shanghai

Lhasa

The Industrial Revolution

Inventions like the cotton gin made a need for more inventions. Can you think of any of them? The spinning jenny was one. Because more cotton could be seeded by the gin, bigger machines were needed to make thread. As thread production increased, weavers needed machines to make cloth faster. And on it went.

Why do you think nations want bigger and better machines to make more things faster? It is because they make money by selling the things. The more they make, the more they can sell. The more they sell, the richer they become. The richer they become, the more powerful they are.

A table leg made from imported mahogany wood

After a while, nations with bigger and better machines could not grow enough cotton or find enough iron or cut enough wood to keep all the machines busy. So they began to look for such things in other places. When a country buys goods from another country, it *imports* the goods, or brings them in. Imported goods have to be paid for, however. Can you think of a reason not to import goods to make things from?

The nations that were making things, called *industrial nations,* began to take over other places that had lots of wood or rubber or people to work in factories. If they owned or ruled the places, they would not have to pay for the rubber and the wood, and they would not have to pay the workers much either. When richer nations tried to take over these places, trouble always began; sometimes wars started. Do you think the inventors of the cotton gin and spinning jenny had any idea how their inventions would "echo" later?

Imperialism

Look at the map. What are some of the countries in Europe? Why do you think countries like England and France sent some of their people to other countries, such as South Africa and China? What were some of the reasons that people wanted to go live in China and Africa? One reason was money; the Boers found gold, and soon many others wanted it. China had silks and tea, goods which brought much money.

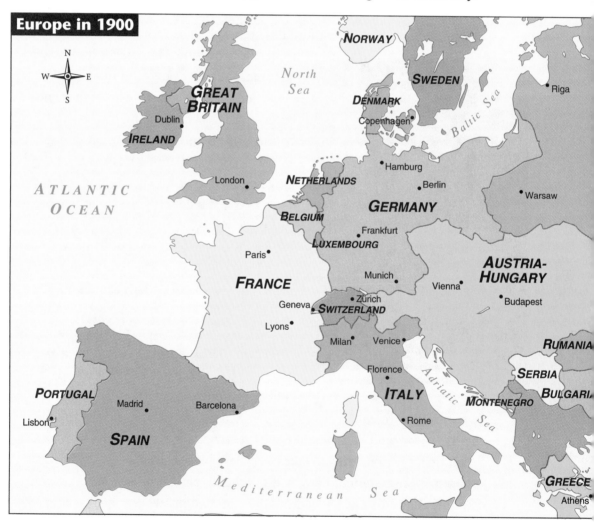

Another reason was that the people in Europe felt they were better than other people. They thought they should teach their ways to the Chinese, the Indians, the Boers, and others. Do you think missionaries felt this way? Some of them did. Some, though, wanted only to serve God.

Yet another reason Europeans went to other countries is nationalism. If a country like England did not own lands somewhere else, it looked weak and small to the other countries. So most nations tried to get

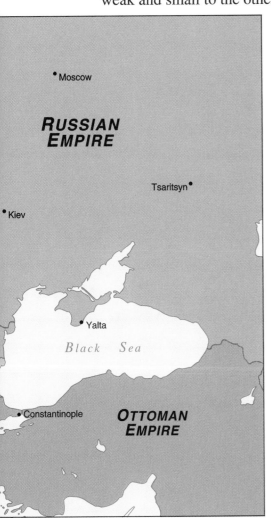

colonies, or territories. England had colonies all over the world. What happened to her colonies in the New World in 1776?

Why do you think most colonies try to get free of the country that established them or that took them over? Sometimes, as in the case of the Boers, they have their own government and customs. In other cases, such as in America, colonists grow away from the old country. They begin to think of themselves as a separate people. Why do you think the Chinese did not want others to rule them? Perhaps it was partly because they did not want their ways to change. Another reason was that most Chinese thought of themselves as better than all foreigners.

What do you think happens when many countries try to get the same land? Suppose three people want a bike that you own. How might they try to get it? One may offer to buy it. One may try to take it. Another may try to prove that it should be his by law. What would you do with your bike?

A country that has colonies is called an *empire*. Getting or keeping colonies is *imperialism*. Both terms come from an old word that means "command." What does that definition tell you about the way empires were usually made?

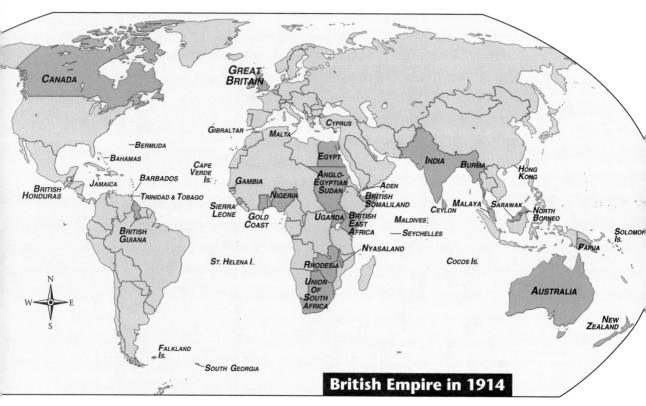

British Empire in 1914

Look at the map. How many colonies did England have by 1914? What do you think people meant when they said that the "sun never sets on the British flag"? They meant that the colonies were so spread out over the world that in at least one of them, it would be daytime at any hour during the twenty-four hours in a day.

Today, few countries still own colonies. Most colonies have become their own nations. How many years ago did the American colonies become the United States of America? What do you know about the American colonies' struggle to become a nation?

12

By the People

A modern farm, in a long American tradition

The United States of America has been a country for more than two hundred years. During that time it grew from a few tiny colonies huddled beside the Atlantic Ocean to fifty states spanning the continent of North America. Farms and factories filled the land. Millions of immigrants came to find work and a new home. But the United States was not the only country where land and work and homes could be found. What made the United States seem better than other countries? Of all the new homes people could have chosen, why choose America?

One important thing that made this country the best choice for so many was the kind of government it had. Our *Founding Fathers,* the early leaders of the United States, did not like the old governments in England and other European countries. So they made a different kind of government, unlike any other, for the new country. But what is a government?

A *government* is a system of rules and authority. Every group of people has some kind of government. Of course, countries have governments. So do states, cities, towns, and even businesses and schools. Each group has rules it must follow. Each group has leaders with the *authority,* or power, to help it follow the rules.

A policeman helps enforce the laws.

250

Think about your school. Can you name some of the rules of your school? Who helped to make those rules? Probably the principal and teachers made many of them. What would happen in your school if your principal did not make rules? It is a good thing he does. You obey the rules at school because you accept his authority.

Your town has rules too. There are rules about how you should cross the street, where you can ride your bike, and what you should do when you see something you want in a store. Who made those rules? The leaders of your town's government did. Can you guess who made the rules for the United States?

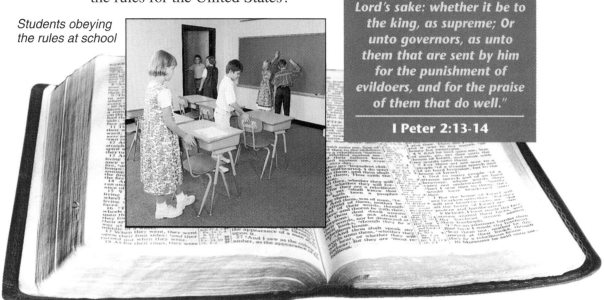

Students obeying the rules at school

"Submit yourselves to every ordinance of man for the Lord's sake: whether it be to the king, as supreme; Or unto governors, as unto them that are sent by him for the punishment of evildoers, and for the praise of them that do well."

I Peter 2:13-14

Rules help to make our schools, towns, and country a safe and orderly place if everyone obeys them. What makes a person obey all the rules? Perhaps you obey rules because you know you will be punished if you do not. That is enough reason for some. But Christians have another reason for obeying rules. God's Word tells us that we must obey the rules made by people in authority.

It might seem that all governments are the same. All governments have rules, or *laws*. And they all have people with authority to make and carry out the rules, but not all governments make and enforce laws the same way. Do you know how the government of the United States is different from other governments?

A Democratic Government

The government of the United States is a type of democracy. *Democracy* comes from two Greek words. The first, *demos,* means "the people." *Kratos* means "authority or government." What can you say about a democracy, then? It is a government by the people.

In a democracy, the people work together to make important decisions. Together they choose their leaders. Together they make the laws for their government. Not everyone needs to agree on a law or a leader. But more than half the people must. When more than half the people make a decision, all the people accept it. We call this process the principle of *majority rule.*

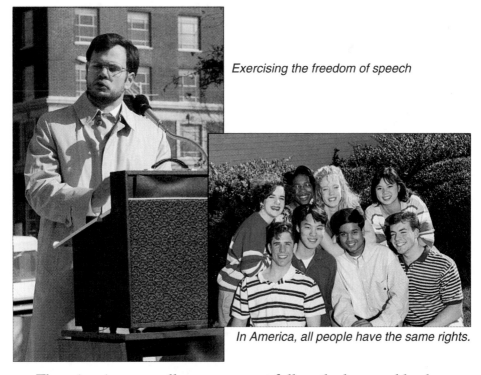

Exercising the freedom of speech

In America, all people have the same rights.

The *minority,* or smaller group, must follow the laws and leaders chosen by the majority. What would happen if they did not? But the people need to be careful about the laws they make. Because everyone will have to obey the laws, the people cannot make laws that might be unfair to a few.

Equality is another important principle of democracy. All people are equal in a democracy. That does not mean that they have equal wealth, or education, or physical strength. We know that God created each person special and different. Instead it means that the government thinks of everyone as the same. It does not give special protection or power to a person because he is rich and famous, or poor and unknown, or somewhere in between.

One last principle makes a democracy special: freedom. A democratic government gives the people freedom to do many things other kinds of government do not. They have the freedom to worship and serve God as they believe they should. They are free to make their own decisions. And they are free to choose their own laws and leaders.

The First Democracy

Democracy is not a new idea. Do you remember where the word *democracy* comes from? It comes from two Greek words; the Greeks were the first people to have a democratic government.

The people of Greece were artists, writers, and thinkers. People who lived in the city of Athens were especially talented in these ways. Athenians studied history,

The Greeks voted by dropping bronze disks into a ballot box.

math, science, and medicine. They built some of the most beautiful buildings in the world. Others wrote stories and poems that are still read today. Athenians set up a great culture about five hundred years before Christ was born.

Greek democracy began in the city of Athens. Every free man of that city helped to make laws and choose leaders. The men met every ten days or so to vote on new laws. Do you think slaves could take part in this democracy? They could not, and neither could women. But more people had a voice in Athens's democracy than in any other government of the time.

The democracy in Athens did not last. Other countries took over the Greek cities. They made the Greek people obey their laws and follow their kings. But the words and ideas of the Greek people "echoed" around the world and across more than two thousand years. They were an example of a government in which the power was in the hands of the people.

254

Two Kinds of Democracy

Democracy—government by the people—can take one of two forms. It can be a *pure,* or *direct, democracy.* In a pure democracy, all the citizens, or members, meet together to decide on their laws. The government in the Greek city of Athens was a pure democracy. The town meetings held in some places in New England even today could be called pure democracy. Pure democracy works best when the people are few and they live close together. What problems would a large number of people have in a pure democracy?

Campaign rally for George Bush

Every citizen should vote.

Large groups of people can also have a democratic government. It is a democracy by the people's *representatives.* The citizens in this kind of democracy choose people to make the laws for them. The representatives listen to the citizens who have chosen them, and they make laws the citizens agree with. This kind of democracy is called a *representative,* or *indirect, democracy.* Can you guess what kind of democracy the United States has?

The American Democracy

On May 25, 1787, men from thirteen states met in the State House in Philadelphia. Four years before, the states had won a war against England. With that victory, they won the right to make their own laws. But now the states were fighting among themselves; they could not agree on what laws to follow. The states sent their best leaders to Philadelphia to work on the problem.

The problem was not easy to solve. The new country had not made one good government. Instead, each state had its own government. Each state acted like a separate country. The states needed a government that would help them to work together, but the men did not want a government like the one in England.

Who made the laws in England and in most other countries in Europe? A king made the laws. The people could not choose their king. All kings were born into a king's family. Once a man became king, he was king until he died. Then his son became the king. Why do you think the men from the states did not want this kind of leader?

The men wanted the chance to choose their own leaders. They wanted the people to have a say about their laws. And they wanted to be able to pick new leaders if they did not agree with the laws their leaders made.

It took many months, but the men finally solved the states' problem. Together they made a plan for a strong national government. The plan allowed the national government to make laws that all the states must follow. But the plan also let each state's government make some of its own laws. Do you think this was a good idea? Now the democratic thing to do was to ask the citizens what they thought.

Signing the Constitution
by Howard Chandler Christy

The men took their plan back to the people. The citizens in each state read and talked about the plan. Some thought that the national government needed more authority. Others thought the states gave too much authority away. Finally the time came to vote on the plan.

The citizens of each state decided how they felt about the plan. If the majority of the states liked the plan, it would become the law. What do you think happened? Every state accepted the plan. It was now the most important law of the new country, the United States.

The Constitution

The plan the men wrote in Philadelphia is known as *the Constitution*. The Constitution does more than set the rules for the government of America. It protects the rights of all the citizens. Its laws help to guard freedom.

The Constitution says that the government should be divided into three parts, or *branches*. Each branch has its own job to do. And each branch checks up on the other branches to be sure they are doing their jobs right. With the authority of the government divided in this way, no one person or group of people can get power over the whole country.

The *legislative* branch writes the laws. The United States Congress makes up this branch. The legislative branch is the only one divided again into two smaller parts. Do you know the names of the two parts?

The first part is made up of 435 people. The citizens of the United States choose these people every two years. They are the citizens' representatives, and the whole group is called the *House of Representatives*. The map below shows how many representatives each state sends to Congress.

The second part of Congress is the *Senate*. The men and women of the Senate are also the citizens' representatives, but we call them senators. Senators serve their states for six years. The citizens of each state choose two senators. How many senators are there all together?

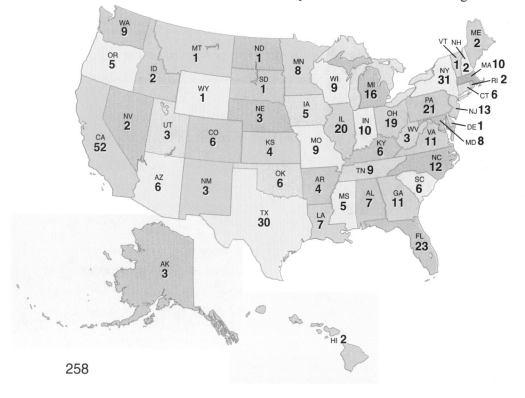

- Suggests legislation
- Calls special sessions
- Vetoes bills

President

- Impeaches and removes officials, including the president
- Approves or rejects treaties and presidential appointees
- Overrides vetoes

- Appoints judges
- Grants pardons

- Rules on constitutionality of executive actions
- Interprets treaties

Supreme Court

- Determines constitutionality of laws
- Interprets laws and treaties

- Regulates types of appeals

Congress

- Establishes lower federal courts
- Determines the number of Supreme Court judges
- Impeaches judges

Shared Powers of Government

One person makes up the *executive* branch—the president. It is his job to see that the laws made by the Congress are obeyed. He represents the United States when he meets with leaders from other countries. And he is in charge of the army, the navy, the air force, and the marine corps. Many people help the president to do his job.

The last branch is the *judicial* branch. Nine judges make up the Supreme Court. It is their job to explain the laws. They must be sure the laws do not take away the freedoms promised in the Constitution.

Can you think of ways each of the three branches of government could check the work of the others? The president checks the laws the Congress writes. He must sign them before they can become the law of the land. Together he and the Congress check on the Supreme Court by choosing the men and women who will be judges. And the Supreme Court checks on the other two branches by determining whether their actions and laws follow the Constitution.

To Read a Flow Chart

1. Get Notebook page 95 and a pencil.

2. Name the shapes on the Notebook page. When these three shapes are connected with arrows, they make a *flow chart*. A flow chart is a sequence of written directions. Have you ever seen a flow chart?

3. The oval signals a start or stop on a flow chart. What shape is a symbol for instruction and directions? Look at the diamond shape on the flow chart. This shape is called a *decision box*. It asks a question. Your answer will help you decide what to do next.

This is the chosen book.

4. Read the flow chart. Answer *No* to the question. Follow the arrow. What do you do next? This time answer *Yes*. What happened this time?

5. Think about something you do in steps. On the back of your Notebook page, make a flow chart to show the process.

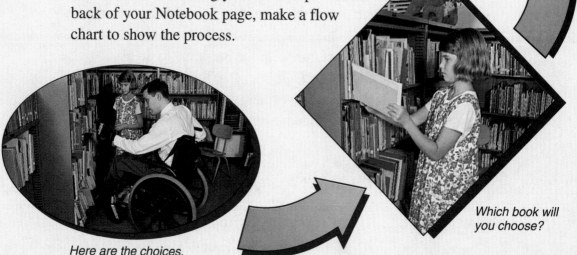

Which book will you choose?

Here are the choices.

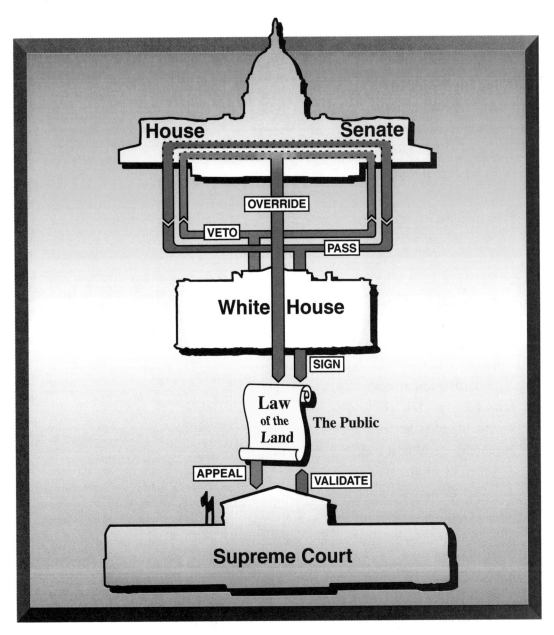

All three branches of the government work together to make sure the country's laws protect the citizens' freedom. A bill, an idea for a new law, must take several steps to become a law. Each branch has a part. Which branch do you think has the most important job?

The Bill of Rights

The Constitution solved the problem of making the new country. But more than that, it has kept the country working for more than two hundred years. The men who wrote the Constitution made sure that it could change as the country changed. The changes that have been made since the Constitution was first written are called *amendments*.

The first ten amendments are special. They were added to the Constitution soon after it was accepted by all the states. The first Congress wrote these amendments because the citizens asked for them. They wanted the Constitution to name the rights the government could not take away. These ten amendments are called the *Bill of Rights*.

The Bill of Rights was added to the Constitution in 1791. Since then, seventeen more amendments have been added to the Constitution. The Thirteenth Amendment ended slavery in all the states. What war was fought before this amendment was added? The Fifteenth Amendment gave all men the right to vote, no matter what their race or skin color. Where can you find a list of all the amendments?

262

A Citizen's Part

Writing good laws and protecting the freedoms of its citizens are the *responsibilities,* or duties, of a good government. Citizens expect their government to fulfill its duties. In return, good citizens should fulfill certain responsibilities. Can you think of some responsibilities of a good citizen?

The first responsibility of a citizen should not be difficult to guess. Citizens must obey the laws their

What law is this man obeying?

government makes. No one can force a citizen to obey the laws. It is his choice. A good citizen obeys the law because it is the right thing to do. The laws of our states and country are written to protect us and all other citizens.

Most citizens do not enjoy their second responsibility. But a good citizen pays taxes, even when he wishes he did not have to. *Taxes* are money given to keep the government working. The money helps to pay for things the government does for its citizens. Taxes pay representatives for their work in the government. Tax money also pays for libraries, parks, and roads. Do you know other things the government uses taxes for?

Taxes help pay road builders.

A good citizen does one more thing: he gets involved. The government will have problems that need to be solved. Spending more money on schools is one problem the government might face. How to help people without jobs is another. Can you think of more problems for the government? Citizens do what they can to help solve these problems.

How can a citizen know whether an action will solve a problem? He must do his best to learn all he can. In school, he can find out how a democracy works. He should listen to the news reports and read the newspaper. Then he must decide what he believes about the things he has heard. He can vote for the man or woman who offers the best solution.

Voting is the easiest and most important way for a citizen to get involved. Today, citizens eighteen or over have the right to vote. But voting is more than a right; it is a responsibility too. Voting allows all to help in making decisions for the country. What would happen if people did not vote? The decisions would be made by a few people. How would that be bad for the country?

Voting is a right—and a privilege.

264

105 0408

This Ballot Stub shall be removed
Mgr. before Ballot is placed in the Ball

Initials of Box Mgr.

To cast a write-in ballot, the name o
candidate and the office must be filled i
stub.

Candidate | Office

PLACE HOLES
OVER POSTS

INSERT CARD

THIS SIDE UP

Elizabeth Cady Stanton/Susan B. Anthony
(1815-1902)   (1820-1906)

As a young girl, Elizabeth Cady studied law books in her father's office. Because she was a woman, she could not become a lawyer. But her studies helped her to understand that the laws did not treat women the same as men. In 1848 Stanton planned a women's meeting in her hometown of Seneca Falls, New York, to discuss the laws and to make a list of rights they believed they should have, including the right to vote.

Stanton met Susan B. Anthony about three years later. In Anthony's family, men and women were treated equally. It was hard for her to understand why all women were not. Both women worked for women's *suffrage,* or the right to vote. They believed that if women could vote, they could change the unfair laws.

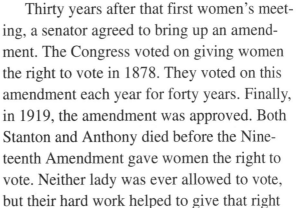

Elizabeth Cady Stanton

Susan B. Anthony

Thirty years after that first women's meeting, a senator agreed to bring up an amendment. The Congress voted on giving women the right to vote in 1878. They voted on this amendment each year for forty years. Finally, in 1919, the amendment was approved. Both Stanton and Anthony died before the Nineteenth Amendment gave women the right to vote. Neither lady was ever allowed to vote, but their hard work helped to give that right to many others.

A statue of Jefferson at the University of Virginia

The Founding Fathers—men like George Washington, James Madison, and Thomas Jefferson—wanted a country where all the people could have a say. At first it was an experiment. No one was sure such a government could last.

What made our democratic government work? The people did: people who were born in the United States and spent their whole lives here; people who came here from other countries looking for freedom and equality for themselves and their children; people who, after years of slavery, were finally free too. All these people believed in the principles of the Constitution. Together they made it work.

Each American must do his part to make sure that the government keeps working. It is every citizen's responsibility to protect the freedoms promised in the Constitution. All citizens must remember what that freedom meant in America's past and what it means to the future.

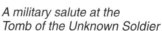

A welcoming parade for soldiers returning from war

A military salute at the Tomb of the Unknown Soldier

Resource Treasury

Presidents

	President	Vice President	In Office	Political Party
1.	George Washington	John Adams	1789-97	None
2.	John Adams	Thomas Jefferson	1797-1801	Federalist
3.	Thomas Jefferson	Aaron Burr George Clinton	1801-9	Democratic-Republican
4.	James Madison	George Clinton Elbridge Gerry	1809-17	Democratic-Republican
5.	James Monroe	Daniel Tompkins	1817-25	Democratic-Republican
6.	John Q. Adams	John C. Calhoun	1825-29	Democratic-Republican
7.	Andrew Jackson	John C. Calhoun Martin Van Buren	1829-37	Democratic
8.	Martin Van Buren	Richard M. Johnson	1837-41	Democratic
9.	William H. Harrison	John Tyler	1841	Whig
10.	John Tyler		1841-45	Whig
11.	James K. Polk	George M. Dallas	1845-49	Democratic
12.	Zachary Taylor	Millard Fillmore	1849-50	Whig
13.	Millard Fillmore		1850-53	Whig
14.	Franklin Pierce	William R. King	1853-57	Democratic
15.	James Buchanan	John C. Breckinridge	1857-61	Democratic
16.	Abraham Lincoln	Hannibal Hamlin Andrew Johnson	1861-65	Republican, Union
17.	Andrew Johnson		1865-69	Union
18.	Ulysses S. Grant	Schuyler Colfax Henry Wilson	1869-77	Republican
19.	Rutherford B. Hayes	William A. Wheeler	1877-81	Republican
20.	James A. Garfield	Chester A. Arthur	1881	Republican
21.	Chester A. Arthur		1881-85	Republican
22.	Grover Cleveland	Thomas A. Hendricks	1885-89	Democratic
23.	Benjamin Harrison	Levi P. Morton	1889-93	Republican
24.	Grover Cleveland	Adlai E. Stevenson	1893-97	Democratic
25.	William McKinley	Garret A. Hobart Theodore Roosevelt	1897-1901	Republican
26.	Theodore Roosevelt	Charles W. Fairbanks	1901-9	Republican
27.	William H. Taft	James S. Sherman	1909-13	Republican

	President	Vice President	In Office	Political Party
28.	Woodrow Wilson	Thomas R. Marshall	1913-21	Democratic
29.	Warren G. Harding	Calvin Coolidge	1921-23	Republican
30.	Calvin Coolidge	Charles G. Dawes	1923-29	Republican
31.	Herbert Hoover	Charles Curtis	1929-33	Republican
32.	Franklin D. Roosevelt	John N. Garner Henry A. Wallace Harry S Truman	1933-45	Democratic
33.	Harry S Truman	Alben W. Barkley	1945-53	Democratic
34.	Dwight D. Eisenhower	Richard M. Nixon	1953-61	Republican
35.	John F. Kennedy	Lyndon B. Johnson	1961-63	Democratic
36.	Lyndon B. Johnson	Hubert H. Humphrey	1963-69	Democratic
37.	Richard M. Nixon	Spiro Agnew Gerald Ford	1969-74	Republican
38.	Gerald Ford	Nelson Rockefeller	1974-77	Republican
39.	Jimmy Carter	Walter Mondale	1977-81	Democratic
40.	Ronald Reagan	George Bush	1981-89	Republican
41.	George Bush	Dan Quayle	1989-93	Republican
42.	Bill Clinton	Al Gore	1993-	Democratic

George Washington

1

1789-97

Born:
Feb. 22, 1732

Died:
Dec. 14, 1799

Place of birth:
Westmoreland County, Virginia

Little-known fact:
He owned a set of false teeth carved from rhinoceros ivory.

John Adams

2

1797-1801

Born:
Oct. 30, 1735

Died:
July 4, 1826

Place of birth:
Braintree, Massachusetts

Little-known fact:
He lived longer than any other president—nearly ninety-one years.

Thomas Jefferson

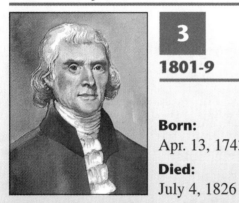

3

1801-9

Born:
Apr. 13, 1743

Died:
July 4, 1826

Place of birth:
Shadwell, Virginia

Little-known fact:
He loved to cook and introduced ice cream, waffles, and macaroni to the United States.

James Madison

4

1809-17

Born:
Mar. 16, 1751

Died:
June 28, 1836

Place of birth:
Port Conway, Virginia

Little-known fact:
He was the first president who wore long trousers.

James Monroe

5

1817-25

Born:
Apr. 28, 1758

Died:
July 4, 1831

Place of birth:
Westmoreland County, Virginia

Little-known fact:
When he ran for re-election in 1820, only one vote was cast against him.

John Quincy Adams

6

1825-29

Born:
July 11, 1767

Died:
Feb. 23, 1848

Place of birth:
Braintree, Massachusetts

Little-known fact:
As president, he got up as early as four o'clock in the morning to write in his diary.

Andrew Jackson

7

1829-37

Born:
Mar. 15, 1767

Died:
June 8, 1845

Place of birth:
Waxhaw, South Carolina

Little-known fact:
He reared eleven children during his lifetime, none of whom were his own.

Martin Van Buren

8

1837-41

Born:
Dec. 5, 1782

Died:
July 24, 1862

Place of birth:
Kinderhook, New York

Little-known fact:
He created the White House "Blue Room."

William Henry Harrison

9

**Mar. 4, 1841-
Apr. 4, 1841**

Born:
Feb. 9, 1773

Died:
Apr. 4, 1841

Place of birth:
Berkeley, Virginia

Little-known fact:
He did not make a single major decision during his time in office.

John Tyler

10

1841-45

Born:
Mar. 29, 1790

Died:
Jan. 18, 1862

Place of birth:
Greenway, Virginia

Little-known fact:
He had fifteen children— more than any other president.

James Knox Polk

11

1845-49

Born:
Nov. 2, 1795

Died:
June 15, 1849

Place of birth:
Mecklenburg County,
North Carolina

Little-known fact:
His inaugural address was the first
to be communicated via telegraph.

Zachary Taylor

12

**Mar. 4, 1849-
July 9, 1850**

Born:
Nov. 24, 1784

Died:
July 9, 1850

Place of birth:
Orange County, Virginia

Little-known fact:
His legs were so short that he
required help mounting his horse.

Millard Fillmore

13

1850-53

Born:
Jan. 7, 1800

Died:
Mar. 8, 1874

Place of birth:
Locke, New York

Little-known fact:
He refused an honorary degree from
Oxford University in England; he
felt that he was not entitled to it.

Franklin Pierce

14

1853-57

Born:
Nov. 23, 1804

Died:
Oct. 8, 1869

Place of birth:
Hillsborough, New Hampshire

Little-known fact:
He was arrested for running a woman
down while driving his carriage, but
he was never proved guilty.

James Buchanan

15

1857-61

Born:
Apr. 23, 1791

Died:
June 1, 1868

Place of birth:
Cove Gap, Pennsylvania

Little-known fact:
He gave sauerkraut-and-mashed-potato parties at his Pennsylvania home.

Abraham Lincoln

16

1861-65

Born:
Feb. 12, 1809

Died:
Apr. 15, 1865

Place of birth:
Hardin County, Kentucky

Little-known fact:
He gave his famous Gettysburg Address while suffering from smallpox.

Andrew Johnson

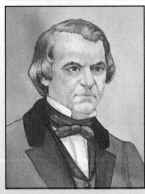

17

1865-69

Born:
Dec. 29, 1808

Died:
July 31, 1875

Place of birth:
Raleigh, North Carolina

Little-known fact:
He taught himself how to read, and a girlfriend taught him how to write.

Ulysses Simpson Grant

18

1869-77

Born:
Apr. 27, 1822

Died:
July 23, 1885

Place of birth:
Point Pleasant, Ohio

Little-known fact:
One of his favorite breakfasts during the Civil War was a vinegar-soaked cucumber.

Rutherford Birchard Hayes

19

1877-81

Born:
Oct. 4, 1822

Died:
Jan. 17, 1893

Place of birth:
Delaware, Ohio

Little-known fact:
He sometimes locked himself in the bathroom in order to concentrate on his work.

James Abram Garfield

20

**Mar. 4, 1881-
Sept. 19, 1881**

Born:
Nov. 19, 1831

Died:
Sept. 19, 1881

Place of birth:
Orange, Ohio

Little-known fact:
After his assassination, the concerned public raised over $300,000 for his wife and children.

Chester Alan Arthur

21

1881-85

Born:
Oct. 5, 1829

Died:
Nov. 18, 1886

Place of birth:
Fairfield, Vermont

Little-known fact:
He enjoyed sleigh rides down Pennsylvania Avenue.

Grover Cleveland

22

1885-89

Born:
Mar. 18, 1837

Died:
June 24, 1908

Place of birth:
Caldwell, New Jersey

Little-known fact:
His inauguration was the first at which fireworks were used.

Benjamin Harrison

23

1889-93

Born:
Aug. 20, 1833

Died:
Mar. 13, 1901

Place of birth:
North Bend, Ohio

Little-known fact:
His grandfather was President William Henry Harrison.

Grover Cleveland

24

1893-97

Born:
Mar. 18, 1837

Died:
June 24, 1908

Place of birth:
Caldwell, New Jersey

Little-known fact:
He was the only president to get married in the White House.

William McKinley

25

**Mar. 4, 1897-
Sept. 14, 1901**

Born:
Jan. 29, 1843

Died:
Sept. 14, 1901

Place of birth:
Niles, Ohio

Little-known fact:
He was the last president who had fought in the Civil War.

Theodore Roosevelt

26

1901-9

Born:
Oct. 27, 1858

Died:
Jan. 6, 1919

Place of birth:
New York, New York

Little-known fact:
A cartoon about him inspired a popular toy—the teddy bear.

William Howard Taft

27

1909-13

Born:
Sept. 15, 1857

Died:
Mar. 8, 1930

Place of birth:
Cincinnati, Ohio

Little-known fact:
He is the only American to have held the highest executive office and the highest judicial office.

Woodrow Wilson

28

1913-21

Born:
Dec. 28, 1856

Died:
Feb. 3, 1924

Place of birth:
Staunton, Virginia

Little-known fact:
He and his wife exchanged more than one thousand love notes during twenty-nine years of marriage.

Warren Gamaliel Harding

29

**Mar. 4, 1921-
Aug. 2, 1923**

Born:
Nov. 2, 1865

Died:
Aug. 2, 1923

Place of birth:
Corsica, Ohio

Little-known fact:
His dog, Laddie Boy, delivered the president's newspapers every day.

Calvin Coolidge

30

1923-29

Born:
July 4, 1872

Died:
Jan. 5, 1933

Place of birth:
Plymouth, Vermont

Little-known fact:
He took the oath of office at 2:45 A.M. by the light of a kerosene lamp at a Vermont farmhouse.

Herbert Clark Hoover

31

1929-33

Born:
Aug. 10, 1874

Died:
Oct. 20, 1964

Place of birth:
West Branch, Iowa

Little-known fact:
He never accepted a salary as president and spent his own money on entertaining.

Franklin Delano Roosevelt

32

1933-45

Born:
Jan. 30, 1882

Died:
Apr. 12, 1945

Place of birth:
Hyde Park, New York

Little-known fact:
He had a swimming pool and a movie theater built in the White House.

Harry S Truman

33

1945-53

Born:
May 8, 1884

Died:
Dec. 26, 1972

Place of birth:
Lamar, Missouri

Little-known fact:
He lived in Blair House while the White House was renovated (1948-52).

Dwight David Eisenhower

34

1953-61

Born:
Oct. 14, 1890

Died:
Mar. 28, 1969

Place of birth:
Denison, Texas

Little-known fact:
His ability to paint but not draw led to a "paint-by-numbers" fad.

John Fitzgerald Kennedy

35

1961-63

Born:
May 29, 1917

Died:
Nov. 22, 1963

Place of birth:
Brookline, Massachusetts

Little-known fact:
He was the first president born in a hospital.

Lyndon Baines Johnson

36

1963-69

Born:
Aug. 27, 1908

Died:
Jan. 22, 1973

Place of birth:
Stonewall, Texas

Little-known fact:
He was the first president to fly all the way around the world visiting other governments.

Richard Milhous Nixon

37

1969-74

Born:
Jan. 9, 1913

Died:
Apr. 22, 1994

Place of birth:
Yorba Linda, California

Little-known fact:
He was the first president to visit all fifty states.

Gerald Rudolph Ford

38

1974-77

Born:
July 14, 1913

Died:
—

Place of birth:
Omaha, Nebraska

Little-known fact:
He was the first vice president not elected by the people to become president (chosen by Nixon).

James Earl Carter

39

1977-81

Born:
Oct. 1, 1924

Died:
—

Place of birth:
Plains, Georgia

Little-known fact:
He was the first president to walk from the Capitol to the White House ($1\frac{1}{2}$ miles) after the inauguration.

Ronald Wilson Reagan

40

1981-89

Born:
Feb. 6, 1911

Died:
—

Place of birth:
Tampico, Illinois

Little-known fact:
He was a popular movie star for more than twenty years (1937-64) before becoming president.

George Herbert Walker Bush

41

1989-93

Born:
June 12, 1924

Died:
—

Place of birth:
Milton, Massachusetts

Little-known fact:
He invited tennis champions to play with him on the White House tennis courts.

William Jefferson Clinton

42

1993-

Born:
Aug. 19, 1946

Died:
—

Place of birth:
Hope, Arkansas

Little-known fact:
His hobbies include playing the tenor saxophone, jogging, and doing crossword puzzles.

States

Definition of terms:

community, social, and personal services: every type of work in which individuals help individuals without growing, mining, manufacturing, or distributing goods

government: refers to all people employed in running the state and money spent by the state

wholesale and retail trade:
wholesale trade—sale of goods in large quantities for lower prices

retail trade—sale of goods or commodities in small quantities directly to consumers

finance, insurance, and real estate:
finance—refers to banking

insurance—buying and selling of insurance policies

real estate—buying and selling of land, including all natural resources and permanent buildings on it

---

Alabama December 14, 1819

22

Capital: Montgomery
Nickname: Yellowhammer State
State tree: Southern pine
State song: "Alabama"
Largest city: Birmingham
Economic strengths:
Paper products, chemicals, and textiles
Interesting fact:
The state has a statue built in honor of the boll weevil.

Camellia

Yellowhammer

Alaska   January 3, 1959

49

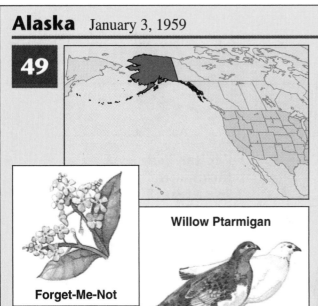

Capital: Juneau
Nickname: The Last Frontier
State tree: Sitka spruce
State song: "Alaska's Flag"
Largest city: Anchorage
Economic strengths:
Petroleum and government
Interesting fact:
Alaska's 6,640-mile coastline is longer than the coastlines of all the other forty-nine states put together.

Forget-Me-Not

Willow Ptarmigan

Arizona   February 14, 1912

48

Saguaro Cactus Flower

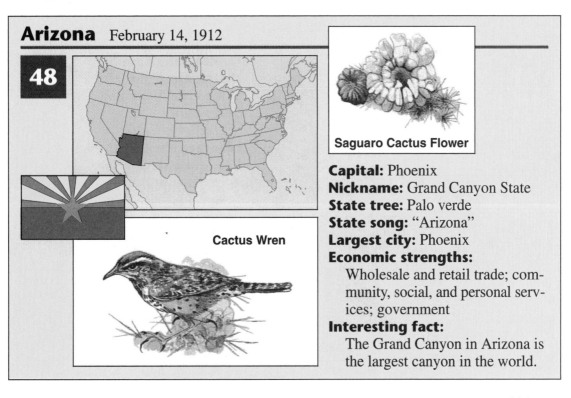

Cactus Wren

Capital: Phoenix
Nickname: Grand Canyon State
State tree: Palo verde
State song: "Arizona"
Largest city: Phoenix
Economic strengths:
Wholesale and retail trade; community, social, and personal services; government
Interesting fact:
The Grand Canyon in Arizona is the largest canyon in the world.

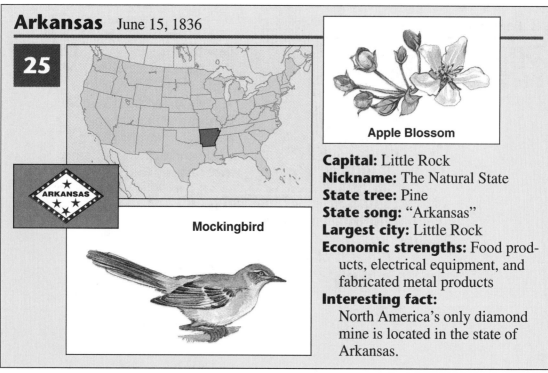

Arkansas June 15, 1836

25

Apple Blossom

Mockingbird

Capital: Little Rock
Nickname: The Natural State
State tree: Pine
State song: "Arkansas"
Largest city: Little Rock
Economic strengths: Food products, electrical equipment, and fabricated metal products
Interesting fact:
North America's only diamond mine is located in the state of Arkansas.

California September 9, 1850

31

Capital: Sacramento
Nickname: Golden State
State tree: California redwood
State song: "I Love You, California"
Largest city: Los Angeles
Economic strengths:
Community, social, and personal services; finance, insurance, and real estate; wholesale and retail trade
Interesting fact: The largest living things in the world—sequoia trees—are located in California.

California Valley Quail

Golden Poppy

CALIFORNIA REPUBLIC

Colorado August 1, 1876

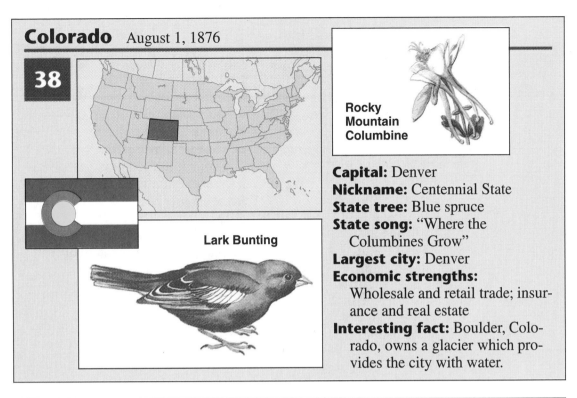

38

Rocky Mountain Columbine

Lark Bunting

Capital: Denver
Nickname: Centennial State
State tree: Blue spruce
State song: "Where the Columbines Grow"
Largest city: Denver
Economic strengths:
Wholesale and retail trade; insurance and real estate
Interesting fact: Boulder, Colorado, owns a glacier which provides the city with water.

Connecticut January 9, 1788

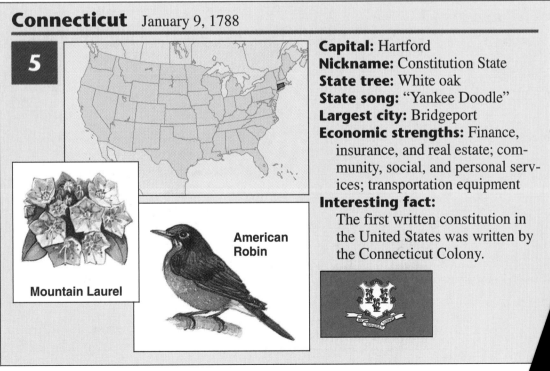

5

Capital: Hartford
Nickname: Constitution State
State tree: White oak
State song: "Yankee Doodle"
Largest city: Bridgeport
Economic strengths: Finance, insurance, and real estate; community, social, and personal services; transportation equipment
Interesting fact:
The first written constitution in the United States was written by the Connecticut Colony.

American Robin

Mountain Laurel

Delaware   December 7, 1787

1

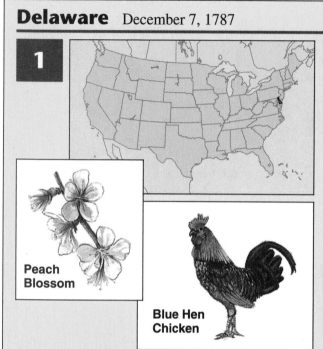

Peach Blossom

Blue Hen Chicken

Capital: Dover
Nickname: First State
State tree: American holly
State song: "Our Delaware"
Largest city: Wilmington
Economic strengths:
   Chemicals, food products, and transportation equipment
Interesting fact:
   Delaware was the first state to accept the Constitution, thereby making it the first state.

Florida   March 3, 1845

27

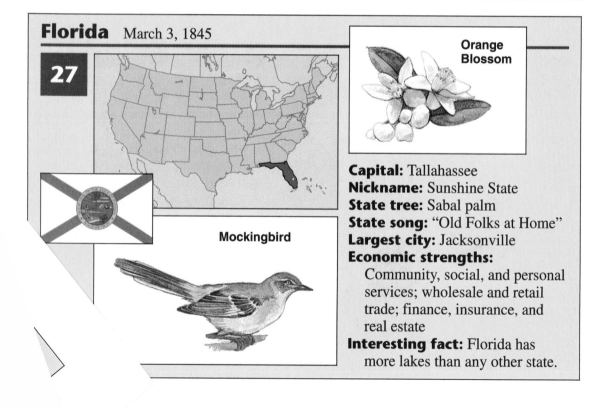

Orange Blossom

Mockingbird

Capital: Tallahassee
Nickname: Sunshine State
State tree: Sabal palm
State song: "Old Folks at Home"
Largest city: Jacksonville
Economic strengths:
   Community, social, and personal services; wholesale and retail trade; finance, insurance, and real estate
Interesting fact: Florida has more lakes than any other state.

Georgia January 2, 1788

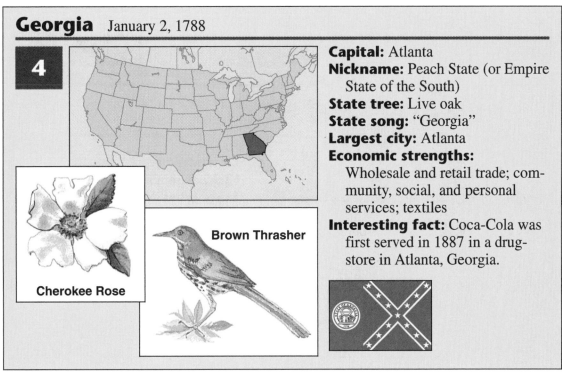

4

Cherokee Rose

Brown Thrasher

Capital: Atlanta
Nickname: Peach State (or Empire State of the South)
State tree: Live oak
State song: "Georgia"
Largest city: Atlanta
Economic strengths:
Wholesale and retail trade; community, social, and personal services; textiles
Interesting fact: Coca-Cola was first served in 1887 in a drugstore in Atlanta, Georgia.

Hawaii August 21, 1959

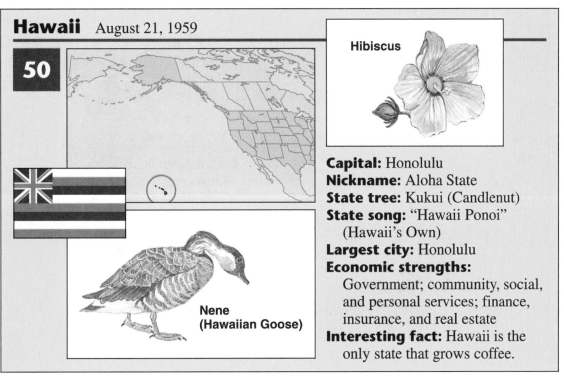

50

Hibiscus

Nene (Hawaiian Goose)

Capital: Honolulu
Nickname: Aloha State
State tree: Kukui (Candlenut)
State song: "Hawaii Ponoi" (Hawaii's Own)
Largest city: Honolulu
Economic strengths:
Government; community, social, and personal services; finance, insurance, and real estate
Interesting fact: Hawaii is the only state that grows coffee.

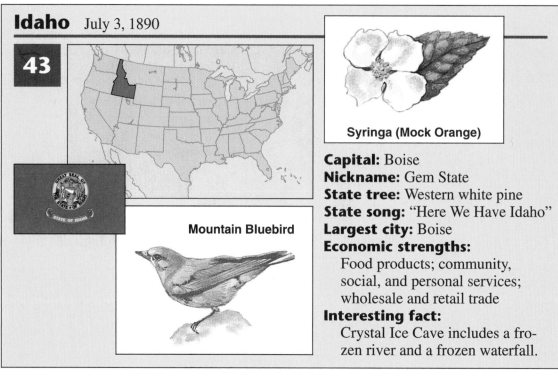

Idaho July 3, 1890

43

Syringa (Mock Orange)

Mountain Bluebird

Capital: Boise
Nickname: Gem State
State tree: Western white pine
State song: "Here We Have Idaho"
Largest city: Boise
Economic strengths:
Food products; community, social, and personal services; wholesale and retail trade
Interesting fact:
Crystal Ice Cave includes a frozen river and a frozen waterfall.

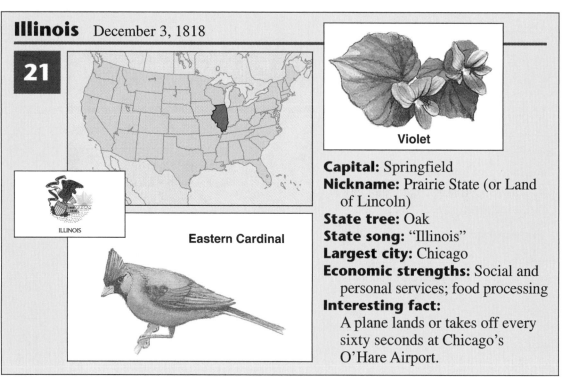

Illinois December 3, 1818

21

Violet

ILLINOIS

Eastern Cardinal

Capital: Springfield
Nickname: Prairie State (or Land of Lincoln)
State tree: Oak
State song: "Illinois"
Largest city: Chicago
Economic strengths: Social and personal services; food processing
Interesting fact:
A plane lands or takes off every sixty seconds at Chicago's O'Hare Airport.

286

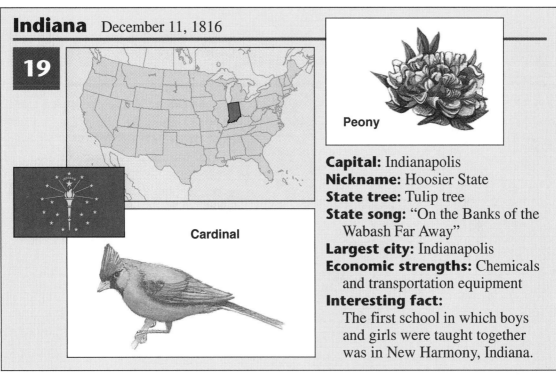

Indiana   December 11, 1816

19

Peony

Cardinal

Capital: Indianapolis
Nickname: Hoosier State
State tree: Tulip tree
State song: "On the Banks of the Wabash Far Away"
Largest city: Indianapolis
Economic strengths: Chemicals and transportation equipment
Interesting fact:
The first school in which boys and girls were taught together was in New Harmony, Indiana.

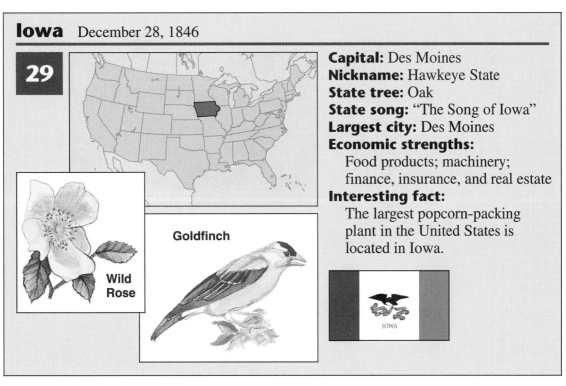

Iowa   December 28, 1846

29

Capital: Des Moines
Nickname: Hawkeye State
State tree: Oak
State song: "The Song of Iowa"
Largest city: Des Moines
Economic strengths:
Food products; machinery; finance, insurance, and real estate
Interesting fact:
The largest popcorn-packing plant in the United States is located in Iowa.

Wild Rose

Goldfinch

IOWA

Kansas   January 29, 1861

34

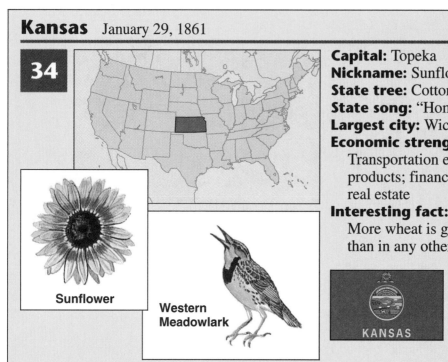

Capital: Topeka
Nickname: Sunflower State
State tree: Cottonwood
State song: "Home on the Range"
Largest city: Wichita
Economic strengths:
   Transportation equipment; food products; finance, insurance, and real estate
Interesting fact:
   More wheat is grown in Kansas than in any other state.

Sunflower

Western Meadowlark

KANSAS

Kentucky   June 1, 1792

15

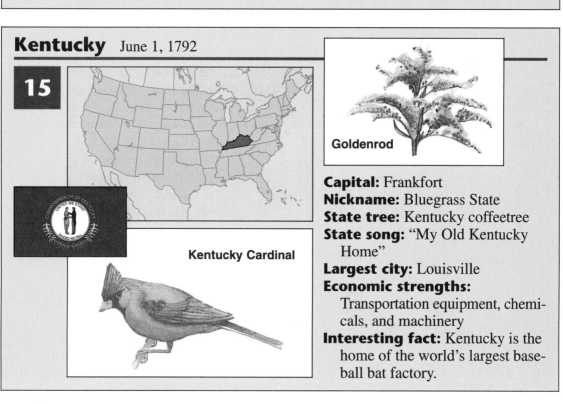

Goldenrod

Kentucky Cardinal

Capital: Frankfort
Nickname: Bluegrass State
State tree: Kentucky coffeetree
State song: "My Old Kentucky Home"
Largest city: Louisville
Economic strengths:
   Transportation equipment, chemicals, and machinery
Interesting fact: Kentucky is the home of the world's largest baseball bat factory.

Louisiana April 30, 1812

18

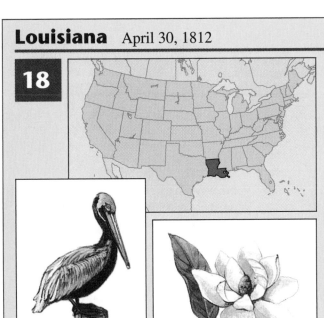

Capital: Baton Rouge
Nickname: Pelican State (or Sportsman's Paradise)
State tree: Bald cypress
State song: "Give Me Louisiana"
Largest city: New Orleans
Economic strengths:
Community, social, and personal services; chemicals; processing petroleum and coal products
Interesting fact: The world's longest bridge—the Lake Pontchartrain Causeway—is in New Orleans; it is almost twenty-four miles long.

Pelican

Magnolia

Maine March 15, 1820

23

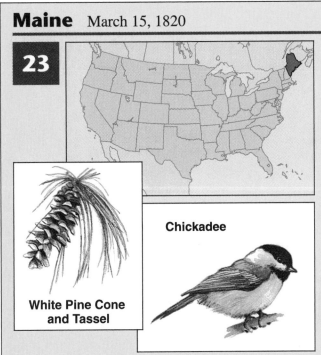

Capital: Augusta
Nickname: Pine Tree State
State tree: White pine
State song: "State of Maine Song"
Largest city: Portland
Economic strengths:
Community, social, and personal services; paper products; finance, insurance, and real estate
Interesting fact:
Maine once belonged to an English family. The Massachusetts Colony bought it for six thousand dollars in 1677.

Chickadee

White Pine Cone and Tassel

Maryland April 28, 1788

7

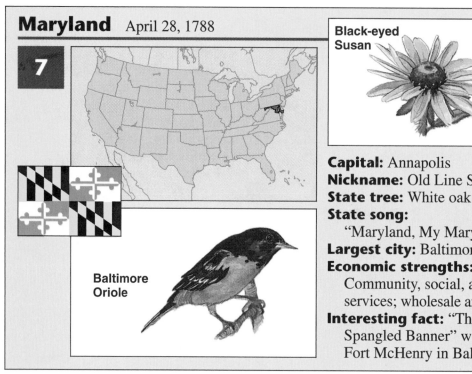

Black-eyed Susan

Baltimore Oriole

Capital: Annapolis
Nickname: Old Line State
State tree: White oak
State song:
"Maryland, My Maryland"
Largest city: Baltimore
Economic strengths:
Community, social, and personal services; wholesale and retail trade
Interesting fact: "The Star-Spangled Banner" was written at Fort McHenry in Baltimore.

Massachusetts February 6, 1788

6

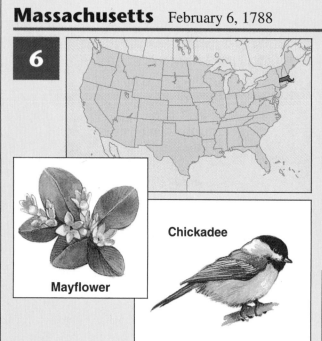

Chickadee

Mayflower

Capital: Boston
Nickname: Bay State
State tree: American elm
State song:
"All Hail to Massachusetts"
Largest city: Boston
Economic strengths:
Community, social, and personal services; scientific instruments; electrical equipment
Interesting fact:
Massachusetts had a number of "firsts": the first college, first railroad, first subway, and first basketball game.

Michigan January 26, 1837

26

Capital: Lansing
Nickname: Wolverine State
State tree: White pine
State song:
  "Michigan, My Michigan"
Largest city: Detroit
Economic strengths:
  Transportation equipment,
  machinery, and fabricated metal
  products
Interesting fact:
  Michigan is touched by four of
  the five Great Lakes.

Apple Blossom

Robin

Minnesota May 11, 1858

32

Showy
Lady Slipper

Common Loon

Capital: St. Paul
Nickname: Gopher State
State tree: Norway pine
State song: "Hail! Minnesota"
Largest city: Minneapolis
Economic strengths:
  Machinery; finance, insurance,
  and real estate; community,
  social, and personal services
Interesting fact:
  Minnesota produces more butter
  than any other state.

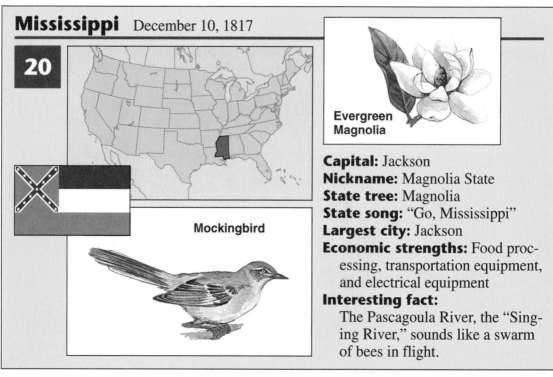

Mississippi December 10, 1817

20

Evergreen Magnolia

Mockingbird

Capital: Jackson
Nickname: Magnolia State
State tree: Magnolia
State song: "Go, Mississippi"
Largest city: Jackson
Economic strengths: Food processing, transportation equipment, and electrical equipment
Interesting fact:
The Pascagoula River, the "Singing River," sounds like a swarm of bees in flight.

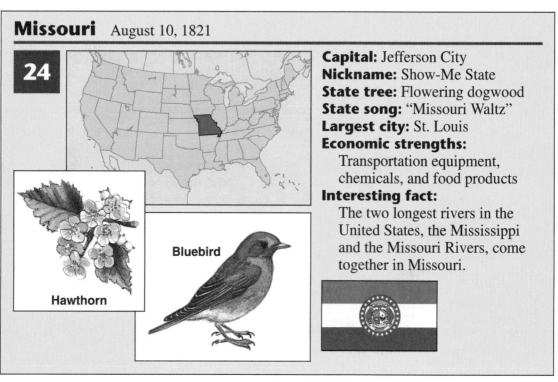

Missouri August 10, 1821

24

Capital: Jefferson City
Nickname: Show-Me State
State tree: Flowering dogwood
State song: "Missouri Waltz"
Largest city: St. Louis
Economic strengths:
Transportation equipment, chemicals, and food products
Interesting fact:
The two longest rivers in the United States, the Mississippi and the Missouri Rivers, come together in Missouri.

Hawthorn

Bluebird

Montana   November 8, 1889

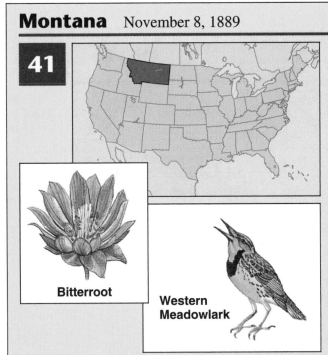

41

Capital: Helena
Nickname: Treasure State
State tree: Ponderosa pine
State song: "Montana"
Largest city: Billings
Economic strengths:
Finance, insurance, and real estate; community, social, and personal services; wholesale and retail trade
Interesting fact:
The first woman elected to Congress was from Montana.

Bitterroot

Western Meadowlark

Nebraska   March 1, 1867

37

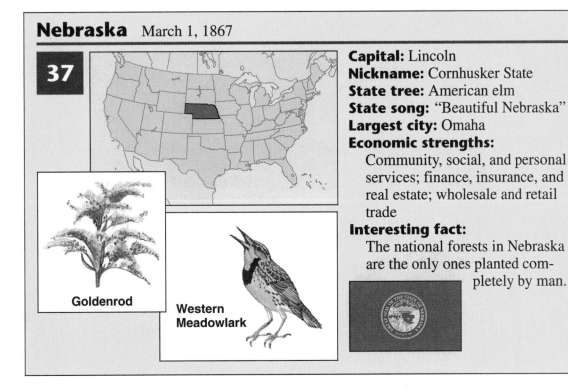

Capital: Lincoln
Nickname: Cornhusker State
State tree: American elm
State song: "Beautiful Nebraska"
Largest city: Omaha
Economic strengths:
Community, social, and personal services; finance, insurance, and real estate; wholesale and retail trade
Interesting fact:
The national forests in Nebraska are the only ones planted completely by man.

Goldenrod

Western Meadowlark

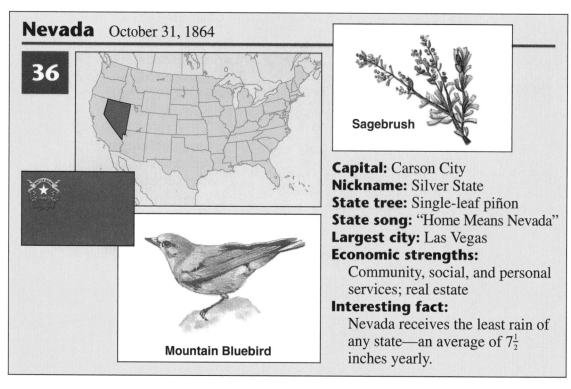

Nevada   October 31, 1864

36

Sagebrush

Capital: Carson City
Nickname: Silver State
State tree: Single-leaf piñon
State song: "Home Means Nevada"
Largest city: Las Vegas
Economic strengths:
  Community, social, and personal
  services; real estate
Interesting fact:
  Nevada receives the least rain of
  any state—an average of $7\frac{1}{2}$
  inches yearly.

Mountain Bluebird

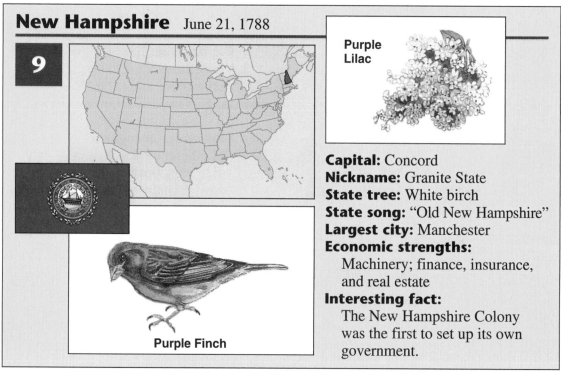

New Hampshire   June 21, 1788

9

Purple
Lilac

Capital: Concord
Nickname: Granite State
State tree: White birch
State song: "Old New Hampshire"
Largest city: Manchester
Economic strengths:
  Machinery; finance, insurance,
  and real estate
Interesting fact:
  The New Hampshire Colony
  was the first to set up its own
  government.

Purple Finch

New Jersey December 18, 1787

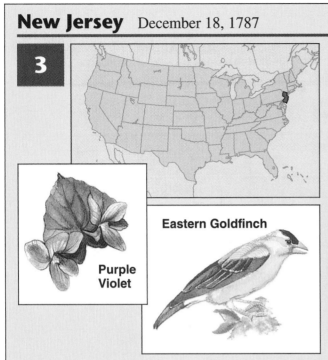

3

Capital: Trenton
Nickname: Garden State
State tree: Red oak
State song: None
Largest city: Newark
Economic strengths:
Finance, insurance, and real estate; community, social, and personal services; chemicals
Interesting fact:
New Jersey has more people per square mile than any other state.

Purple Violet

Eastern Goldfinch

New Mexico January 6, 1912

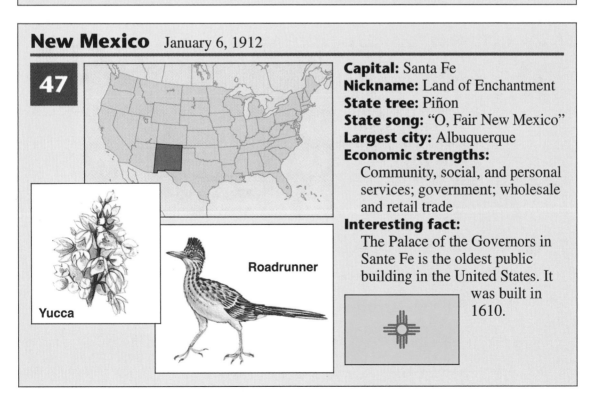

47

Capital: Santa Fe
Nickname: Land of Enchantment
State tree: Piñon
State song: "O, Fair New Mexico"
Largest city: Albuquerque
Economic strengths:
Community, social, and personal services; government; wholesale and retail trade
Interesting fact:
The Palace of the Governors in Sante Fe is the oldest public building in the United States. It was built in 1610.

Yucca

Roadrunner

New York July 26, 1788

11

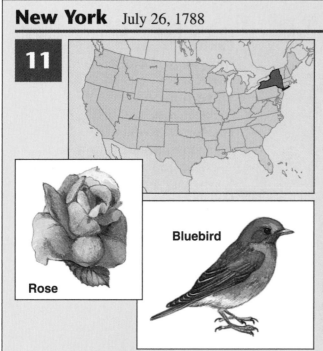

Rose

Bluebird

Capital: Albany
Nickname: Empire State
State tree: Sugar maple
State song: "I Love New York"
Largest city: New York City
Economic strengths:
Community, social, and personal services; finance, insurance, and real estate; wholesale and retail trade
Interesting fact:
The biggest and busiest port in the United States is in New York.

North Carolina November 21, 1789

12

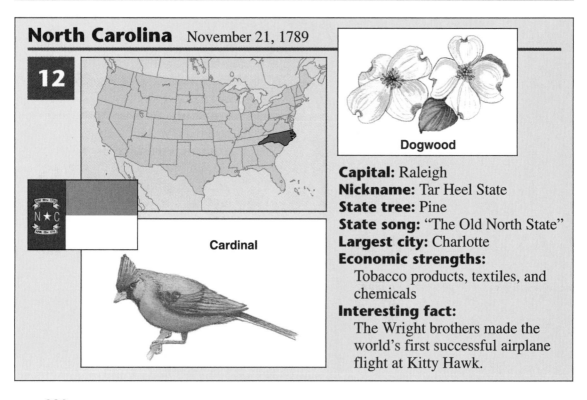

Dogwood

Cardinal

Capital: Raleigh
Nickname: Tar Heel State
State tree: Pine
State song: "The Old North State"
Largest city: Charlotte
Economic strengths:
Tobacco products, textiles, and chemicals
Interesting fact:
The Wright brothers made the world's first successful airplane flight at Kitty Hawk.

North Dakota November 2, 1889

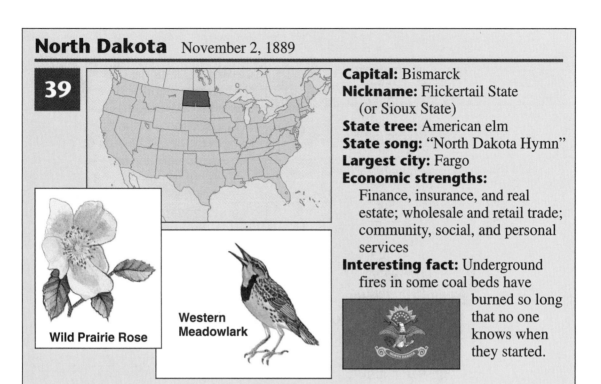

39

Capital: Bismarck
Nickname: Flickertail State (or Sioux State)
State tree: American elm
State song: "North Dakota Hymn"
Largest city: Fargo
Economic strengths:
Finance, insurance, and real estate; wholesale and retail trade; community, social, and personal services
Interesting fact: Underground fires in some coal beds have burned so long that no one knows when they started.

Wild Prairie Rose

Western Meadowlark

Ohio March 1, 1803

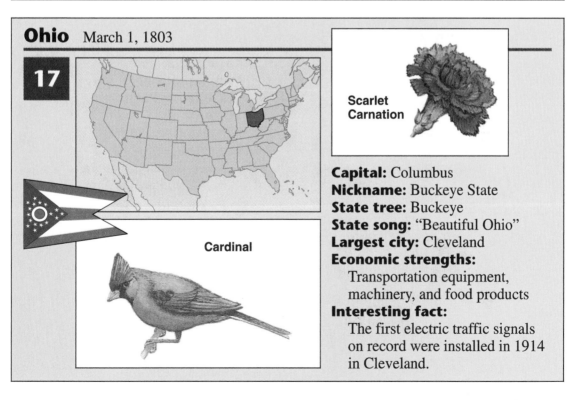

17

Scarlet Carnation

Capital: Columbus
Nickname: Buckeye State
State tree: Buckeye
State song: "Beautiful Ohio"
Largest city: Cleveland
Economic strengths:
Transportation equipment, machinery, and food products
Interesting fact:
The first electric traffic signals on record were installed in 1914 in Cleveland.

Cardinal

Oklahoma November 16, 1907

46

Scissor-tailed
Flycatcher

Mistletoe

Capital: Oklahoma City
Nickname: Sooner State
State tree: Redbud
State song: "Oklahoma!"
Largest city: Oklahoma City
Economic strengths:
Community, social, and personal services; wholesale and retail trade; government
Interesting fact:
More Native Americans live in Oklahoma than in any other state.

Oregon February 14, 1859

33

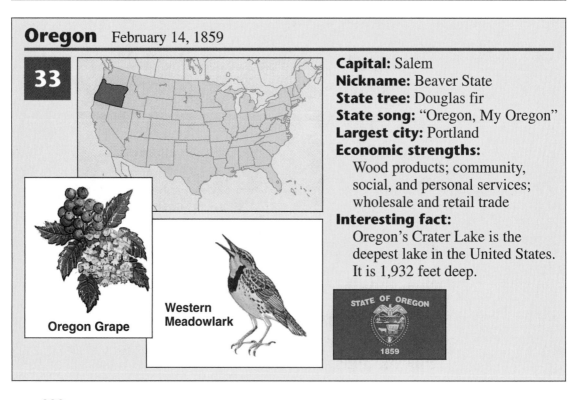

Oregon Grape

Western
Meadowlark

Capital: Salem
Nickname: Beaver State
State tree: Douglas fir
State song: "Oregon, My Oregon"
Largest city: Portland
Economic strengths:
Wood products; community, social, and personal services; wholesale and retail trade
Interesting fact:
Oregon's Crater Lake is the deepest lake in the United States. It is 1,932 feet deep.

Pennsylvania December 12, 1787

2

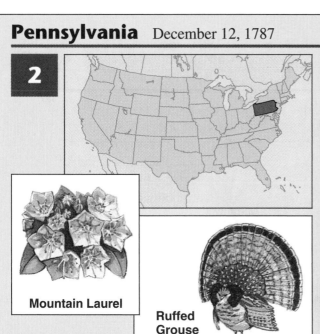

Capital: Harrisburg
Nickname: Keystone State
State tree: Hemlock
State song: None
Largest city: Philadelphia
Economic strengths:
Community, social, and personal services; food products; chemicals
Interesting fact:
The chocolate and cocoa factory in Hershey, Pennsylvania, is the largest one in the world.

Mountain Laurel

Ruffed Grouse

Rhode Island May 29, 1790

13

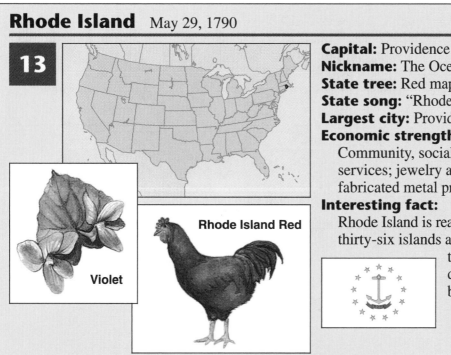

Capital: Providence
Nickname: The Ocean State
State tree: Red maple
State song: "Rhode Island"
Largest city: Providence
Economic strengths:
Community, social, and personal services; jewelry and silverware; fabricated metal products
Interesting fact:
Rhode Island is really made up of thirty-six islands and a mainland that is nearly divided in two by a bay.

Rhode Island Red

Violet

South Carolina May 23, 1788

8

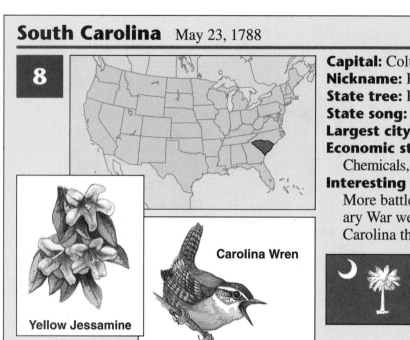

Capital: Columbia
Nickname: Palmetto State
State tree: Palmetto
State song: "Carolina"
Largest city: Columbia
Economic strengths:
  Chemicals, textiles, and machinery
Interesting fact:
  More battles of the Revolutionary War were fought in South Carolina than in any other state.

Yellow Jessamine

Carolina Wren

South Dakota November 2, 1889

40

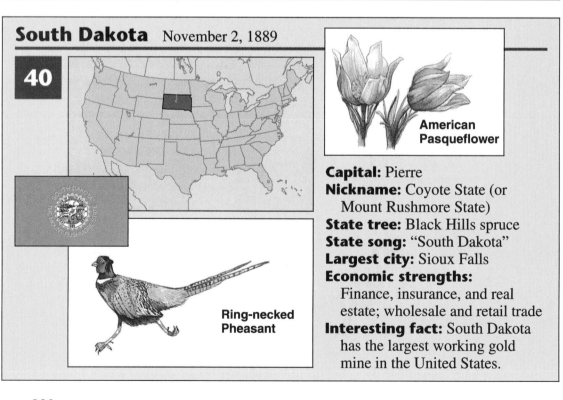

American Pasqueflower

Capital: Pierre
Nickname: Coyote State (or Mount Rushmore State)
State tree: Black Hills spruce
State song: "South Dakota"
Largest city: Sioux Falls
Economic strengths:
  Finance, insurance, and real estate; wholesale and retail trade
Interesting fact: South Dakota has the largest working gold mine in the United States.

Ring-necked Pheasant

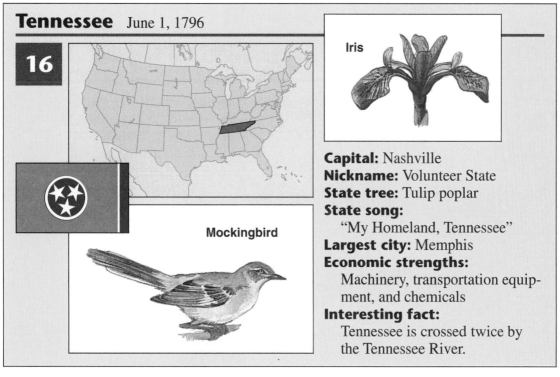

Tennessee June 1, 1796

16

Iris

Capital: Nashville
Nickname: Volunteer State
State tree: Tulip poplar
State song:
   "My Homeland, Tennessee"
Largest city: Memphis
Economic strengths:
   Machinery, transportation equipment, and chemicals
Interesting fact:
   Tennessee is crossed twice by the Tennessee River.

Mockingbird

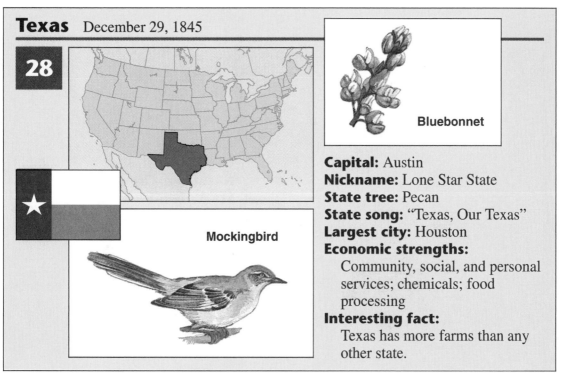

Texas December 29, 1845

28

Bluebonnet

Capital: Austin
Nickname: Lone Star State
State tree: Pecan
State song: "Texas, Our Texas"
Largest city: Houston
Economic strengths:
   Community, social, and personal services; chemicals; food processing
Interesting fact:
   Texas has more farms than any other state.

Mockingbird

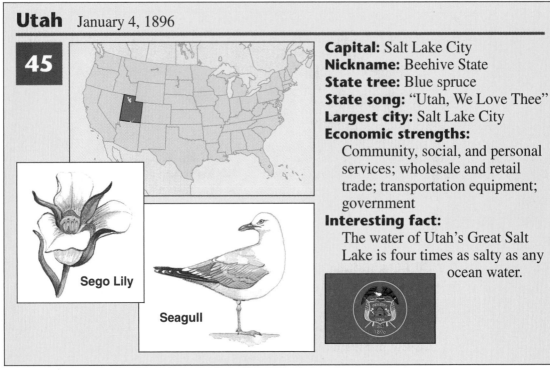

Utah   January 4, 1896

45

Capital: Salt Lake City
Nickname: Beehive State
State tree: Blue spruce
State song: "Utah, We Love Thee"
Largest city: Salt Lake City
Economic strengths:
Community, social, and personal services; wholesale and retail trade; transportation equipment; government
Interesting fact:
The water of Utah's Great Salt Lake is four times as salty as any ocean water.

Sego Lily

Seagull

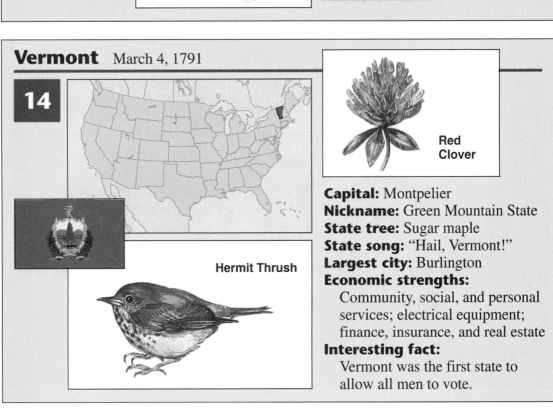

Vermont   March 4, 1791

14

Red Clover

Hermit Thrush

Capital: Montpelier
Nickname: Green Mountain State
State tree: Sugar maple
State song: "Hail, Vermont!"
Largest city: Burlington
Economic strengths:
Community, social, and personal services; electrical equipment; finance, insurance, and real estate
Interesting fact:
Vermont was the first state to allow all men to vote.

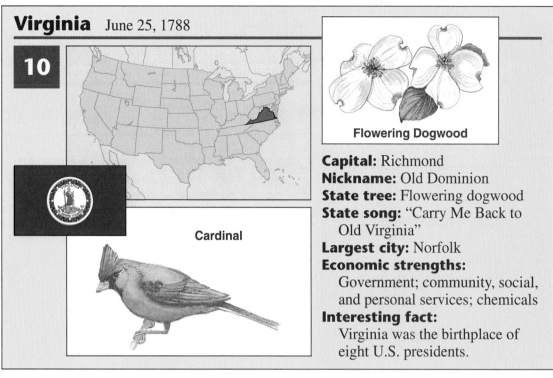

Virginia June 25, 1788

10

Flowering Dogwood

Cardinal

Capital: Richmond
Nickname: Old Dominion
State tree: Flowering dogwood
State song: "Carry Me Back to Old Virginia"
Largest city: Norfolk
Economic strengths:
Government; community, social, and personal services; chemicals
Interesting fact:
Virginia was the birthplace of eight U.S. presidents.

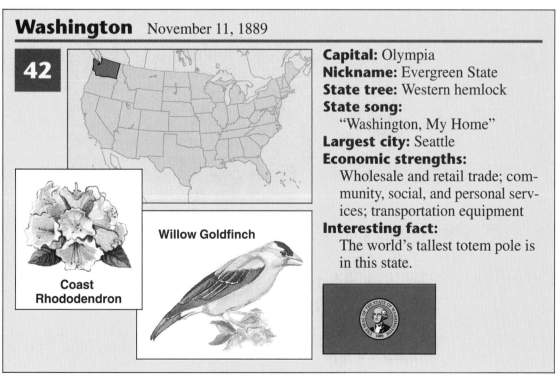

Washington November 11, 1889

42

Coast Rhododendron

Willow Goldfinch

Capital: Olympia
Nickname: Evergreen State
State tree: Western hemlock
State song:
"Washington, My Home"
Largest city: Seattle
Economic strengths:
Wholesale and retail trade; community, social, and personal services; transportation equipment
Interesting fact:
The world's tallest totem pole is in this state.

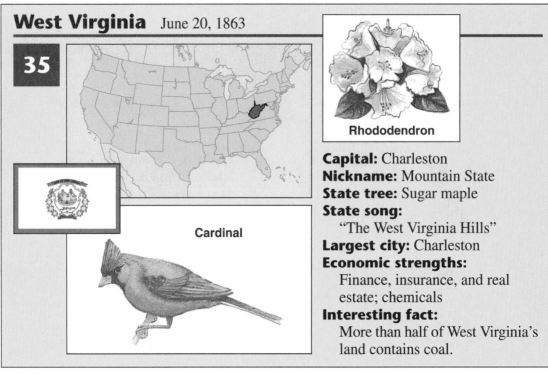

West Virginia June 20, 1863

35

Rhododendron

Capital: Charleston
Nickname: Mountain State
State tree: Sugar maple
State song:
"The West Virginia Hills"
Largest city: Charleston
Economic strengths:
Finance, insurance, and real estate; chemicals
Interesting fact:
More than half of West Virginia's land contains coal.

Cardinal

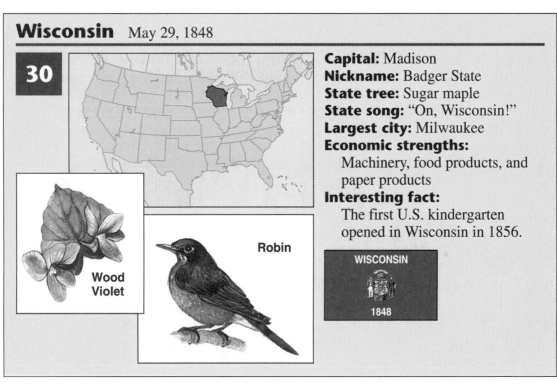

Wisconsin May 29, 1848

30

Capital: Madison
Nickname: Badger State
State tree: Sugar maple
State song: "On, Wisconsin!"
Largest city: Milwaukee
Economic strengths:
Machinery, food products, and paper products
Interesting fact:
The first U.S. kindergarten opened in Wisconsin in 1856.

Wood Violet

Robin

WISCONSIN

1848

Wyoming July 10, 1890

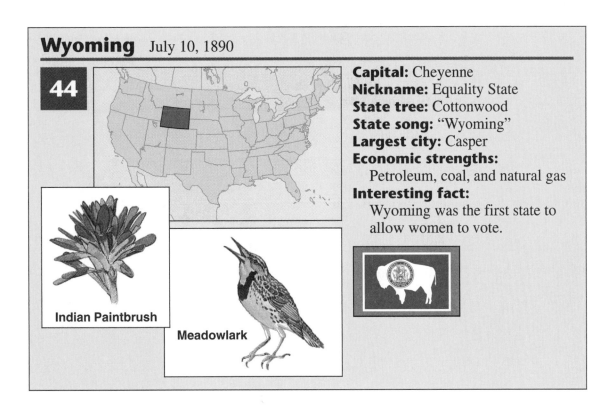

44

Capital: Cheyenne
Nickname: Equality State
State tree: Cottonwood
State song: "Wyoming"
Largest city: Casper
Economic strengths:
Petroleum, coal, and natural gas
Interesting fact:
Wyoming was the first state to
allow women to vote.

Indian Paintbrush

Meadowlark

Symbols

The Statue of Liberty

The Statue of Liberty, or *Liberty Enlightening the World,* was a gift from France to the United States in 1884. Made of copper and standing on an enormous pedestal of steel and granite, Miss Liberty has become a symbol of the United States and a beacon of freedom for people all over the world.

The statue presents liberty as a proud lady, draped in a graceful, loose robe. In her right hand, she lifts on high a glowing torch. Her crown bears seven spikes, representing the seven seas and seven continents. In her left arm, she cradles a tablet that bears the date

The Statue of Liberty raises her torch above New York Harbor.

of the Declaration of Independence. At her feet lies a broken chain, symbolizing that unjust rule is gone. As millions of immigrants entered the United States seeking freedom and opportunity, their first image was of the Statue of Liberty. Seeming to speak for the "Lady with the Lamp," the poem "The New Colossus" by Emma Lazarus was inscribed on a bronze plaque on the pedestal of the monument.

> ". . . Give me your tired, your poor,
> Your huddled masses yearning to breathe free,
> The wretched refuse of your teeming shore.
> Send these, the homeless, tempest-tost to me.
> I lift my lamp beside the golden door!"

The Pledge of Allegiance

The Pledge of Allegiance is a promise of loyalty to the United States. Bostonians James B. Upham and Francis Bellamy wrote the original pledge. School children first recited the Pledge of Allegiance in 1892 as they commemorated the 400th anniversary of the discovery of America. In 1923 and 1924, the National Flag Conference expanded the wording of the pledge. In 1942 Congress sanctioned the use of the Pledge of Allegiance with the display of the flag. Then in 1954 Congress added the words "under God" to the pledge.

The Pledge of Allegiance reads:

I pledge allegiance to the flag of the United States of America and to the Republic for which it stands, one Nation under God, indivisible, with liberty and justice for all.

Washington, D.C.

Washington, D.C., is the capital of the United States, serving as the headquarters of the federal government and a symbol of the country's history. Washington, D.C., is the only American city or town that is not part of a state; it covers all of the District of Columbia, a section of land under the rule of the federal government.

Jefferson Monument (above) and Washington Monument (right)

Capitol Building

Lincoln Memorial

White House

In 1791 President George Washington chose the site for the city, along the Potomac River, between Maryland and Virginia. He hired Pierre Charles L'Enfant, a French engineer, to draw up the plans for the city. L'Enfant's plan made the Capitol building the center of the city with streets leading out from it like spokes on a wheel. Every year, millions of visitors from all over the world visit Washington, D.C., learning of America's government and her history. Some of the most-visited points of interest include the Capitol, the White House, the Washington Monument, the Lincoln Memorial, and the Smithsonian Institution.

Uncle Sam

During the War of 1812 Sam Wilson's packing plant supplied meat in boxes that were stamped "U.S.," for America's soldiers. Though it was the abbreviation for United States, U.S. also came to mean "Uncle Sam," sometimes referring to Sam Wilson and sometimes a nickname for the United States government.

James Montgomery Flagg's famous painting of Uncle Sam inspired young men to enlist in the U.S. Army during World War I.

The figure of Uncle Sam with his white beard, red and white striped trousers, and tall top hat covered with stars and stripes has come to symbolize the United States of America. Probably the most famous picture of Uncle Sam is the one on a World War I recruitment poster. Uncle Sam is pointing his finger and saying "I want you!"

Ellis Island

Ellis Island is located in New York Harbor, less than half a mile north of Liberty Island, where the Statue of Liberty stands. Ellis Island is named for the merchant and farmer Samuel Ellis, who owned the island in the late 1700s. The United States government bought the island in 1808 and, after the construction of thirty-five buildings, began using it as an immigration station in 1892.

Can you imagine how these immigrants felt upon their arrival on Ellis Island?

For more than twelve million immigrants, Ellis Island was their first glimpse of America with her promise of freedom and opportunity. Newcomers were questioned by government officials and examined by doctors before being allowed to enter the United States. Most of the immigration station at Ellis Island closed down in 1924, and the station was completely closed in 1954. In 1965, Ellis Island became a national historic site, part of the Statue of Liberty National Monument.

Days

Memorial Day

Memorial Day, also called Decoration Day, is a holiday in the United States to honor those who died in war while serving the United States. In 1971 a federal law declared that Memorial Day would be celebrated on the last Monday in May.

On Memorial Day, many communities have parades and special ceremonies to honor the nation's war dead. People often place flowers and small American flags on the graves of military personnel.

Labor Day

Labor Day is a holiday honoring working people. Matthew Maguire, a machinist from New Jersey, and Peter J. McGuire, a carpenter from New York City, are credited with suggesting this holiday. In September 1882, the two men took part in the nation's first Labor Day parade. The earliest parades were held in New York City and Philadelphia, but in 1887 Oregon became the first state to make Labor Day a legal holiday. Then in 1894, President Grover Cleveland signed a bill that made Labor Day a national holiday.

Many people celebrate Labor Day with a picnic.

In the United States, Puerto Rico, and Canada, Labor Day is celebrated on the first Monday in September. Though some organizations sponsor Labor Day festivities, most people enjoy time off from work for rest and relaxation.

313

Victorian Christmas Customs

The first Christmas greeting card was made in 1843. Sending cards did not become popular, however, until many years later.

Christmas cards were originally little cards that children decorated for their parents. They soon developed into elaborate creations; they were often decorated with satin, fringed silk, and plush. Sometimes the cards were even jeweled.

314

Colors of Christmas

Traditional colors of Christmas, which became popular in the late 1800s, are red and green. Green represents the continuance of life through the winter and the Christian belief in eternal life through Christ. Red symbolizes the blood that Jesus shed at His Crucifixion.

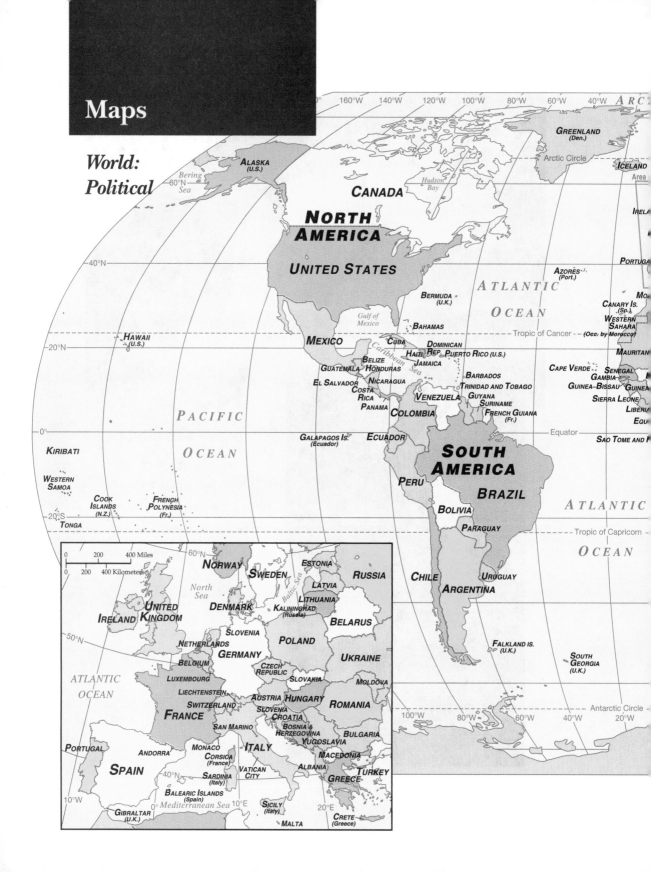

Maps

World:
Political

OCEAN · 40°E · 60°E · 80°E · 100°E · 120°E · 140°E · 160°E · 180° · 80°N

60°N

RUSSIA

ASIA

40°N

Sea of Okhotsk

Bering Sea

AY SWEDEN FINLAND
ESTONIA
LATVIA
ARK LITHUANIA
POLAND BELARUS
ERMANY CZECH
EUROPE SLOVAKIA UKRAINE
IX. REP. HUNGARY MOLDOVA
Z. AUS. ROMANIA
OATIA
ITALY YUGO. BUL
S.& HER. ALB. MACEDONIA
GREECE TURKEY
MALTA CYPRUS SYRIA
UNISIA LEBANON
RIA ISRAEL
Black Sea
GEORGIA
ARMENIA
AZERBAIJAN
TURKMENISTAN

KAZAKSTAN

Caspian Sea

UZBEKISTAN

KYRGYZSTAN

MONGOLIA

TAJIKISTAN

CHINA

N. KOREA
S. KOREA

Sea of Japan

JAPAN

PACIFIC

OCEAN

LIBYA EGYPT
NIGER CHAD SUDAN
AFRICA
CENTRAL AFRICAN REPUBLIC
CAMEROON
GABON CONGO ZAIRE
NDA
ola) RWANDA
BURUNDI

SAUDI ARABIA

IRAQ
JORDAN
KUWAIT
BAHRAIN QATAR
U.A.E.
OMAN

IRAN

AFGHANISTAN

PAKISTAN

Arabian Sea

INDIA

NEPAL
BHUTAN

BANGLADESH

BURMA (MYANMAR)

LAOS
THAILAND
VIETNAM
CAMBODIA

HONG KONG (U.K.)

TAIWAN

East China Sea

20°N

South China Sea

N. MARIANA IS. (U.S.)

GUAM (U.S.)

PHILIPPINES

MARSHALL ISLANDS

ERITREA YEMEN
DJIBOUTI
ETHIOPIA
UGANDA SOMALIA
KENYA
TANZANIA

SRI LANKA

MALDIVES

SEYCHELLES

BRUNEI

MALAYSIA
SINGAPORE

PALAU

FEDERATED STATES OF MICRONESIA

INDIAN

INDONESIA

0°

NAURU KIRIBATI

PAPUA NEW GUINEA

TUVALU

ANGOLA ZAMBIA
MALAWI
COMOROS
ZIMBABWE MADAGASCAR
NAMIBIA MOZAMBIQUE
BOTSWANA
MAURITIUS
REUNION (Fr.)

OCEAN

SOLOMON ISLANDS

VANUATU

FIJI

NEW CALEDONIA (Fr.)

20°S

SOUTH AFRICA
SWAZILAND
LESOTHO

AUSTRALIA

Coral Sea

N
W E
S

1000 · 2000 Miles
0
0 · 1000 · 2000 Kilometers

NEW ZEALAND

Tasman Sea

40°S

60°S

20°E · 40°E · 60°E · 80°E · 100°E · 120°W · 140°W · 160°W

ANTARCTICA

80°S

180°

317

The United States: Political

WASHINGTON

OREGON

IDAHO

MONTANA

NORTH DAKOTA

SOUTH DAKOTA

WYOMING

NEVADA

UTAH

COLORADO

NEBRASKA

KANSAS

CALIFORNIA

ARIZONA

NEW MEXICO

OKLAHOMA

TEXAS

ALASKA

318

NEW HAMPSHIRE

VERMONT

MAINE

MASSACHUSETTS

RHODE ISLAND

NEW YORK

CONNECTICUT

MINNESOTA

MICHIGAN

WISCONSIN

PENNSYLVANIA

NEW JERSEY

IOWA

OHIO

DELAWARE

ILLINOIS

INDIANA

W. VIRGINIA

VIRGINIA

MARYLAND

MISSOURI

KENTUCKY

NORTH CAROLINA

ARKANSAS

TENNESSEE

SOUTH CAROLINA

ALABAMA

GEORGIA

LOUISIANA

MISSISSIPPI

FLORIDA

N

W   E

S

HAWAII

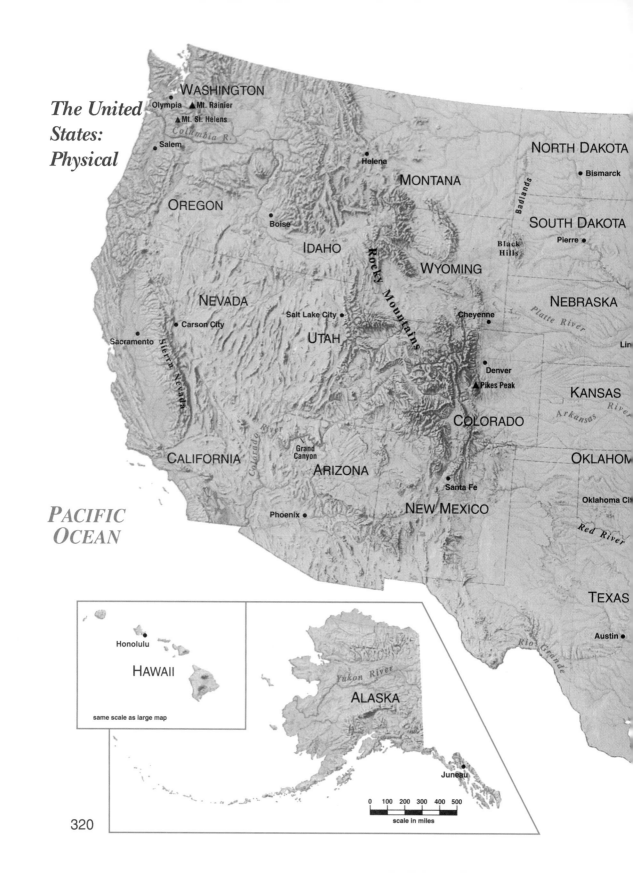

The United States: Physical

WASHINGTON
Olympia ▲ Mt. Rainier
▲ Mt. St. Helens
Columbia R.
Salem

OREGON

Boise

IDAHO

NEVADA

Carson City

Sacramento

Sierra Nevada

CALIFORNIA

Colorado River

Grand Canyon

ARIZONA

Phoenix

Helena

MONTANA

Rocky Mountains

WYOMING

Salt Lake City

UTAH

Cheyenne

Denver

▲ Pikes Peak

COLORADO

Santa Fe

NEW MEXICO

NORTH DAKOTA
Bismarck

Badlands

SOUTH DAKOTA
Pierre

Black Hills

NEBRASKA

Platte River

Lin

KANSAS

Arkansas River

OKLAHOM

Oklahoma Cit

Red River

PACIFIC OCEAN

TEXAS

Austin

Rio Grande

Honolulu

HAWAII

same scale as large map

Yukon River

ALASKA

Juneau

0 100 200 300 400 500

scale in miles

320

INNESOTA

Lake Superior

MICHIGAN

Lake Huron

WISCONSIN

St. Paul

MADISON

Madison

• Lansing

Lake Michigan

IOWA

Des Moines

ILLINOIS

INDIANA

OHIO

Lake Erie

NEW YORK

L. Ontario

Columbus

Indianapolis

Green Mtns.

MAINE

Augusta •

White Mtns.

• Montpelier

NEW HAMPSHIRE

Concord •

VERMONT

Albany • Boston •

MASSACHUSETTS

Providence •

Hartford •

RHODE ISLAND

CONNECTICUT

PENNSYLVANIA

Harrisburg •

Trenton •

NEW JERSEY

Dover •

DELAWARE

Annapolis •

Washington, D.C.

MARYLAND

Springfield •

Ohio River

Missouri River

eka

Jefferson City •

Frankfort •

WEST VIRGINIA

Charleston •

Richmond •

VIRGINIA

Appalachian Mountains

MISSOURI

KENTUCKY

Raleigh •

ATLANTIC OCEAN

ARKANSAS

Mississippi River

• Nashville

Great Smoky Mtns.

TENNESSEE

NORTH CAROLINA

SOUTH CAROLINA

Columbia •

Little Rock •

• Atlanta

Montgomery •

GEORGIA

N

W   E

S

• Jackson

ALABAMA

MISSISSIPPI

Baton Rouge •

LOUISIANA

• Tallahassee

FEET

12,000

9,000

5,000

2,000
1,000
500
0—

GULF OF MEXICO

FLORIDA

0   100   200   300   400   500

scale in miles

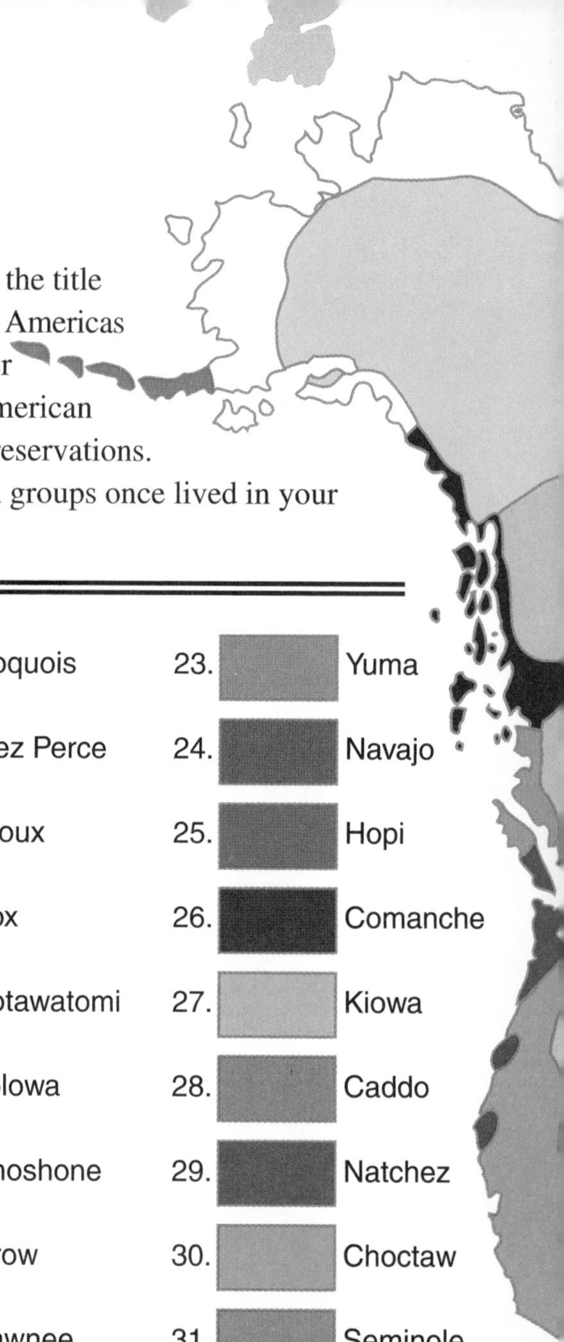

Indian Nations of Long Ago

The American Indians have truly earned the title *Native Americans,* for they have been in the Americas for thousands of years. As settlers from other places spread from coast to coast, Native American territory shrank, driving many groups onto reservations.

Look at the map. What Native American groups once lived in your area? Do they still live there today?

=== **Key** ===

1. Aleut
2. Eskimo
3. Hare
4. Dogrib
5. Tlingit
6. Nootka
7. Chipewyan
8. Cree
9. Lillouet
10. Blackfoot
11. Algonquin
12. Iroquois
13. Nez Perce
14. Sioux
15. Fox
16. Potawatomi
17. Tolowa
18. Shoshone
19. Crow
20. Pawnee
21. Shawnee
22. Pedee
23. Yuma
24. Navajo
25. Hopi
26. Comanche
27. Kiowa
28. Caddo
29. Natchez
30. Choctaw
31. Seminole
32. Carib
33. Arawak

323

Glossary

apartheid (ə - pärt′ hīt) a rule that kept black South Africans from voting and from living and working wherever they wanted

Bill of Rights the first ten amendments to the Constitution

capital wealth that is owned and used by one person or a group of people working together

climate the normal condition of the atmosphere near the earth's surface in a particular place

Constitution a set of rules for the government, protecting the rights of all citizens

culture the way of life of the people who live in a certain place

democracy a government by the people

economy the way a country handles its money and resources

emigrants people who move away from their old country to live in a new place

equator an imaginary line halfway between the North and South Poles dividing the earth into two half spheres

factory a place where goods are made

government a system of rules and authority

House of Representatives one part of Congress, made up of 435 people; representatives are chosen every two years

immigrants people who come into a new country

imperialism getting or keeping colonies

industry the production and sale of goods

international date line an imaginary line running from the North Pole to the South Pole passing through the Pacific Ocean

laws rules that governments have

manufacture to make raw material into a finished product, usually by machine

meridians of longitude a set of imaginary lines that run along the globe from north to south

North Pole the northernmost point on the earth

parallels of latitude a set of imaginary lines circling the globe from east to west; each line is parallel to the equator

prime meridian an imaginary line running from the North Pole to the South Pole passing through England and the Atlantic Ocean

profit an amount that is more than the original cost of something

pure democracy also called a direct democracy; all the citizens or members meet together to decide on their laws

representative democracy also called an indirect democracy; the citizens choose people to make the laws for them

Senate one part of Congress, made up of one hundred people called senators

South Pole the southernmost point on the earth

tradition a practice or a belief that is handed down from generation to generation

unions groups of workers who join together, or unite, to help each other

INDEX

Photograph Credits

The following agencies and individuals have furnished materials to meet the photographic needs of this textbook. We wish to express our gratitude to them for their important contribution.

Suzanne R. Altizer
American Antiquarian Society
American Cyanamid Company
American Telephone and Telegraph (AT&T) Archives
Architect of the Capitol
Arkansas Department of Parks and Tourism
Nathan Arnold
Bancroft Library
Banner of Truth Trust
Johanna Berg
Boeing Commercial Airplane Company
Rose Brouhard
George R. Buckley
Ron and Kathy Burget
Judith Caballero
Canadian Pacific Limited
Chicago Convention and Tourism Bureau
Chicago Historical Society
George R. Collins
Connecticut Department of Economic and Community Development
Corel Corporation
Terry M. Davenport
Eastman Chemicals Division
Eastman Kodak Company
Ellis Island Immigration Museum
Farm Bureau Management Corporation
Dave Fish

Carson Fremont
Zoltán Gaal
General Motors
Georgia Department of Trade and Industry
GeoSystems Global Corporation
Gospel Fellowship Association
Independence National Historical Park
Albert Isaak
Victor Jackson
Brian D. Johnson
G. David Koonts
Kansas Department of Economic Development
Mr. and Mrs. David Larson
Library of Congress
Lynn Historical Society
Marine Diamond Corporation
Maryland Department of Economic and Community Development
John F. Matzko
Gerald McKenney
Mark McKenney
Michigan Travel Bureau
Milwaukee Public Museum
Montana Department of Commerce
Museum of the City of New York
National Aeronautics and Space Administration (NASA)
National Archives
National Collection of Fine Arts, Washington, D.C.

National Park Service
Nebraska Department of Economic Development
New Mexico Tourism and Travel Division
New York Convention and Visitors Bureau
New York Historical Society
New York Public Library
Norwegian Embassy
Ohio Historical Society
J. Norman Powell
Wade K. Ramsey
Karen Rowe
Royal Photographic Society
Science and Society Picture Library
South African Consulate General
South Dakota Tourism
Tuskegee Institute Archives
Union Pacific Railroad Museum Collection
United Nations
University of Illinois at Chicago
Unusual Films
U.S. Space and Rocket Center
Ward's Natural Science Establishment
Washington Convention and Visitors Association
Dawn L. Watkins
David Wilson
John Wolsieffer
World Bank Photo
Yale University Art Gallery

Cover
Dawn L. Watkins (left), Corel Corporation (right), Union Pacific Railroad Museum Collection (bottom)

Title Page
Union Pacific Railroad Museum Collection

Chapter 1
National Park Service 1; NASA 2 (both); George R. Collins 3; Unusual Films 8; Corel Corporation 10 (all), 16 (right, bottom), 18 (both); Maps created by GeoSystems Global Corporation 11, 12-13, 14-15, 20; John Wolsieffer 14; World Bank Photo 16 (top left); Ward's Natural Science Establishment 19 (inset); Norwegian Embassy 19

Chapter 2
William Williams Collection, United States History, Local History and Genealogy Division, The New York Public Library, Astor, Lenox, and Tilden Foundations 21, 38-40; National

Archives 23; Mr. and Mrs. David Larson 24, 43 (both); Dawn L. Watkins 26 (top), 33 (bottom); Unusual Films 26 (bottom), 33 (top), 46 (right); Corel Corporation 27; New York Historical Society 28; Library of Congress 30 (left), 37, 44 (both), 47; John F. Matzko 30 (right), 40; Albert Isaak 31; Ellis Island Immigration Museum 32, 41; Museum of the City of New York 34-35; National Park Service 38 (left); Maps created by GeoSystems Global Corporation 42; Johanna Berg 45; Judith Caballero 46 (bottom); Carson Fremont 48

Chapter 3

Rose Brouhard 49; Ellis Island Immigration Museum 51; Library of Congress 52, 53 (right); University of Illinois at Chicago, The University Library, Jane Addams Memorial Collection 53 (left); Corel Corporation 57, 60 (top); David Wilson 58; Maps created by GeoSystems Global Corporation 59, 64; Unusual Films 60 (bottom), 62; Zoltán Gaal 61; Dawn L. Watkins 63 (both)

Chapter 4

Unusual Films 67, 69; National Park Service 68; Library of Congress 73, 80; Maps created by GeoSystems Global Corporation 82; Gospel Fellowship Association 83; Unusual Films 84 (both); Terry M. Davenport 85; Banner of Truth Trust 87

Chapter 5

Brian D. Johnson 89, 117 (bottom); J. Norman Powell 91 (top); United Nations 92 (bottom); Corel Corporation 92 (top), 96 (bottom), 104 (top), 110 (bottom), 116 (top), 117 (top); Connecticut Tourism, Department of Economic and Community Development 93 (bottom); George R. Collins 93 (top), 95 (bottom), 98 (top), 100 (top); Independence National Historical Park 94 (bottom); Maryland Office of Tourist Development, Department of Economic and Community Development 96 (top); National Park Service 97 (top), 99 (top), 105 (top), 110 (top), 112 (bottom), 113 (bottom), 115 (bottom); Dawn L. Watkins 97 (bottom); G. David Koonts 99 (bottom); Terry M. Davenport 100 (bottom), 106 (top); U.S. Space and Rocket Center 101 (top); Arkansas Department of Parks and Tourism 102 (top); Georgia Department of Trade and Industry 102 (bottom); Ohio Historical Society 103 (top); Michigan Travel Bureau 103 (bottom); Chicago Convention and Tourism Bureau 104 (bottom); Gerald

McKenney 105 (bottom); South Dakota Tourism 107 (bottom); Nebraska Department of Economic Development 108 (top); Kansas Department of Economic Development 108 (bottom); George R. Buckley 111 (bottom), 113 (top); Mark McKenney 112 (top); Ward's Natural Science Establishment 115 (top); Karen Rowe 116 (bottom); Ron and Kathy Burget 118 (top); Victor Jackson 118 (bottom)

Chapter 6

Eastman Kodak Company 119; Unusual Films 121 (all), 138, 139; Science Museum/Science and Society Picture Library 123; Library of Congress 124, 125 (both), 129, 135 (left), 137 (both); Yale University Art Gallery, Mabel Brady Garvan Collection 126; Chicago Historical Society 128; Lynn Historical Society 130; Dawn L. Watkins 133; Milwaukee Public Museum 135 (right); Wade K. Ramsey 136; Tuskegee Institute Archives 140; Terry M. Davenport 141 (both)

Chapter 7

Unusual Films 143, 144, 145 (top), 146-47, 147, 153 (both), 154, 155, 157 (top), 159; Dawn L. Watkins 148 (top left, bottom), 149 (bottom), 150 (top, bottom right), 152 (top), 160; George R. Collins 145 (bottom), 148 (top right); Marine Diamond Corporation 149 (top); Boeing Commercial Airplane Company 150 (bottom left); Suzanne R. Altizer 152 (bottom); Nathan Arnold 157 (bottom); World Bank Photo 158 (top left, right); General Motors 158 (bottom left)

Chapter 8

American Cyanamid Company 161; Unusual Films 162 (both), 172; George R. Collins 163; Dawn L. Watkins 164; Science Museum/Science and Society Picture Library 166, 167; Maps created by GeoSystems Global Corporation 169, 174, 176; Wade K. Ramsey 171 (both); Eastman Chemicals Division 175; National Archives 177, 182 (left); Library of Congress 178, 179, 180, 183 (left), 184; Eastman Kodak Company 182 (right); Union Pacific Railroad Museum Collection 183 (center); Ellis Island Immigration Museum 183 (right)

Chapter 9

Union Pacific Railroad Museum Collection 185, 186, 187; Bancroft Library 188-89; Canadian Pacific Limited 190; Museum of the City of New York 192; National Archives 193, 195, 208; National Collection of Fine Arts, Washington, D.C. 198; Maps created by GeoSystems Global Corporation 199; Montana Department of Commerce 200 (bottom); Commerce and Industry Department, New Mexico Tourism and Travel Division 201 (background); Brian D. Johnson 201 (inset); Kansas Department of Economic Development 203; Library of Congress 207, 209

Chapter 10

Eastman Kodak Company 211; American Antiquarian Society 214; National Archives 215; Library of Congress 221, 226 (bottom left); AT&T Archives 222; Unusual Films 225 (both), 227 (both); NASA 228

Chapter 11

The Royal Photographic Society, Bath 229, 235, 236; National Park Service 230; Library of Congress 233, 239, 243; South African Consulate General 237; Maps created by GeoSystems Global Corporation 238, 241, 246-47, 248; Carson Fremont 240, 244; Dawn L. Watkins 245

Chapter 12

Unusual Films 249, 251, 253 (right), 260 (all), 262, 263 (both); Farm Bureau Management Corporation 250 (top); George R. Collins 250 (bottom); Dawn L. Watkins 251 (background); Suzanne R. Altizer 253 (left), 255 (both), 264; Architect of the Capitol 256-57; Library of Congress 265 (right); National Archives 265 (left); Washington Convention and Visitors Association 266 (bottom); Corel Corporation 266 (top, middle)

Resource Treasury

Dave Fish 267, 308 (bottom right); New York Convention and Visitors Bureau 306; Unusual Films 307, 313, 314; George R. Collins 308 (bottom left); National Park Service 308-9, 309; National Archives 310; Lewis W. Hine Collection, United States History, Local History and Genealogy Division, The New York Public Library, Astor, Lenox, and Tilden Foundations 311; Dawn L. Watkins 312, 315 (both); Maps created by GeoSystems Global Corporation 316-17